WOMEN IN UNIFORM

Jane Waller trained as a sculptor before moving into ceramics, which she studied at Hornsey and at the Royal College of Art. She divides her time between writing and ceramics. Her first book, *A Stitch in Time*, helped to launch the current revival of interest in hand-knitting. Jane has also written novels for children and her book *Handbuilt Ceramics* will be published by Batsford this year.

Michael Vaughan-Rees, Jane's husband, started writing for publication when he had the idea for their previous book *Women in Wartime: The Role of Women's Magazines 1939–1945* (Optima, 1987). But as a linguist, lecturer and language teacher he has spent much of his time writing, in a career that has taken him throughout Europe and North Africa.

Jane and Michael have lived in Waterloo for many years, and were active in the campaign to save the Oxo Tower from destruction and to prevent a wall of office blocks being built in the area. They have the largest private collection in Britain of women's magazines from the Second World War.

WOMEN IN UNIFORM

**Jane Waller
and Michael Vaughan-Rees**

PAPERMAC

First published 1989 by
PAPERMAC
a division of Macmillan Publishers Limited
4 Little Essex Street London WC2R 3LF
and Basingstoke

Associated companies in Auckland, Delhi, Dublin, Gaborone,
Hamburg, Harare, Hong Kong, Johannesburg, Kuala Lumpur,
Lagos, Manzini, Melbourne, Mexico City, Nairobi, New York,
Singapore and Tokyo

A CIP catalogue record for this book is available from
the British Library

ISBN 0-333-48896-2

Typeset by Wyvern Typesetting Ltd, Bristol

Printed in Great Britain by
WBC Print Ltd, Bristol

To all women in the allied countries
who served in uniform during the Second World War

Contents

Acknowledgements

Our warm thanks to the following:

The Director and staff of the Imperial War Museum, especially Dr Christopher Dowling and Mrs Ann Commander; for their help and advice.

The editors of *Woman's Weekly*, *Home and Country*, *The Wren Magazine* and *Together Again* (the magazine of the Transatlantic Brides & Parents Association); for putting us in touch with most of the contributors to the book.

Dorothy Smith; for inviting us to the WAAF reunion at Selsey, which set the whole thing rolling.

Mrs Paddy Wall of the Association of Wrens, as well as various branch secretaries (especially Patricia Pern who invited us down to a meeting at Hastings).

Pamela Winfield (author of *Sentimental Journey* and *Can I forget you*); for friendly advice.

To the following for permission to quote from their unpublished accounts: Claire Lowry (for 'The Wren Who Wanted to Sing'); Maria Narishkin-Dembicki (for 'Just Mookie, Adventures & Misadventures of a Jenny Wren'); Mollie Crisford (for 'Our Brethren Shield in Danger's Hour'); Mary Morris (for allowing us to quote freely from her wartime diaries, the basis of her recently completed 'A Woman At War').

Our thanks, finally, to all the women whose accounts, letters and diaries form the basis of this book, especially those who lent us precious photographs and other mementos of the war years.

Picture Acknowledgements

Illustrations are reproduced by permission of the following: Mrs Lilian M. Bader, Mrs C. Flower, Mrs M. Margery Leigh, Jane Waller, Michael Vaughan-Rees, Topham Picture Library, The Hulton Picture Company, Popperfoto, The Lee Miller Archive and The Imperial War Museum.

The authors and publishers would also like to acknowledge the generous help of other ex-service women who offered their assistance.

x

Abbreviations

AA	anti-aircraft (*also* ack-ack)	LACW	Leading Aircraftwoman
ACW	Aircraftwoman	LCP	Landing Craft Personnel
AFS	Auxiliary Fire Service		
AKS	Army Kinematograph Service	LCT	Landing Craft Tanks
ARP	Air-Raid Precautions	LFB	London Fire Brigade
ATS	Auxiliary Territorial Service	MGB	motor gun boat
		MO	Medical Officer
BEF	British Expeditionary Force	MT	Motor Transport
		MTB	motor torpedo-boat
BGH	British General Hospital	NA	Nursing Auxiliary
		NAAFI	Navy, Army and Air Force Institutes
C-in-C	Commander-in-Chief	NCO	non-commissioned officer
CNR	Civil Nursing Reserve		
CO	Commanding Officer	NFS	National Fire Service
CO	Conscientious Objector	O	Officer (e.g., 3/O=Third Officer)
COS	Chief of Staff		
CPO	Chief Petty Officer	OCTU	Officer Cadets Training Unit
ENSA	Entertainments National Service Association	OTC	Officers' Training Course
FANY	First Aid Nursing Yeomanry	OP	operative
		OPS	operations
FFI	free from infection	OR	other ranks
GD	general duties	PMRAFNS	Princess Mary's Royal Air Force Nursing Service
GI	American serviceman (*from* Government Issue)		
		PO	Petty Officer
HAA	heavy anti-aircraft	PO	Plotting Officer
HMS	His Majesty's Ship	POW	prisoner of war
HMT	His Majesty's Troopship	PX	post exchange, i.e., canteen/stores on American bases
i/c	in charge		
LAC	Leading Aircraftman		

QAIMNS	Queen Alexandra's Imperial Military Nursing Service (QA for short)	SOE	Special Operations Executive
QARNNS	Queen Alexandra's Royal Naval Nursing Service (QA for short)	SS	Steamship
		TA	Territorial Army
		TAF	Tactical Air Force
		USAAF	United States Army Air Force
RA	Royal Artillery		
RAF	Royal Air Force	VAD	Voluntary Aid Detachment
RAMC	Royal Army Medical Corps	WAAC	Women's Army Auxiliary Corps
RASC	Royal Army Service Corps	WAAF	Women's Auxiliary Air Force
RDF	Radio Direction-Finding	WAPC	Women's Auxiliary Police Corps
REME	Royal Electrical and Mechanical Engineers	WL	Women's Legion
RMS	Royal Mail Steamer	WLA	Women's Land Army
RSM	Regimental Sergeant-Major	WO	Warrant Officer
RT	Radio Telegraph	WRAF	Women's Royal Air Force
RWS	Restaurant and Welfare Superintendent	WRNS	Women's Royal Naval Service
		WTC	Women's Timber Corps
SD	special duties (WAAF clerk SD=plotter)	WVS	Women's Voluntary Service

British women often give orders to men. The men obey smartly and know it is no shame. For British women have proved themselves in this war. They have stuck to their posts near burning ammunition dumps, delivered messages afoot after their motor cycles have been blasted from under them. They have pulled aviators from blazing planes. They have died at their gun-posts, and as they fell another girl has stepped directly into the position and 'carried on'. There isn't a single record of any British woman in uniformed service quitting her post, or failing in her duty under fire. When you see a girl in uniform with a bit of ribbon on her tunic, remember that she didn't get it for knitting more socks than anyone else in Ipswich.

Extract from a booklet issued by the US War Department to every American soldier entering Britain and quoted by Godfrey Winn in Scrapbook of Victory, 1945.

I had two ex-Wrens to lunch recently, Babs Smith (Orme), and Margot Hathaway; and of course our experiences and memories vary greatly. As a hairdresser Margot worked much more regular hours than we boats-crew, and did not come into contact with the men and the ships in the same way. In fact she said, 'listening to you and Babs talking, I feel I was in a completely different WRNS to you two'. So I don't doubt that a lot of your readers will be saying, 'It wasn't like that at all!' But believe me, it was.

Pamela Burningham (née Desoutter), ex-deckhand, letter to the authors.

Introduction

It's easy to remember when we decided to write this book. We were at the Imperial War Museum for the launch of *Women in Wartime*, our study of women's magazines during World War Two. The room was full of women of a certain age, with a certain glint in the eye and that erectness of bearing that tells of drill, uniform and authority. One of them, as she waited for her copy to be signed, said, 'Fine book, I'm sure; but why don't you write about *us* next time?'

It took us a while to decide who the 'us' should be. After attending a reunion of over 600 former wartime Waaf we realised that a book could be written just about that particular service. The same, presumably, could be said for the ATS and the WRNS. But there are such books already, with others on the way, no doubt. We rejected the idea of writing about women in general since this would be far too cumbersome, as well as overlapping with much of our previous book. Finally we decided that we would look at the experiences of women who served in uniform; in the NAAFI as well as the services, in the cities and on the land.

Some of our information comes from accounts deposited at the Imperial War Museum, but the greater part of it is from the women themselves. Hundreds wrote in response to letters appearing in *Woman's Weekly, Home and Country, Wren Magazine* and *Together Again* (the magazine of the Transatlantic Brides & Parents Association); others we talked to by arrangement – at reunions or in their homes – or as a result of chance meetings, whether in the local shop or over coffee and baklava in Greece.

The range of background of our informants represents with some accuracy the relative numbers involved during the war. Thus we have more accounts from other ranks than from officers, from Ats than from Wrens and from nurses than from members of the Timber Corps. One category that may be represented out of proportion to their original numbers, however, is that of the volunteers who chose their particular uniform before the Act introducing full conscription was passed in December 1941. But that may be due to their looking back with particular pride on their contribution to the war effort.

Not all the stories are of smiling, comradely determination to get the better of old Adolf and make the world safe for democracy. Yes, the happy times are recalled; but so are the indignities, the injustice and the pain. And more of the negative side would doubtless have emerged if we had sought information from women so disillusioned with their days in uniform that they would not wish voluntarily to recall them. (This means that we hear from military policewomen, but not from deserters, from those who observed breakdowns, not from those who underwent them.)

A number of quotations come from diaries or letters, but the majority of women rely on their memory which, in most cases, can summon up the past in intricate detail. In fact we have received so many accounts, often running to thirty, forty pages or more, that we have not been able to quote from every one. And rather than try to cram everyone in we have chosen, in a number of cases, to follow women through the years; from first putting on uniform, through training, at work and play and on to demob. To those women who have not been quoted from or mentioned by name we would like to express our warmest thanks. Everyone's contributions have helped us to understand a little bit more about what it was like to be a young woman in uniform at that crucial moment in our history. And we would like to stress that all the accounts, whether quoted from or not, are being handed over to the Imperial War Museum as part of their World War Two archives.

Some omissions are particularly regrettable. Although we include material from ex Ats, Waaf and Wrens now living in Commonwealth countries, we have not been able to deal with such bodies as the Canadian Women's Army Corps Unit or the New Zealand Women's Army Auxiliary Corps. A trickle of letters came in from women serving in such organisations, but not enough to do justice to what deserves a separate book.

ONE

Joining Up

I remember my mother; she hated it; she loathed it; she was so cross with me for volunteering! And I can see her now. She stood at the gate; my father took me along to the bus with the case and – she was only a little lady – she just looked over the top of the gate, and I kissed her and she said: 'And if you don't like it you needn't come crying home to me!'

 EILEEN CAVEY, formerly Leading Aircraftwoman Hall

Nearly half a million women served in the forces during the Second World War.

Some were reluctant to join, awaiting conscription and then only choosing service life because it seemed better than work in the factory or on the land. Others volunteered for a variety of motives: simple patriotism, the example of relatives or friends, the desire to do something different or to leave behind the restrictions of family or work.

By the time war was declared, on 3 September 1939, some 20,000 women had already volunteered for the auxiliary forces. But what they often found in those early days was a great deal of enthusiasm mixed with equal quantities of muddle and ignorance.

This was hardly surprising since the longest-established of the women's services, the ATS (Auxiliary Territorial Service) was not officially formed until September 1938, the month of the Czechoslovakia crisis. The WRNS (Women's Royal Naval Service) was re-formed in March 1939, while the WAAF (Women's Auxiliary Air Force) was not separated from the ATS until late June, a matter of weeks before the outbreak of war.

With what we now know of the rôles that women were to play over the next six years, it seems remarkable that the establishment of the auxiliary forces was delayed so long. The example of the First World War showed that women would be needed in case of hostilities. Some 5,000 had served in the WRNS and about the same number in the WRAF (Women's Royal Air Force), while 38,000 joined the WAAC (Women's Army Auxiliary Corps), 9,000 of them serving in France.

But all three branches were disbanded when peace came, and neither the Government nor the service chiefs seemed in any hurry to re-establish them. As late as August 1937 the Cabinet's thinking was that sufficient women could be recruited as civilians through the Ministry of

Labour in case of war, thus making the formation of separate women's forces unnecessary.

There were, however, some women's organisations which bridged the two wars and acted as lobbyists for the mobilisation of women while providing a pool of experienced women for the new services once formed. To start with, there were the various associations of women war veterans, hundreds of whose members were keen to rejoin or otherwise help out their old services. (Beatrice (Brownie) Browne was told that she would be of most use coming into the new WRNS headquarters and sorting through the sacks of unanswered mail, since Mrs Laughton Mathews – the recently appointed Director – hadn't even been allocated a typist.)

Then there were two long-established voluntary bodies, the Women's Legion, and the First Aid Nursing Yeomanry or FANY. Out of the Legion grew two organisations which disbanded once the auxiliary services were in existence: the Emergency Service (whose original task was to train potential women officers for any future war) and the Motor Transport Section.

The FANY, meanwhile, carried on its training programme with no funding and little interference from the Government – as, indeed, it had been doing since its formation in 1909. Throughout the war one section – partly in uneasy alliance with the ATS – concentrated on Motor Transport. A second, independent wing became involved, as we shall see later, in supporting various secret operations.

These organisations were run by some remarkable women, all of whom worked incessantly during the mid- to late thirties, writing memos, collaring Members of Parliament, chairing committees and – what they did best – addressing meetings. The most indomitable of these was Dame Helen Gwynne-Vaughan. During the First World War she had been Chief Controller of the WAAC, later being transferred to the newly formed WRAF. In July 1939, when the powers-that-be finally conceded that the ATS needed a woman to run it, she was appointed Director. But some months earlier she was still stomping around the country, talking to groups of women who were increasingly aware that war was on its way and frustrated that no mechanism existed for them to prepare for it.

One of these was Molly Gale (Sutherland), later sergeant-major and commissioned in 1947. On learning that a women's service had been formed, she wrote off for details and was

notified to obtain forms from the nearest TA Drill Hall, but they hadn't heard of the ATS and really didn't want to know. I finally traced them to the Army Recruiting Office. After the officers were trained we were enrolled at a meeting held in the Central Halls, Glasgow, on 2 February 1939. Dame Helen Gwynne-Vaughan and Staff attended, she wearing her WW1 uniform, which didn't particularly impress us. No decision had yet been made about uniforms, and when they eventually were issued they were available in only three sizes, small, medium and large, the skirts were too long and military tailors had made the uniforms, with the result that the buttons were on the wrong side.

At about the same time, Mary (later Squadron Officer) Ker was worried about being untrained for any wartime job and contacted a friend for advice.

She said a meeting had been called in Aldershot to form 'The Women's Voluntary Services' and I should go with her. We did this, and Dame Helen Gwynne-Vaughan came down and addressed us and said there was no future in this and to go back and contact our nearest ATS recruiting officer. This I did, only to be told there was nothing near Woking where I lived.

This was not untypical. The ATS had been formed hurriedly and lacked trained personnel at every level, from recruiting staff upwards. Much of the confusion of these early months was in fact shared by the men of the Territorial Army, now being mobilised in some haste. But in the case of the ATS this was compounded by the fact that co-operation from the Regular Army was often grudgingly given. Yet, as Molly Gale says,

The first years, when we were all volunteers, laying the future foundations of the women's services, were a wonderful experience. We had to prove we were capable of becoming members of an establishment that up till then had been all-male.

The prime need in those first months was for officers and senior NCOs. Mary Ker was finally told that an RAF company of ATS was being formed and was sent to Chelsea Barracks for a week's intensive officer training where she amused the crowds (if not the Guards Sergeant-Major) by using her left hand when 'saluting to the left'. Molly Gale, meanwhile, joined the 11th Glasgow Company (attached to 54th Anti-Tank Regiment, Royal Artillery) as a private in February 1939 and was promoted to Section Leader (Sergeant) just two months later. This, she tells us, was because she was a lieutenant in the Guides 'and knew Drill, Discipline and Duty'. Many of her fellow-Ats were Guiders, and she believes that this helped them to overcome any lack of organised training from their male counterparts.

Our TA units were not sure how to cope with us and on the whole left us alone, the Adjutant keeping a fatherly eye on the Company to ensure we didn't disgrace the Regiment, especially as our first public appearance was to be at the Annual TA Parade on the first Sunday in May 1939. The public were taken by surprise when we appeared; the remarks by the bystanders, especially the old soldiers, were amusing. We acquitted ourselves well; no fault could be found with the drill. Not so sure about the uniforms issued on the Friday before the Parade. We were told not to alter them (am afraid I

3

shortened my skirt). So began the spit and polish that was to continue for so many years.

The WAAF uniform was first seen in public at another parade two months later, on 2 July, when ten women from each of the companies then in existence marched past the King and Queen in Hyde Park. One of those marching was Lesley Nightingale (née West, later Flight Officer), who had been teaching at a London school at the time of the Munich crisis in 1938.

> One of the parents at the school, the wife of a major at Woolwich, came to the school to talk about the Women's Legion, a Motor Transport organisation which eventually incorporated with the FANY, of which she had been a member at the end of the '14–'18 war. Several of us in the neighbourhood joined the re-formed Company of the WL and trained as motor mechanics at the MT workshops, Woolwich. We camped at Aldershot and drove many kinds of motor vehicle. We were subsequently transferred to a Balloon Centre where an RAF company of the recently formed ATS was being inaugurated. This was one of the forty-eight officer- and NCO-producing units which were distributed all over the country.

Not all of the early volunteers were seen as officer or NCO material, and many were not sent for until the actual outbreak of war. But others did receive some form of training. Eileen Scott-Martin (née Flynn) joined up in early 1939 and spent a fortnight under canvas at a camp in Lainden, Essex, in the first half of August. About the 20th, only a week after getting back home, she was called up and taken by bus to Saxmundham in Suffolk. It was that last beautiful summer of peace, and she recalls thinking what great fun it all was. Two Sundays later, along with other Roman Catholics, she went to Aldeburgh some seven miles away to attend mass. After the service they were just about to climb back in the lorry when a man in a flat over one of the nearby shops opened his window and turned up the radio so that they could hear a message from the Prime Minister. They stood in silence to learn that we were at war with Germany; then, as Eileen says, 'we all looked to the skies – why, I don't know – and all of us just had the urge to get back to camp as soon as possible'.

The reason why they looked up was simply that the British people, led by the Government, feared that a devastating attack would come from the air that first day. If it had, there would have been little that the women of Britain could have done about it.

The authorities had hummed and hawed until the last minute, with the result that the women's services, at the start of the war, were deficient in practically every area. Not only was the mechanism for enlistment somewhat creaky, but also new recruits were often presented with the most primitive equipment and pitched into their duties with little or no preparation.

Grace Houghton (Dewey) joined the ATS on the day before war was declared and found herself called up just six days later. 'We had no training,' she writes. 'We were all sent to gun-site 10 ATS. For many weeks we slept on hard boards in our tents, then we were given palliasses which we filled with straw.'

There are many similar instances of lack of equipment and only cursory training. More frustrating still were the cases of enthusiastic, sometimes trained, volunteers drumming their heels in holding-camps, being given meaningless tasks, or postings and counter-postings, often viewed with great suspicion by their male counterparts.

A combination of energy and adaptability saw that things improved, however. Even from the start there were groups and individuals who saw clearly what was needed. The FANY, for example, were both trained and prepared to produce highly qualified driver-mechanics and just got on with the job (in the face of much opposition from the ATS high command, one must add). In addition, the regular armed forces were not Colonel Blimps to a man, outraged at the very thought of women in uniform. Much of the later success of the ATS in air defence was due, as Shelford Bidwell has pointed out, to 'the foresight of General Pile who, ahead of his time, believed that women were capable of many skilled tasks around the battery position, which in due course led to the establishment of mixed batteries'.

But improvements were slow in coming, and there was not the great rush of volunteers that had been hoped for. In the very first days, yes; Molly Gale (who had received training in Enlistment Documentation) writes that on the day after war was declared there were queues round the Glasgow Army Recruiting Office and that the police had to come and control them. Yet by the end of 1939 only a further 20,000 or so women had joined the forces – hardly a headlong rush.

Some may have been put off by lack of firm information at certain recruiting offices in the early days, while others may not have been interested in the very few trades then available for women. Many more were likely to have encountered strong opposition from their parents, as is clear from the accounts we have of women who volunteered in the face of such opposition.

Daphne Fagg (Utteridge) was working in an office in Rochester and during her lunch-hour one day went into the recruitment office in Chatham, and told them she wanted to join the WAAF. 'As I was not yet eighteen,' she writes, 'they said I would have to get permission from my dad and gave me a form for him to sign. At first he said no, but I said if he didn't it would ruin my life, so I won the day.'

Another future Waaf, Peggy Wells (Brannan), proved less persuasive. 5

At the outbreak of war I was just seventeen years old, and fortunately I had passed my driving test, for they were stopped for the duration. The women's section of the forces had begun with the ATS, but when they started the WAAF I couldn't wait to join as a driver, but my parents wouldn't give their consent, so as you were unable to join without it I had to wait until I was eighteen.

Those who overcame parental opposition or waited until they no longer needed parental consent then had to decide which branch of the service to join. The WRNS, from quite early on, was the hardest to get into; at their wartime peak they numbered no more than 74,000, compared with 170,000 Waaf and 198,000 Ats. Because of this they were able to impose a strict two-week probationary period for new Wrens and eventually limit recruitment to women having family connections with the Navy. This very exclusivity made the WRNS the first choice of many volunteers, and some accounts show that there was a decided pecking order in the minds of many outsiders. Peggy London (Thomson) chose the Air Force because she 'liked the colour. Didn't fancy the Army (too rough) and the WRNS were very difficult to get into'. Hazel Williams (Jenner), who also ended up in the WAAF,

> tried to join the Wrens, but they didn't accept girls who didn't have any connection with the Navy. I didn't make any attempt to join the ATS, which weren't a very attractive service to join. A saying went that the Wrens were the tops, WAAF a reasonable second, but the ATS – Yuk! We were a snobbish lot, I regret to say.

Joan Stewart (Hole) confirms that many people viewed the ATS as the least desirable of the three services. 'I opted from the very beginning for the ATS,' she says.

> People, even soldier friends, begged me not to join, to consider the WRNS or WAAF. The ATS certainly had a very bad press at the time, though I'm blessed if I know why, unless it was that there were more jobs of a lowly nature to be done.

The reason may well have been that the ATS was the prime target for allegations of immorality in the women's services which swept Britain during the first two years of the war. (As they had in the first war, when it was alleged that the WAAC provided the inmates of official army brothels.) According to John Costello:

> Wild rumours about an epidemic of pregnancies and VD in the auxiliary services in 1941 generated a flood of protests from worried parents; churchmen preached against wartime morals from the pulpit, and questions were tabled in Parliament. So vociferous had the outcry become that, on 2 November 1941, at the height of the Blitz, Churchill's Cabinet, which was concerned about its plans for female conscription, announced that a

Beatrice 'Brownie' Browne in her First World War uniform. She was one of many women who flocked to join up in the months before the Second World War.

Barbara Edwards (Martin) in 3rd Officer uniform. Barbara started out as a PO coxswain, and later became a Boarding Officer.

Veronica Christie (Ronnie Moody) showing her stoker's 'props'.

Daisy Baldwin (Henderson). Leading Wren (Durban 1943). Petty Officer Wren, Capetown, 1944.

Hazel Williams (Jenner) aged seventeen and a half. Hazel tried to join up at fourteen and a half and finally made it at seventeen. She was to become a plotter at Tangmere.

Dora Sibley. Started off as a cook and ended the war as a Squadron Officer running No. 2 WAAF Convalescent Home.

Joyce Ashton (White). As a corporal she wasn't allowed to serve with her warrant officer husband.

An ATS driver

Ats on parade, some not yet issued with uniform.

Waaf being kitted out.

parliamentary committee would investigate 'amenities and welfare conditions in the women's services'.

The committee reported six months later that 'there was no justification for the vague but sweeping charges of immorality which have disturbed public opinion' and produced statistics to demonstrate that the incidence of VD and of illegitimacy was lower in all women's services than in the population as a whole. But many people – including servicemen – were still prepared to believe the worst.

Young women, then, needed great determination if they were to go ahead with their plans to enter service life. Many volunteered in the face of parental opposition (in some cases forging signatures on consent forms); and all risked the odium of being seen as 'officers' groundsheets', 'pilots' cockpits' or any of the other obnoxious epithets circulating at the time.

And that was before they had even left home.

Why did they do it, then? For some the onset of the Blitz gave them personal reasons to want to fight back at the enemy. Margaret Hunt (Bettle) volunteered for the ATS at seventeen just after her house received a direct hit in an air raid.

> I was getting ready for bed at the time, and my life was saved by a wardrobe propping up the ceiling which had collapsed on top of it. We lost everything except our lives, and as I lay there covered in plaster I thought: They're not getting away with that! That was what made me want to go on a gun-site, so I could get back at them!

Barbara Charters (Hurst), who was nineteen years old the day war was declared, continued working in an office in Liverpool for about eighteen months. 'As I went back and forth each day,' she says, 'I would see once beautiful buildings burning fiercely and some just a pile of rubble after the night's air raids. That finally decided me to volunteer for the WAAF.'

Others had been even more closely affected by the war. One Wren was already a widow, her engineer-officer husband one of the earliest merchant navy casualties. One Waaf had lost her childhood sweetheart, shot down piloting a lumbering Wellington in one of the first bombing raids. Another had lost her only brother and, when her mother said she was sorry she didn't have another son to send, thought 'there was only me left at home, so I'd better go'.

Some had escaped from countries now occupied by the enemy. Yvonne George left Holland the day the Germans marched in and arrived in England courtesy of the Dutch navy, since the first boat was torpedoed under her. Jean Spear (Nicoll) also fled Holland, ending up as a WAAF flight sergeant, despite the lack of a British education. Jill Carter (Magnus) left Jersey just ahead of the Germans, arriving in England with no papers, which delayed her entry into the WRNS for a year while the family's security classification was sorted out.

A few were separated from their family by the fortunes of war. Dora (later Squadron Officer) Sibley was listening to the wireless in her father's house in Chester Square one day, her husband being stuck in West Africa for the duration, when she heard that the WAAF needed cooks. 'I can cook,' she announced, and went off to Ad Astral House to volunteer.

Fourteen-and-a-half-year-old Hazel Williams was staying with her grandparents in England, her parents having sent her away from Spain, still in the throes of civil war. 'My grandfather was a very military-minded man,' she writes, 'having served in the Boer War and World War I.'

> So he and I tried to join up several times – he putting his age back and I forward. But to no avail, and in the end we became the oldest and youngest fire-watchers in the village. . . . We all moved to South London where I joined the first branch of the Girls Training Corps in Chelsea. The FANY officers who ran this movement trained us in first aid, the receiving and sending of Morse and how to march. . . . We wore navy skirts, white stiff linen tunics, berets and leather belts, and were nicknamed 'Hitler's Maidens', for we looked quite tough. It was because of my year's training with the GTC that I was accepted at seventeen and a quarter (instead of seventeen and a half) by the WAAF when I volunteered at Ad Astral House.

Many followed the example of husbands, boyfriends or fiancés already serving with the forces. In the case of future Wren Vera Selwood (then Boyce) this meant leaving the sanctuary of Canada in July 1941 and joining a convoy of eighty-seven ships which took three weeks to go from Halifax to Liverpool, travelling north among the icebergs to avoid U-boats.

Some need not have entered the forces at all, being in 'reserved occupations' judged as essential for the war effort. Marjorie Gaston (Kite) describes herself as a 'volunteer conscript' since she resigned from her safe bank job, thereby making herself liable for call-up. Others, in non-reserved occupations, saw conscription looming up and decided to volunteer for a specific service rather than risk being directed to more uncongenial work.

Whatever their reasons, few of the many thousands of volunteers realised what they were letting themselves in for.

Imagine you are a young woman of seventeen or eighteen, maybe younger if you lied about your age. You've got your travel warrant and have just said a tearful goodbye to your mum and younger sisters. The train is packed already, mostly with men in khaki, air force and navy blue, so you have to stand all the way to King's Cross, but at least you've met two other girls from your home town heading the same way as you (which you're thankful for, because you've never travelled alone like this before; in fact this is the farthest you've ever been away from home except on the occasional week's holiday with the family). You arrive tired and coughing from the pall of cigarette smoke filling even the corridors of the train and get out clutching the piece of paper which tells you how to get to Paddington. Once there, you ask which is your train and eventually find the right platform and the right train, already packed with other girls of your age, all shapes and sizes, some drab, some manicured, some shy, some brassy, some already in tears. The train sets off, passing through anonymous stations, all signs removed for the duration, arriving hours later. You all clamber out, wondering what to do, when suddenly . . .

> out of nowhere a ruff voice shouted. 'Come on, speed it up!', the bloody drill sergeant sprinted effortlessly to the rear of the gasping, panting column of women. 'Alright, girls!' she cryed out, smiling over the 25 new ATS girls, fall in!, she shouted, we're just going to trot round the park, so follow me. Le – ight! Le – ight, we stopped at the zoo, eating lunch army rations then the sergeant yelled out Ok girls, off we go!!! Le – ight, le – ight! the army barracks was just a little way down the road. I staggered up to them gates which was around the barracks, my comrades moaning and groaning, the sergeant calling out keep going girls you'll thank me for it later, I said Have a heart Serg! Keep moving faster faster one two she yelled we finaly made it back. The next day out on the parade ground, Sergeant called out feet together come on girls she shouted, up up get some height into it, up up my chest was a flamming cavern of agony she supose to make us fit not give us a bloody heart attack, the next day we started up again, the fog swirled over the heads of the marching women thick fog yellow metallic on the tongue I coudn't see the head of the column only the swinging lantern carried by the leader, this 5.30 am, walk to breakfast was just about the worst part of the day when my morale was low and thoughts of home rose painfully in my mind.

Not everyone was pitched into service life quite as abruptly as Erica Donellan (née Dimmock) now of Gonzales, Louisiana; but few found the first days enjoyable, and all have vivid memories of the moment of leaving home. Hazel Williams (no longer a 'Hitler's Maiden') set off early one morning:

> Seventeen and a half, very naïve with my little suitcase. I shall always remember my mother, tears streaming down her face, at the door. Then she called me back and said: 'Don't sit on any strange lavatory seats, and' – pointing to her bosom – 'don't let any man touch you there!' So that was the only advice I had on joining up. . . .

Her destination was Ad Astral House in London where they were put into coaches to go to Euston Station and on to Bridgnorth in Shropshire 13 for initial processing. 'The journey took ages,' she says, 'for as our train was just for girls joining the WAAF we kept on being put into sidings, while more important trains rushed by. When we got to Crewe we had another long wait – all sitting down on the platform floors, drinking huge cups of tea.'

Eileen Hazell had what she describes as a 'memorable' journey. The train was constantly held up owing to air raids, during which they stayed in complete darkness. She had to change several times, arriving in Aldershot after the last bus had gone. Some soldiers gave her a lift to Command HQ, telling her of the perils of joining the ATS. But when she arrived all the offices were locked up for the night.

A guard on duty pointed out the officers' living-quarters and suggested I ring and wake someone up. This I did, and was greeted by a very sleepy and not too happy CO who said: 'You're the last to arrive, Catt. I don't know where to put you at this late hour.' I felt awful and wished the ground would open up. However, someone was called and I was ushered into a small room where someone was already asleep, given the remaining bed and told to be ready for Roll Call at six the next morning. I made my bed by a dim light, washed in icy water and crawled between the army blankets. Amazingly I slept, to be rudely awakened by my companion who was already dressed. Well, I did eventually make it to the mess, freezing, disillusioned and desperate for a bite to eat, having eaten nothing since breakfast the day before.

It was rare for women to arrive alone at their first camp. Most, like Doris Wallington (Holmes), came by lorry or coach, having been met at the nearest railway station.

We eventually arrived at Wrexham to find there was a large army lorry to take us to camp. We had to clamber in as best we could, trying not to expose our lacy undies or ladder stockings, and as the lorry bucketed along the country roads we had to hang on for dear life. But worse was to come.

Worse, indeed. The introduction to their huts could be bad, with the realisation that they could be sleeping with thirty or forty others, in iron bunk beds, on hard three-part 'biscuit' mattresses, with a stove that couldn't be lit until early evening and the ablutions 200 yards away across a frozen field. But all this was nothing compared with what for many women remains their most humiliating memory of the war: the first mass medical examinations.

For Eve Sugden (Durman), 'convent educated and fairly modest, it was quite an experience to be in the same room with sixty naked women'. And Shirley Aston (Webb), who had volunteered for the ATS along with her twin sister Stella, describes that first night as 'ghastly – we were all sore from injections, and not used to sleeping with a lot of girls in one large room. Also our medical examinations had horrified us; we were very

14

modest in those days. Having to parade naked appalled us (I'd never even seen my twin naked!).'

Perhaps the most demeaning part of the procedure was the dreaded FFI, or Free From Infection (graphically described by another former Waaf as looking for 'bugs, scabies and babies'). Margaret Adams (Parfitt) says that this made her first day 'rather traumatic, as I was found to have "nits" on arrival. I was immediately plastered with a horrible concoction which smelt like paraffin, so of course I and a couple of others in the same situation felt a bit like lepers.'

But not everything about the introduction to service life was miserable. To some of these children of the Depression it was an improvement on what they were used to. Margaret Adams, after recovering from her nits, found she had a real treat in store.

As I was under eighteen I was told (with a couple of others) that we must drink a pint of milk a day, so every mid-morning and afternoon we went to the cook-house and had our half-pint of milk. We were called the 'milk-babies', and the milk – why, me coming from a large family (I was the youngest of fifteen children) had never had such luxury.

While Joan Stewart, when two girls were pointed out to her 'as being about to be thrown out of the Army because "they had been found in bed together" could not understand why two girls should want to share a bed when they could enjoy the luxury of a bed to themselves. To me a single bed was paradise.'

Some found themselves with more spending money than they had ever imagined. Grace Houghton had been working in a carpet factory where her pay 'was 7 shillings [35p], my mother had 6 shillings [30p] so I had 1 shilling [5p]. Then to have 9 shillings [45p] pay from the Army all to myself and all food found, I thought I was rich.'

Peggy Wells was happy to have found freedom from the restraints of home life. 'I am not meaning to be nasty to my family,' she writes,

but being the only girl in a family of three brothers all much older than me really meant that I had four fathers! And my brothers were more strict than my father. I know they had my interests at heart, but there were times it was a bit too much. I had to be in by nine, and if I was just a little bit late I had the third degree; what was more annoying, they could just go out with no questions asked or what time to be in, so you can imagine, upon joining up, the luxury of being allowed out until ten and the odd late pass to 2359; it was enough to turn your head! Plus ten whole shillings [50p] a week!!

And for those who joined up later, having experienced life in the Blitz-torn cities, the services proved comparatively restful. Queenie Stearn, a civil servant, had been on compulsory overtime from 1939 to 1943. She was on duty five nights a fortnight at St Mary Abbots Hospital First Aid Post and every Saturday night took her turn fire-watching, getting by on very little sleep during the London Blitz. Eventually, when the Government decided to release 10 per cent of female civil servants for the forces as an example to the country, she applied to go and was accepted by the WRNS. 'I found the life much easier than that I'd been having in London where I'd lived in a bed-sitter and had to get my own meals and do my own washing. Communal living is easy to take when you're young.'

But for many it was difficult to take to start with. In quite a few huts, barracks, cabins or tents young women on their first night in the services would lie awake, arms throbbing from their inoculations, listening to sobs in the dark, wondering what was in store for them.

TWO
Initial Training

What faced most new recruits was a tough basic induction period, usually followed by some form of specialised training. Fledgling Wrens (from March 1941 onwards) were on probation for the first two weeks and could withdraw – or be asked to leave – at any time. As 'Pro-Wrens' they were issued with drab blue dresses and overalls and only received their full uniform on satisfactory completion of the course. Ats and Waaf, on the other hand, were kitted out from the start.

A WAAF recruit, for example, would be issued some fifty-six different items of equipment; skirts and tunics, shirts, detached collars and collar-studs, cardigan, tie, cap, black lace-up shoes, various items of under-wear, grey lisle stockings, winceyette pyjamas, greatcoat, mug and irons (knife, fork, spoon), a sewing-kit known as a 'housewife' (pronounced 'hussif'), plus shoe-brushes, tooth-brush, button-stick and button-brush, tin hat, groundsheet, gas-mask, gas-cape and goodness knows what besides. (One ex-Waaf recalls that they found it difficult at first to pack everything into the kit-bag, let alone carry it when full.)

Not that every single item was available in the first few weeks, or even months. Ida Garland (Kirby), who joined the WAAF in December 1939, writes that 'we had no proper uniforms and had to parade in the few items we had. My first and only piece was a WAAF cardigan for several weeks.' Recruiting for the WAAF had, in fact, to stop for a while that October, such was the shortage of kit. And in November supplies of shoes and stockings ran out at the West Drayton depot, which meant that recruits had to march in their civilian shoes, however inappropriate.

Similar shortages of kit affected the ATS. Eileen Hazell describes how after breakfast on her first morning at Aldershot the new recruits were taken to the Quartermaster Stores for kitting out.

Oh, those uniforms – skirts far too long (for us) and thick baggy khaki stockings, itchy underwear and clodhopper shoes – our high-heeled courts to be saved for those special leaves. One item evaded us, though – HATS. Stores were waiting for another issue, so we became known as the Ats without HATS. Even our first leave was taken hatless.

Anything that more or less fitted had to be worn, leading to often   17 incongruous mixtures of civilian and military clothing. 'In my case,' recalls Peggy Wells, 'it was only my cap and shoes (like iron boxes). I must have looked ridiculous. Can you imagine? A new cap which stood up like a chef's hat, a camel coat, check shirt and jumper, with clomping great shoes!'

At least the new recruits were all in the same boat, whether fully kitted out or not. There are many accounts of young women back in their huts, helpless with laughter at the sight of each other in skirts round their ankles or caps perched like peas on heads or coming down over ears. What caused the greatest hilarity was the regulation underwear. As ex-Waaf Mary Winter (Boxer) writes:

> I don't know how many of us had worn corsets with bones in before. *I* certainly hadn't, but you had to wear them because of the suspenders, so you just took the bones out. As for the knickers – 'blackouts', as they were soon called – what a colour! 'Passion-killers' was another name (not always warranted, though, as it proved).

Civilian clothes had to be returned home, either using the recruits' cases or by having them pack everything up in brown-paper parcels. Since their new kit included a gas-mask, they had no further use for their civilian issue, which meant that on at least one WAAF camp – according to Hazel Williams – some old hands had discovered an easy way of making a little money on the side.

> As we walked in, still in our civvies, and with our civilian gas-masks on, I noticed a WAAF NCO and an airwoman standing at the entrance, with dozens of gas-mask cases slung over their shoulders. You can imagine what they looked like, for most women tried to make the cardboard boxes containing their gas-masks look attractive. Thus some of the cases were in real leather, others 'mock-croc' or attractive waterproof covers. As we passed these two women they said to each of us: 'You don't want those civvy gas-masks any more. We'll take them.' What a racket! I wonder how much they made selling the cases taken from each new intake of Waaf?

Once the new recruits had tried on their uniforms and parcelled up their civvies it was time to be introduced to the delights of drill. And this often meant their first encounter with male NCOs. When Connie Poolman (Plumb) went on to the parade-ground for the first time she was confronted by a Regular Army sergeant who announced in a strong Scottish accent:

> 'I'm going to teach you in three weeks what should take three months. Although you're women, I'm going to treat you no different from men.' He told us that we must 'always obey orders and don't complain until after carrying out the order'. It was three weeks of 'Heads up, chins in, chests out'.

18   Joan Thrush (Mullin) found herself in December 1939 being drilled

by a very strict regular RAF sergeant, who made it very clear that he did not approve of women in 'his' service. After marching us into a hangar he bellowed 'Halt!' and we obligingly obeyed. As we did so, the frilly and very non-regulation knickers of the girl in front of me dropped to the ground. Seemingly unperturbed, she stepped out of them and popped them in her pocket.

But there was very little to laugh about in those first few days. Peggy Wells recalls that 'every time when marching you were told to swing your arms you lifted the top of your vaccination scab higher, too, a lovely feeling'; and another Waaf, Mary Palmer (Matthews), describes how while drilling after receiving their inoculations 'a number of the girls passed out and suddenly they were going down like ninepins, but all who were still on their feet had to keep on marching'. The new-issue shoes could cause problems, too. 'While still suffering painful punctured arms,' writes Paula Irwin, 'we now had to contend with the curse of blistered heels. Two of our girls had to report to sick-bay as their bloodied heels showed signs of becoming septic.'

Betty Stanbury (Martin) describes her first few days of basic training in the wilds of Scotland as 'a nightmare, until you got used to being always called by your surname, being taught to march and salute, to wearing khaki issue, endless medicals inside and out'. While another former At, Hilda Mason, remembers being 'completely bewildered. I never knew where I should be or at what time; I paraded with whichever section was nearest.'

And, as if pain and bewilderment were not enough, many raw recruits had to contend with the extremes of English weather. Each of the first three winters of the war was terrible, particularly that of 1939–40 when facilities were at their most primitive. When Peggy Wells arrived at the WAAF camp of Innsworth, Gloucestershire, she jumped from the lorry into two feet of snow, then found herself having to go outside in a blizzard to find the ablutions hut. Dorothy 'Ossie' Osbon found the same camp so cold on her first day in January 1942 that she kept her gloves on while queuing up for food, only to hear a voice thundering out: 'Airwoman, take those gloves off!' 'Two hours in the WAAF and my first telling-off,' she thought to herself. That same winter Ann Secretan woke up at Aldermaston to find not only that there was a layer of ice covering the fire-buckets inside the huts, but also that the very edges of their pillows had frozen. (In the winter of 1939–40 WAAF other ranks had no great-coats, by the way; it was the King – seeing them shivering on parade in East Anglia – who ordered that greatcoats be issued to all ranks.)

Not all recruits spent the full initial training period at the recruitment depot, however. In the case of the WAAF this was possible in the early part of the war, but as numbers increased, particularly following the introduction of conscription, they would spend no more than three or four

19

days in camp and be sent elsewhere for the rest of this initial period. And the name that comes up in account after account is Morecambe, where every boarding-house seems to have been commandeered by the WAAF for the duration.

'Lancashire in winter was patriotism indeed,' writes Eve Sugden from Virginia, USA. 'We drilled every morning on the wet and windy front, trying to believe that people really came here voluntarily in peacetime for fun.' Lilian Shattock (Lynch) recalls with distaste 'running in squads along Morecambe front with jackets off, collars undone, grey lisle stockings rolled down to ankles with grey gym-shoes. Most degrading, and this in January!'

When not being drilled they were marched to theatres or dance-halls for lectures. Some were on bland subjects such as the history of the RAF and WAAF and the various ranks in both services. But many, according to Pat Sparks (Pattison), were 'about things like VD and sexual relationships, which were never discussed by most of us in civvy life. Lots of times we didn't even understand the lectures.' Gabrielle Reilly (LACW Garman) remembers that 'they got us off to a confusing and embarrassing start the first morning by showing us two films, *The Birth of a Baby* followed by a film about venereal disease. The latter was pretty incomprehensible, but they were enough to put you off family life for good.'

There was little to do in the evenings. Waaf were not allowed to go more than five miles from Morecambe, and all the RAF were in Blackpool. Most of the boarding-houses were pretty unwelcoming, with grim landladies and dire food. ('The food was inedible, but we ate it all the same,' writes Dorothy Hobson (Parker) from Gulgong, New South Wales. 'We had rice pudding for dinner, and any left over would be mixed with porridge and served for breakfast, and any left over would be called rice pudding and served for dinner and so on.')

But the weeks soon passed, the arms stopped throbbing, and most women began to take a pride in their uniform and even some pleasure in being able to drill with increased ease. Pat Sparks was instructed by Flight Sergeant Fox, 'a regular airman of many years' standing. His voice broke when he shouted "E Squadron, you're marvellous!" once we had attained his high standard.'

Eventually it was time for Passing-Out Parade, with the British weather true to the last. Peggy Wells's intake 'assembled on the pier to be inspected by the "Queen Bee" herself, the Honourable Trefusis Forbes, the WAAF Commandant. We waited and waited, but she didn't arrive, so we were disbanded. Maybe it was as well as we were blue with cold and our buttons green with the salt from the sea.' Dorothy Hobson remembers that it was very cold. 'And as we stood to attention big flakes of snow covered us; we were like frozen snow-women.'

20   It required great resilience to last out in such conditions, and the

majority did, indeed, pull through. But some did not. Mary Ker, who spent five months as an officer at the Innsworth training depot, recalls with sadness the young women 'who couldn't take it and had severe mental breakdowns, and yet they had so wanted to do their bit for the war and all at that time were volunteers'.

Probationer Wrens seemed to suffer less hardship. There was not so much emphasis on drill, they knew from the start that they could withdraw from the course if it proved too tough, and the training took place not in frozen barracks or along wind-swept promenades but in colleges such as Greenwich, Westfield, Westley and Mill Hill.

To Priscilla Inverarity (Fuller) it seemed, if anything, like an extension of boarding school.

> When I arrived at Greenwich College we were welcomed by a messenger who informed us that we had to gargle. Then we had to visit 'nurse' and have our hair inspected and combed. Having completed these rather peculiar acts we were taken to an office and names and addresses had to be given, not only ours but next of kin in case we were involved in action. We were then told to go to the 'mess' and collected vast cups of rather weak sweet tea and met some other girls. . . . Later we had to attend lectures on how honoured we were to be accepted by the Navy and we had to live up to a very high standard of behaviour and hard accurate work . . . one mistake in a number or degree or place-name could lose the War, and that would be on our conscience for the rest of our lives! We were also told that if we didn't do well enough we could be sent home. Every morning we had 'Muster', in other words we had to parade in a courtyard and be inspected by a group of rather terrifying Wren officers, who ticked us off if they thought our hair was too long or our shoes were not sparkling with polish. There were more and more lectures on every subject, including Sex and how we should behave with our boyfriends. Every morning we were wakened by some sort of bell or loudspeaker. A dash to the wash-basins and a quick wash before dressing in haste and down to breakfast where we had to hand in a ticket which entitled us to a rather dreadful meal. We stood behind our chairs while an officer said grace and we were warned that we had to finish everything that was put on our plates. . . .
>
> We were on a fortnight's probation and after that we could decide if we wished to continue or if THEY thought we were suitable. It was hard going as there was so much to remember, like standing to attention when an officer came into the room or flattening yourself against a wall if you passed an officer in a corridor. Finally we were selected and issued with our uniforms . . . very scratchy jacket and skirt (the dye came off on your petticoat), three shirts and a few collars which had to be attached with studs, front and back. . . . We were inspected before going on 'shore leave' and if we weren't clean and tidy our pass was stopped. Some of the officers were unnecessarily strict and obviously enjoyed looking for faults, whereas others were strict but fair. What a relief it was to become an officer myself!

21

There was great emphasis on domestic work. Eve Canvin (then Lynch), whose husband had been lost at sea, was one of 'an eager and slightly apprehensive bunch of girls' who were sent from Mill Hill to Whitehall

> where we were presented with mops, buckets, cloths and ladders, and it was our job to wash the walls and paintwork of the longest, highest corridor I had seen. It was quite hilarious to see us, and hear the backchat with the amused matelots and young naval officers passing down the corridor. It was excellent therapy for any private grief or homesickness and as our intake was from various types of background shook us on to an even level.

Another Wren describes how at Mill Hill they were 'divided into three groups doing general domestic work, ablutions or washing-up, apart from the inevitable square-bashing and lectures about the Royal Navy'.

Such lectures were given great emphasis, as the WRNS has always been extremely proud of its close connection with the Senior Service. Mollie Crisford describes how as her course went on

> the Pro-Wrens' notebooks were rapidly filling up with information to Read, Learn and Inwardly Digest. As well as the ships in the commands there were pages of Naval Abbreviations, Naval and WRNS ranks, the different colours worn between Naval Officers' Gold Braid, and also General Knowledge about the College, the names of all the Chief Wrens of each category, where they were to be found, and the names of all the Officers, etc.

At the end of two weeks they had a one-and-a-half-hour written examination, following which they were formally enrolled as Wrens and had to 'fill up a lengthy questionnaire stating that they would be amenable to Naval Discipline, and put the Service before Family ties'. Only then would they be kitted up, emerging as real Wrens.

The FANY, too, insisted on a preliminary vetting period before accepting volunteers. 'I cope' was their motto, and it did indeed need a combination of guts and intelligence merely to get through the initial training period. Ruth Middleton (Graham Wood) applied in the autumn of 1944, when

> one was sent to the training school at Chicheley Hall, Newport Pagnell, for very vigorous basic training. Here we had to polish floors, were drilled and marched on the parade-ground, taught map-reading and first aid, lectured on FANY history, given psychological and occupational tests, exams to pass, and subjected to extremely strict discipline. Not until the end of the course were we told whether or not we had been selected. The standard was very high, and some dropped out and others were asked to leave.

Kay Kerrvish (formerly Warriner) trained after being allowed to finish her degree. After Chicheley her intake

> moved to St John's Wood to be kitted out. We were very proud to receive our uniform – especially our officer-type Sam Browne belts and hats which

came from Scott's of Piccadilly, as did our distinctive berets with the red flash which distinguished us from the ATS.

What new recruits did then – whether in khaki, navy or air force blue – depended on various factors: their results in exams or trade tests, their individual interests; above all, on the needs of the service. For some it would mean immediate postings, but for most servicewomen completing basic training the next step was an intensive course of specialised training.

Choice of Trade

In the very early days, as we have seen, there was little provision for any form of training. The jobs open to women were limited therefore to those involving skills which female volunteers might be expected to possess already. According to Sadie Nias (Thomas), who joined the ATS on its formation, 'trades open were cooks, orderlies, clerical workers and a very few drivers (had to be able to drive, no training given)'. The first Wrens were only allowed into five categories involving various forms of clerical or domestic work, and the situation was much the same in the WAAF.

Most of the male service chiefs, it can be assumed, believed at this stage that women should remain in such positions. But the demands of total war were such that by 1945 women were serving in literally hundreds of capacities, many involving skills unknown in 1939. As the war progressed provision had to be made, therefore, not only for the specialised training of new recruits in a wide variety of areas but also for the updating of skills and the retraining of women in new skills.

This did not mean that all recruits were presented with a huge list of trades and asked to select the most congenial. Categories closed, new ones opened, and what was available at any given moment was usually a matter of chance, as can be seen from the following accounts.

There wasn't really much more than Hobson's Choice . . . there were only three trades on offer that week, balloon operator, MT driver or wireless operator. The first two seemed too much like hard work in winter, and as we passed a Morse aptitude test (wearing earphones and determining the length of certain sounds emitted) we were in. (*Mary Winter, WAAF*)

I was told that the vacancies at the time were for cooks or sparking-plug testers, so in spite of not knowing what a sparking plug was, or even what it was used for, I opted to be a tester. I was twenty years old and felt this was a great adventure. (*Ivy Humphries (Smith), WAAF*)

I was very eager to be a Boat's Crew Wren and pressed the point at Mill Hill. At first I was told there was no possibility, and gardening was suggested as

23

an alternative. Then I was asked if I liked mechanical things, because a new category (Boat Driver) was starting, and I jumped at that. (*Margaret Boggis*)

The interviewers thought me an ideal candidate for various jobs which would have meant spending most of my time in secret underground rooms, but I had had enough of being underground in shelters during the Blitz. So my choice was limited to being a cook or a motor-driver. I told them my cooking would be considered sabotage, and I had always wanted to drive. (*Eve Sugden, WAAF*)

Interviews and aptitude tests to decide which job would be the most appropriate took place either at the recruiting office or during basic training. Elsie Harper (Barnett) can remember going to the ATS recruitment centre and being given a test

which relied on the ability to sort out different shapes and words and also to do simple arithmetic. Considering that two years previously I had been to grammar school and obtained three credits in the school cert exam, it was not surprising that I got the highest marks possible. I remember the officer expressing surprise at my result and saying I could have a free choice of any trade. However, as I had good maths he suggested that I might like to work with theodolites on firing ranges or become a radio mech. Without really knowing anything about it I chose the latter.

Before conscription came in it was possible for uncongenial proposals simply to be turned down. Peggy Wells was an excellent driver, working for her father's engineering firm. 'Upon going for my interview,' she writes,

the interviewing officer asked if I wouldn't rather be an aircraft hand GD instead of a driver. I gave her a very definite 'no' on that score. I knew exactly what that could mean: anything from cleaning the ablutions to office work, depending on how lucky you were. My father was ex-Flying Corps, so I had a rough idea about service life. I told her that I would be classed as a reserved occupation when I reached the age to register, so that if I couldn't be a driver I would go back to that.

Later it was more difficult to turn down the trades suggested, and Babs Howard, who worked as a WAAF recruiting clerk, remembers many women 'disappointed because they couldn't go in for the trade they had set their heart on'. In terms of efficient use of resources it was obviously in the interest of the services to steer as many women as possible towards jobs for which they needed no further training. One Waaf who asked if she could become a despatch rider was told: 'Sorry, not tall enough or heavy enough.' 'A PT instructor, then?' 'Do you really want to get up early in the morning and yell at recruits? What will help the country most is for you to be a shorthand typist as you are already trained.'

24   There were women, however, who successfully managed to resist any

Waaf Dorothy Hobson (Parker) on the front at Morecambe in February 1943 with her oppo Sylvia Brookes. Dorothy (*left*) became an airframe mechanic and now lives in Gulgong, New South Wales.

IN THE BEGINNING.

THE END PRODUCT.

Two drawings by Joan Zeephat who was a topographical draughtsman and served at 522 Ordnance Survey Royal Engineers, Thames Ditton. 'Our job was to help with the planning of the RAF air offensive by revising out-of-date maps [using] photographs taken by reconnaissance planes over enemy territory.'

ATS wireless operator undergoing training at Southern Command, November 1941.

Waaf reporting for duty at a balloon station in June 1940.

pressure to spend the war doing traditionally female jobs. Win Dowd served in the Army Kinematograph Service, driving round camps, home and abroad, showing films to service personnel. Before being called up she had run her own hairdressing business, but

> from what I had seen of the ATS during my basic training before meeting the Selection Officer, I wouldn't have felt I was doing work of national import-ance dressing their hair. I didn't see anyone put in what I would have considered a good day's work. The officer was surprisingly understanding. I told her that I would make a terrible soldier if I was made to do hairdress-ing, but given something interesting and worthwhile to do I would be my usual self-disciplined self.

Joan Stewart was a Post Office telegraphist and had to wait until her job was de-reserved before being able to join the ATS as an MT driver. 'Two things I had always wanted in life and which in civilian life I could see no way of attaining,' she writes.

> I wanted to travel and I wanted to drive. How could I, a trained telegraphist, a teleprinter and a switchboard operator, prevent myself getting called up to do exactly the same job I was doing in civvy street? I decided it was no good telling lies, but managed to blind them with science by putting my occupation down as SC & T (Sorting Clerk & Telegraphist), and nobody knew what it was!

Dorothy Hobson was another switchboard operator who tried to be accepted as a driver. In her case there were no vacancies; but after turning down a lot of other suggestions she agreed to become one of the first WAAF flight mechanics and never regretted it for a minute.

> I just didn't want to carry on doing office work as before. That's why I wanted to be an MT driver in the first place. You see, I could have been a batwoman, a waitress, but I didn't want to do that. I didn't see why I should spend the war pressing some bloke's trousers. Let them press their own, I thought! I don't know how I landed that job. Just a bit of luck.

Special Training

Some women didn't think themselves all that lucky when they found out what was expected of them. Margaret Tansey (Curry) did a five-month course as an Electrician Air Mechanic at Mill Meece in Staffordshire (HMS *Fledgling*) where 'there was a small airfield with various aircraft on which we learned practical work. When at first I saw the interior of the cockpit of a Seafire (naval version of a Spitfire) I was petrified at the sight of the electrical controls and thought I could never cope.'

And when Hilda Mason saw her first predictor (the instrument used   29 for calculating where to aim an anti-aircraft gun) she thought: 'I shall never be able to do this.'

But both survived their initial shock. Hilda Mason soon discovered that using the predictor was a team effort, with each member specialising in one part of the operation; while Margaret passed her finals working on a Barracuda, perhaps the most disliked plane of the whole war – 'quite ancient and an absolute horror', as she describes it.

Not everybody could cope with the demands of a training course, however. According to Dorothy Baker (Cartwright), the strain of trying to absorb all the electrical theory, part of her six-week intensive radar training, drove one of her fellow-Ats to attempt suicide by climbing up a pylon. And Eileen Shaw (Corporal Hemus), before leaving for six months' Wireless Operator training at RAF Compton Bassett, was told: 'Don't worry, because there is a special home in Blackpool if you are affected by the course.'

It was not just the women who were affected, however. Eileen tells us that 'the men . . . were driven to all kinds of actions, the worst being one of the airmen who shot himself outside our billet one night'. Her fellow-Waaf were not pushed that far, though one used to sleepwalk every night, picking up the mail from the hut table and taking it to be posted, while another would sit up in bed, sing and answer questions without remembering a thing next day. Fourteen of the original twenty-four Waaf, these two included, failed to last the course and were returned to other duties.

Most courses were very demanding indeed, and, as the need for skilled personnel increased, considerably more intensive than in the leisurely days of peacetime. Mary Winter was told that before the war the men had been given eighteen months to complete the course at Compton Bassett, three times as long as the Waaf.

> Not only did we have to do a Wireless Operator's course but, it seemed, part of a Wireless Mechanic's course as well. The idea was that in case we should be stationed at a place without a Wireless Mech we could do all our own running repairs. It still seems to me that they asked a lot of us to learn not one but two jobs, all in six months. But we did it. Only one girl in my class failed her final exam, but she retook it in six weeks and then passed it OK.

In other areas, too, women learned that they had to be able not only to operate equipment but also to service it when necessary. Betty Stanbury's three months' intensive Motor Transport training included 'endless lectures on how the vehicles worked; we had to be able to know where the trouble was, should we break down, and how to get it going again'.

Eve Sugden confirms that the WAAF had a similar approach:

30   Our days were filled with theory in the mornings and driving in the

afternoons. We learned to maintain motor vehicles, do minor repairs, even paint them. Our driving was learned on left-over World War I lorries. Our instructors were ex bus drivers, or in our case an ex racing car driver. They must have been men with nerves of steel. We learned to double-declutch, and our dreams at night about where to put our hands and feet tangled the sheets like strait-jackets.

And those destined for convoy work had to acquire a whole range of additional skills. Betty's group

did night driving after we passed our test, quite hazardous with our headlamps almost blacked out, but it was surprising how soon we got used to it. We were delighted when the moon was there to guide us. Did first-aid course and map-reading, no signposts, all had been removed.

The day after Margaret Adams passed her MT course the surviving members of her group

were sent out alone for the first time with a map and map references and had to find our way to a chosen spot and meet up with the others. On our last day we drove in convoy through London and I learned that in convoy you keep your eye on the vehicle behind and, if it stops, you stop; that way the convoy stays together.

Those training as mechanics of various kinds had a similar mix of theory and practice. Dorothy Hobson eventually chose to be a flight mechanic, opting to work on airframes (rather than on engines or as an electrician).

We did all sorts of things on the course. We did basic, which was filling and drilling and putting threads on, both internal and external; we did filing and measuring and making sure it was all absolutely straight; then we spent two weeks on the theory of flight, then on to hydraulics, pneumatics, joinery, fabric work – because a lot of the airframe was covered in Irish linen that was spread all over the frame; some frames were metal and some wooden, then you'd put dope on it to tighten it all up, you'd paint it on to get a smooth surface. We learned how to splice the steel rope, the cables that ran from the control column right through the rudder on the main frame. We had to test all those and we did repairs and inspections – you know, like when you take your car in for a regular check-up.

Alice Bell (Pollitt), an ATS radio mechanic, did the first part of her training at Regent Street Polytechnic and later went on an upgrading course where she was the only woman.

The men did not take me seriously, especially when I could not reach the workbench – I am under five foot three, and the benches had been put in for men much taller than that. A large tool-box was found for me to stand on. Part of the test was to make a box spanner. I was given the number 8 as my identification and when the results were put up Number 8 had the top marks for that section of the course, so I had the last laugh. By the time I went on the second upgrading course I was more readily accepted; I was

31

again the only girl, but I was a Craftswoman Class II and as such had proven my ability.

Gladys King (Yates) was one of the first WAAF mechanics and she, too, recalls outdoing the men she trained with. 'You know when you make a spanner,' she told us, 'there's the grain of the file on the head of the spanner and you're supposed to leave it there? But the men thought they'd be clever and emery-papered it off; so we got full marks and they lost. Yes, we beat them on the practical.'

The men who encountered women learning such unfeminine skills seem to have reacted in a variety of ways, from resentment to simple acceptance. The most common attitude appears to have been one of initial condescension mixed with amused chaffing, turning into approval when it was proved to be deserved.

In June 1943, Barbara Smith (Orme) was one of the first Wrens to be trained as a stoker (up till then women had crewed the boats, but not serviced the engines). Her course involved

practical work on various boats, small petrol-craft, diesel hospital-boats, fishing smacks carrying barrage balloons, etc. The instructors would do what they called 'put crumbs in the engine', and we would have to get them to go again. This first course caused lots of jibes and coarse remarks from the matelots who had never seen a Wren stoker before. It is a tough branch in the RN, and most of us were slightly built.

Margaret Boggis confirms that the first women stokers were something of a novelty.

Though we must have looked awful with navy squares around our heads, the POs and sailors were marvellous to us. There were seven of us at MTE Flathouse. We travelled by bus, arriving at nine o'clock to be greeted by Chief Griffin who lectured us on carburation, lubrication, solid fuel injector pumps and so on. We learned the tag 'suction, compression, POWER, exhaust' or, more succinctly, 'Suck, squeeze, bang, blow'. At 11.30 we broke for lunch. Our quarters supplied us with sandwiches, but the Navy gave us soup and duff which we had to fetch from the galley through the ranks of trainee stokers to shouts of 'Hello, Stokers!', 'Why didn't I join the Wrens?' or 'Look, she's smiling!'

Many of the instructors – who were often NCOs brought out of retirement – are remembered with affection by their former pupils. One Torpedo Wren (whose job included assembling and servicing torpedoes and depth charges) still smiles about the time she

climbed up the rigging to repair a minesweeping light at the top of the mast, not knowing that the ship was berthed under a crane and I should have been taken out on a saddle. After that I learned, of course, and was trained as a crane driver by my Leading Seaman workmate, a marvellous character, a reservist of fifty-one. (He hadn't told me about the saddle because his idea was that I should learn better by making my own mistakes.)

In fact even the grumpiest of old-timers were prepared to concede that women were capable of doing the jobs well; though they might not say so openly. Pamela Burningham worked under a tough old CPO who, to their faces, would say: 'Girls in the navy – whatever next? Flighty young things, can't expect them to do a man's job properly.'

But one day we overheard him and another Chief talking in the Bosun's stores and were surprised to hear him say: 'Don't you criticise them girls. Better than your lads in many ways. Do their jobs well, they do.' So we knew he was an old softie really.

Some women were trained to operate in all-female units. Jean Spear, the refugee from Holland, spent six months at the WAAF balloon school at Chigwell.

The training involved so many skills. Learning all the knots, splicing cables (very hard on the hands), patching balloons. Then came the winch (almost a car, except for the steering-wheel). We were instructed in every detail so that once on remote sites we could maintain and operate the Ford V-8 engine. Then how to operate the winch, paying out to 5,000 feet and bringing it down again. Bedding down and furling fins; no small feat, as these were very large.

Some searchlight crews, too, were exclusively female, but they usually trained alongside men. Kathleen Burton (Batten) 'had been taught the ATS marching style and halt, and when we got to Taunton we had to learn the artillery halt, and you should have seen us falling over each other'.

On searchlights they had to work as a crew of nine. 'We were divided into different groups to learn about the different parts of the lights,' Kathleen explains.

Some learned about Lister diesel engines (they were the ones trained as drivers). Three were trained on radar, how to pick up a plane and follow it on the screen; another had to have good eyesight and learn to do it manually. I was picked to light up the beam and keep it under control with a nice straight edge to it. We had to get inside the lamp and change the carbons ready for use, also practise changing them, leaning on the barrel and using gas pliers to get them out.

According to Freda Spowart (Barlow),

although we had to learn all the jobs we were all given tests and asked our preferences, though not guaranteed to get it. I chose Number 5 and was accepted. This involved getting the beam on target with the help of the radar, the rest of the crew and messages from HQ. It was very hard work and very studious learning all about electricity and maintenance, and a far cry from office work, but I'm proud to say we all passed.

Some Ats, finally – those of the mixed anti-aircraft (ack-ack) batteries – were to work alongside and complement men. Margaret Hunt describes   33 the training as 'arduous and very extensive. I learned how to work a predictor, which was a very large, movable, square-shaped piece of machinery used to feed information to the guns. Our aim was not only to shoot the German aircraft down but to put them off course with our flack.'

The predictor wasn't always available for practice. Then, as Hilda Mason explains,

> a Tate & Lyle sugar-box was mounted on a pedestal and its sides painted with the various dials; this did vaguely resemble the instrument. At times we'd have neither, and the team of six people stood around nothing, thumbs on imaginary buttons or turning imaginary handles, at the same time giving imaginary reports.

During the third month of training they used to go on firing practice, usually at Burrow Head Camp in Scotland. Edna Smith (Bennett) describes how 'a plane would fly past pulling a sleeve, which was a long way back from the plane. The Ats would pick up and get the height, range, etc., and the information would be passed on to the guns who would fire at the sleeve.'

Once their firing practice was over they would go back to their own camp to complete their training and take the final tests.

For women in all the services, to learn that they had passed these tests was a moment of particular pleasure. In all cases it meant a few extra shillings in their pay-packet. For some it led to automatic promotion, to recommendations for commissions, or to offers of jobs as trainers themselves. But what really mattered was the satisfaction of having acquired new skills, many of which had hitherto been considered beyond the reach of women. The day that Alice Bell and her colleagues were entitled to call themselves Radio Mechanics Class III they 'walked down the main road singing "I've got sparks that jingle, jangle, jangle . . ." to the tune of the popular song of that time which was "spurs that jingle . . ." and so on. We were so proud of those red sparks on the right arm for which we had worked so hard.'

How they would cope with the realities of their new jobs is something we will look at in the next chapter.

THREE

On Duty

By the end of the war many of the barriers separating 'men's' from 'women's' work had broken down. Women were ill represented at the higher command levels, it is true, but they had balked at nothing which they had been allowed to undertake.

The nature of this expansion can be illustrated by looking at the increasing number of trades open to members of the WAAF. In the autumn of 1939 there were just five, all of them traditional support services. By the following spring the number had tripled, with women coming in as instrument-repairers for the first time. Three months later there were twenty-six, including instrument mechanics, balloon-riggers and sparking-plug testers. Finally there were over sixty trades open to both RAF and Waaf, from acetylene welder to armourer (guns), clerk (movement control) to draughtsman cartographer, fitter (aircraft) to radar mechanic (computer).

In addition there were about twenty trades open to Waaf only, including some where women had completely taken over from men, usually on a one-to-one basis. And in many highly skilled categories women ended up outnumbering men, or constituting a large minority of the work-force. They formed, for example, 75 per cent of wireless ops, half of all MT and flight mechanics, 45 per cent of radar ops and 33 per cent of radar mechanics.

All three services witnessed this expansion, one which indeed affected officers as well as other ranks. But we have no space to do justice to everyone, and can only hope that the following accounts give some idea of the range of duties undertaken.

Mechanics and Maintenance

Some women mechanics have stories of being treated with suspicion or bemusement at first, though most eventually became accepted.

Wren aircraft checker: We were told to go and check some new American aircraft just in, Corsairs. We sailed into the hangar on our cycles in our bellbottoms, sailor hats and short hair. We asked, 'Are these the Corsairs?' and at the sound of our voices every plane suddenly became alive with American sailors, mouths open. 'Oh, dames!' It was difficult to make them realise we were there to do some serious work.

Jean Spear, WAAF electrician: We were posted to the north of Scotland in January. Men were very suspicious of the two WAAF electricians. So they sent us to a derelict Manchester aircraft minus its perspex. Our task was to strip the conduit; a totally useless job! We were sure it was just dumped after our painstaking efforts with half-frozen fingers to get screws and brackets undone. The aircraft faced the Cromarty Firth, and it was like the Arctic. *[She became seriously ill, recovered then did the group 2 course.]* Passed well and got posted to Church Lawford, near Rugby. Once again men were very much against women technicians, so I landed on the magneto bench. Very boring.

Dorothy Hobson, a flight mechanic (airframe), worked on Oxfords and Blenheims at RAF Grantham: The Flight Sergeant in charge decided to split us three girls and put one in each of three separate groups, which meant that we never had the same day off together. (We worked a rota – seven days on and one day off.) The airmen in our hangar didn't seem very happy to see us, and the Flight Sergeant didn't seem to know what to do with us. Finally I was sent to help an LAC who was taking the tail unit off a Blenheim. I didn't have much to do except pass the right-size tools and run errands to the stores for him, but I learned by watching him work and helped him to fit a new stern frame. I was mostly inside the fuselage holding the nut to stop it turning. I was small, so it was easy for me to fit into small places. . . .

Although we were doing a man's job, and because we were smaller and not so strong as the men, we did some jobs differently. When we had to fit new windows in the cockpit we used less strength than they did and did a good job first time. The men used too much strength and cracked the new panes of perspex/triplex; sometimes they cracked two or three before they completed the job.

Now and then we had to work overtime in the hangar, and on this occasion I was the only Waaf among several men and when we had finished our work we all walked to the cookhouse for a very belated tea. The cookhouse was deserted except for us and one server, and I took my meal and sat down at one of the tables in the Waaf section. One of the men shouted to me: 'Come and sit with us. If you're good enough to work with, you're good enough to eat with.' I picked up my plate and mug of tea and went to sit with them. At long last I felt that they had accepted me as a fellow-mechanic.

After leaving the Repairs Hangar, Vi, Penny and I went to join the other Waafs as it had been decided to have one hangar serviced entirely by Waafs. As we now didn't have any men to help us lift the tail off the floor, we still did it; we bent down on the floor and put our backs under the tail section and it was one, two, three and lift together.

Pat Machray (LACW Moth), flight mechanic (engines): There was no battledress for us, so we had to be kitted out with men's trousers. Being on the short side, they had to be tied up under my armpits and trailed on the ground. I must have looked like Dopey out of *Snow White*. I think that looking like that made the men feel sorry for me, and they taught me a lot about engine overhauls.

When I moved to Moreton-in-Marsh I was attached to a Flight working out on the dispersal, which meant being out in the open carrying out daily inspections (DIs) to check that the engine was fit to fly. This meant responsibility for signing the report sheet (Form 700) to that effect. We were also required to fly with the aircraft on occasion. After experience on Lancasters and Mosquitos I was posted to 11 Operational Training Unit and found myself assigned to a Flight Hut out on the dispersal sites. I was the only WAAF engine mech on the flight and I knew that I had to be as good as, if not better than, the men if I was to be accepted. Although it came hard at times, I had a Flight Sergeant (Chiefy) who seemed determined that I should do so. Working high on scaffold platforms undoing engine cowlings, stripping down components, adjusting and replacing parts was hard enough in the summer, but to change a leaking oil-cooler that had smothered the engine in the midst of winter when you could not feel your frozen fingers was 'no life for a lady'. But I would not have swapped my lot for any other. I suppose we were the closest of all ground crew to those flying – we were dedicated to seeing that the engines which were the lifeblood of the aircraft would not let them down. We watched the pilot run up the engines, verifying that our Form 700 report was justified, an OK thumbs-up, we pull away the chocks from the wheels and wave goodbye.

We worked on three gangs. On training the aircraft are flying round the clock, weather permitting. It was a three-day cycle, one day from eight to six, one day 24-hour shift, third day off duty. The night-flying shift in winter was the worst: aircraft in and out on 'circuits and bumps', being filled up in the middle of the night, crawling along icy mainplanes holding on to frozen petrol-nozzles, filling in hundreds of gallons of high-octane fuel.

I hardly ever saw a WAAF officer at work. One did call at the flight one day and apparently was concerned about conditions for the only WAAF mech, especially as I was doing night-shift with the gang. Chiefy went berserk at her insinuations, and through the Engineering Officer she was seen off with a flea in her ear. In fact I was never more protected in my life than by the boys on shift.

Most flight mechanics, as Pat says, were expected to fly on occasion. Here are two accounts of such flights, one of which ended in disaster.

Maria Narishkin-Dembicki, Wren aircraft mechanic (engines): Armed with the necessary permits, commonly known as 'blood-chits', I presented myself to the Duty Officer seated behind a desk in the corner of the Dive Bombing and Torpedo Bombing Training Squadron hangar, at Machrihanish.

The officer, finding all my 'blood-chits' in order, asked me how much I weighed. I told him that I was not sure, so he had me stand up on to the scale. 'OK. You'll do,' he said to me, and to his assistant he said: 'Enter Miss Ballast one hundred pounds in the log.' 'What does that mean?' I asked.

'You'll see,' said an incredibly tall Telegraphist Air Gunner, leading me out on to the tarmac where several Swordfish biplanes were parked.

'Remove the hundred-pound lead weight. We have a live one in its place,' the TAG said to a mechanic, as he picked me up and plopped me into the rear cockpit, then he climbed in beside me and attached a 'G' string to the back of my Mae West. 'What's that for?' I asked. 'So that we don't drop you somewhere. Wouldn't be very tidy, would it?' he answered.

The pilot was already in the front cockpit, warming up the engine and doing his cockpit checks. When he was ready, we slowly taxied out on to the perimeter track and headed towards the Torpedo Shop where a couple of 'tin fish' were attached beneath the plane.

When we reached the bombing range out at sea, we circled the target a couple of times, gaining height. At the appropriate moment the pilot put the Swordfish's nose down and we began diving at full throttle, wings straining, struts and wires whining and whistling. The G forces almost pushed me down to a sitting position on the floor. I had to hang on to the side of the cockpit to remain standing so that I could see what was going on outside the plane. I felt a sudden jerk beneath my feet as I thought we were about to crash into the water, and the pilot eased the plane upwards and to port, in a banking climb. On the descent my face felt squashed down and pulled out sideways; on the ascent it felt stretched out again.

Our first torpedo missed its mark, so we had to repeat the manoeuvre. The second drop was right on target. The pilot and TAG were jubilant. It was the best practice they'd ever had.

Norah Anderson (Drew) radio mechanic, RN air station, Arbroath: On 2 February 1943, having carried out a routine service and ground test of the wireless equipment as part of the overall servicing of a Walrus seaplane, I went up for a test flight together with a fitter and a rigger who had also worked on the aircraft. We flew out over the North Sea, and I tested the wireless, communicating with base by Morse code. All seemed to be well until the seaplane landed on the water, took off again, failed to gain sufficient height and plunged into the sea.

I remember the noise of the crash, the pain of my head hitting the sea, the terror of hearing and seeing the water rushing into the cabin and the panic of getting to the rear hatch and trying to open it. I never found out the details, but I believe the pilot must have managed to get out and open it from the outside and the next thing was that I found myself in the drink. The plane sank so quickly that the rigger was unable to escape. The water was very cold and fairly rough and, having no Mae West and wearing heavy flying-boots, I found it hard work keeping afloat. The pilot shouted to me, 'Can you swim?' and I replied, 'Yes, thank you, sir – can you?' I remember those words so clearly even after forty-five years, and I even recall thinking that if I had had my hat on I would have saluted him – after all, he was an officer and, anyway, I had been brought up to be polite, courteous and respectful.

Fortunately the local RAF Air–Sea Rescue team must have been following our manoeuvres, because it was quickly out to rescue us from the water – I believe we were about five miles off the coast. I remember being hauled out of the water with the aid of a boathook, my tie being cut off, and the fact that they were using the same type of radio transmitter and receiver as I had been trained on. The launch took us into Montrose harbour, and I recollect being carried ashore wrapped in a blanket and hearing a lady's voice saying in surprise: 'Och, it's a wee girl!' I was taken to the RAF Sick Quarters where I was treated for concussion and multiple bruises and abrasions.

The mechanics who looked after the engines, airframe and electrical parts were vital to the efficient functioning of aircraft. But so were the sparking-plug testers like Ivy Humphries (Smith). A Wellington bomber had twin engines, each with thirty-six plugs all of which had to operate perfectly.

There were six airwomen in plug bay, and we were kept pretty busy. Plugs were cleaned on every routine inspection, after forty hours' flying. As most raids were of eight to ten hours' duration, and approximately ten aircraft on a raid, there was plenty to do. We had three types of plug, KLG, Champion and Bendix, the latter an American plug for the Wellington. Unlike the others, it was not sand-blasted: the centre of the plug was black, and it was fitted into the chuck of a ten-inch lathe and as the plug turned we used extremely fine sandpaper to clean the dirt out. This was what I was doing when I first met my husband. He couldn't believe his eyes!

But not all mechanics worked on aircraft. Jean Rawson (Moir) was a qualified maintenance Wren based at HMS *Attack*, Portland.

As the Wrens Slip Party we were responsible for slipping a 72-foot MTB or MGB. This was done on a cradle that was lowered into the water, and it was up to me as leading hand to get her guided with ropes into the right position. I then operated the hydraulic lift to bring her right out of the water; then with wire hawsers and a donkey engine we had to pull her into a vacant bay where we scrubbed her off from top to bottom. Anywhere where shadow fell was painted white and where light was a blue-grey: the bottoms were done in red anti-fouling. We enjoyed our work, and the Base was always ringing with our singing, all the old Rita Hayworth and wartime songs. Because of our jobs we were allowed to wear bell-bottoms and white square-rig tops, like the men.

Finally, Margery Rosser, a WAAF mechanic working at 61 OTU Rednal, near Shrewsbury, came into closer contact than most servicewomen with the enemy.

One of our jobs was to open up the Spitfires, fill them with petrol and inspect them every morning before the pilots came, and this bitter winter morning – about 7 a.m. – a very sleepy Waaf climbed up to the cockpit of the Spitfire and pulled the perspex back to find a German POW asleep in the cockpit. I, of course, screamed, and I don't know whether he or I was the more surprised. Like our POWs in Germany, he had tried to escape. The petrol-tank was emptied every night, so of course he couldn't fly the machine. He knew he

39

would be caught, so he very sensibly decided to have a kip before he was taken back to his POW camp at Oswestry.

Radar

Radar was developed by Robert Watson-Watt following his classic 1934 paper on 'The Detection and Location of Aircraft by Radio Methods', and in the autumn of 1939 he personally trained the first contingent of WAAF operators. By the time they took up their duties in October a chain of radar stations had been set up, from the south coast to Scotland. The work was highly confidential and, according to Joy Talbot (then Carstairs), they were 'fed tons of carrots to keep up the myth that they vastly improved one's eyesight, to disguise the fact that there was such a thing as radar'.

The south-coast stations were an early target of the Luftwaffe. As a result of such attacks WAAF radar ops were withdrawn from Dover in early August 1940 and posted to Scotland, a move which they resented considerably. But this was the only time that women were given such special treatment. At the peak of the war over 4,000 WAAF officers and airwomen were classified as radar signals officers, supervisors, mechanics and operators.

Joy Talbot describes how radar ops could work closely with pilots without ever seeing them.

> On watch one day we were 'practising' with two Beaufighters for our normal rôle of shooting down enemy aircraft. I was sitting in front of the tube working out the heights of the aircraft which the Controller passed to the 'fighter', and at this time it was 'Angels 9.9'. Suddenly came the voice of the Czech pilot of the 'target' aircraft: 'Check height, please.' This I did and still made it the same, and this was passed back to him. Imagine my amazement when he replied: 'Congratulations, you're bang on!' I never did discover whether the Allies were more polite than our lads, or whether that was the only time I got the height right. Incidentally, we did manage to shoot down forty-nine enemy aircraft!
>
> I remember sitting in a darkened cabin in the middle of a night watch as we sent a Beaufighter after an enemy aircraft, losing contact on the RT and listening to the RT operator calling and calling to try to regain contact, but all there was was silence.

Radar was used to spot the movement not just of aircraft, but also of shipping, which led to the involvement of Wrens, many of whom – like Heather Gibling (Gale) – trained with the WAAF. She eventually trained to become a Fighter Direction Officer (the only Wren officer among forty-five men, two of them captains).

Mollie Crisford describes a group of Wrens undergoing a week's 'radio-location' training in the Chatham 'Tunnel'.

[The officer] showed them the switchboard, manned by a Wren. She showed them how to take an angle and bearing from a given point. She explained how to read a grid position on the map. They were going to be the first Wrens sent to two RAF stations on the coast, to do the radio-location side of plotting. Through the marvels of R–L they would be able to plot the exact position of shipping miles away by watching a ribbon of blue light on a screen.

(She was then posted to the RAF radar station at North Foreland.)

They climbed up to a room in the tower, under the swinging Radar Scanners. It was a small room with a map on one side, taking up half the room, behind which sat the girl on duty, gazing at a square screen . . . [she] would notice an increase in size on the horizontal line of light, known as a 'Blip', then she would turn a wheel that adjusted the huge sweeping sails overhead, until the 'Blip' was at its maximum. Then she would call the girl at the map: 'Read at such and such degrees and so many miles.' The other girl with a ruler on a swivel would mark the place on the map and so be able to trace the progress of planes as they left the coast of France and see where they approached the English coast. There was a direct telephone line to Dover RAF for sending the plots.

One evening an RAF sergeant took the girls to the edge of the cliff and taught them how to fire a rifle and shoot with a sten-gun and throw grenades. They all had their instructions what to do to destroy the radar equipment, if the enemy should invade and capture the equipment.

Finally, Ats working in Anti-Aircraft Command began to use the new system for aiming both guns and searchlights. Elsie Harper was sent on detachment to various heavy ack-ack sites in the Plymouth area.

On site I was responsible for the maintenance and repair of the transmitter and receiver of the Mark II radar which was the main guidance system for the heavy guns. There was some resistance from a few RA Battery Commanders who were almost always astonished to find that their site radar mech was a girl.

Radar at this time was very bulky equipment. The transmitter was housed in a large wooden hut – I would estimate about ten feet by six feet – which rotated so that the huge aerials could transmit in any direction. The receiver some distance away in the field was an even larger rotating box in which four operators worked. Of course this was in the days before transistors, and valves could be very large items. Those in the transmitter were something over two feet tall and could administer a lethal dose of electrical current if touched when the set was switched on. For that reason (as well as for secrecy) the whole of the working parts were behind locked panels, the keys to which could only be used by the radio mech.

Plotters

The plotters formed the link between the radar operators and the officers responsible for ordering the movements of aircraft or ships. By 1940 all Air Force plotters were women. This had been recommended as early as 1936 by Air Chief Marshal Dowding who, thirty years after the start of the war, said that 'Fighter Command relied on the Waaf in the ops room and the radar stations for its very existence, let alone their efficient operation'. This was particularly so during the Battle of Britain, at which time Joan Thrush (Squadron Officer Mullin) was stationed at RAF Wittering.

My duties included plotting the movements of all aircraft in our area, and, on the night that Coventry was so badly bombed, I was on duty at 'the bottom of the table', the 'table' being a very large map of the UK and surrounding waters. I had my back to the Controller, who was in charge of directing our night fighters. It was a very busy night, with unidentified aircraft literally covering the map. One of those that I was plotting was moving rapidly towards Wittering, and the Controller was most anxious to find out whether or not it was friendly. The Observer Corps were unable to help, and as I turned to the Controller to pass on this information there was a massive explosion. Believing the unidentified aircraft to be one of our night fighters returning to base, he had switched on the flare path, and the German bomber – as it turned out to be – was able to pick his targets at random. When we finally returned to our quarters, in the early hours of the morning, we found windows blown in, doors blown off and curtains in tatters. But we cleaned up the mess as best we could, then sat down and, by torchlight, polished our buttons and shoes ready for duty later in the day.

Pat Sparks explains what the routine of an ops room was like:

I worked on a Ground Controlled Interception station. RAF Fighter Command was divided into Groups, Sectors and satellite stations. Bentley Priory at Stanmore was the HQ of Fighter Command, and an Operations Room was set up there by ACM Sir Hugh Dowding. In this Ops room plots were passed by radar stations throughout Britain and also Observer Corps Centres, giving a complete picture of the airways over the country at any given time. Ops rooms were also set up at Sectors and at GCI stations. Plotters were the girls who stood at a table marked with a map, subdivided into grid squares. 'Plots' were passed down the line of command, and from these given positions we placed a metal arrow on the table, giving the fix and directions of a flight. We used metal rods with a magnetic tip, often described as 'croupiers', and kept track of several flights at any given time by moving arrows coloured according to the 'colour change' clock in all Ops Rooms. Each five minutes was divided by red, yellow and blue sections, which then told of any old plots not removed. On busy days we had a monitor who would watch out for this, and also make up the metal plaques which gave the number of the flight ('H' for Hostile or 'F' for Friendly). At Sopley the detail of each flight was also put up on a 'tote' which showed the height, number of aircraft, etc. Above the Ops-Room table was a gallery where the Controller sat watching all movements. We also had cabins where radar screens were operated and our fighter aircraft were controlled from plots on the screen until the Navigator/Radar Op in the plane could see contact on the AI.

We wore headsets with a mouthpiece, like those worn then by telephone operators. These were very unhygienic, and we were supposed to clean them on collecting or returning a set, but the smell of disinfectant under your nose was very unpleasant, so diseases were apt to spread. We worked in air-conditioned rooms which were either underground or supposed to be bomb-proof. None of us was used to the bright strip lighting, nor to complete darkness when on the 'tubes' (radar screens). It was hypnotic watching a beam sweep round, leaving a greenish blip which was a plane (or group of planes). Many of us suffered headaches and eye strain owing to such conditions.

Of course we heard all the RT calls, but at least we knew where our friends were and what they were doing. Like the time Dai had us up a long time at night when his navigation was amiss and he got lost in fog, or Roy pranged his plane on landing. We soon got over our blushes at some of the conversation on the RT, but it wasn't always easy to face the boys after hearing 'my instrument is bent' – which actually meant his radar or AI was not working. We all used RAF slang, of course; everything was 'wizard', a crash was a 'prang', everyone was 'old bean' or was 'browned off' or was 'binding'.

Queenie Stearne, a Wren plotter at Portland Dockyard, says that such work was 'secret and interesting'.

We had signals notifying us of all the shipping expected in the area. The plots were passed with grid references from a nearby radar station, and we moved little model ships along the perspex-covered plotting-table so that the Duty Commander could get a picture of the situation. The decibel response indicated the size of the ship, so there was no danger of confusing a frigate with a battle-cruiser.

Communications

A large number of women were involved in communications, from cypher officers and coders to wireless and teleprinter ops.

Shirley Aston, ATS: We didn't really have a typical day. We'd go on duty, say, from 5 p.m. to 11 p.m., taking our supper with us. Then we'd hand over to the night shift, going on again in the a.m., be off until 1 p.m. the next day, then go on in the afternoon and then all night. When working for an AA group I

43

worked all night; the signals never stopped, and by 3 a.m. you'd feel exhausted, then pick up again.

Eileen Shaw, wireless op, RAF Great Witcombe: We were the control station for a number of stations at home and abroad, and it was here that I was put on a charge. It was Christmas-time and we used to send and receive messages in Morse, but they were also in code. All the other stations were manned by men, and when they knew we were Waaf they used to send TU, which could mean 'Thank you' but in Morse code was X. I had sent a message to a fellow in Africa and ended it with three Xs and thought no more about it. However, the CO was monitoring the messages that day (Christmas Day) and I was hauled up before him. By putting those Xs, the enemy, who were listening, would know that there were women on that station and they would come over and bomb us!

Communications went on round the clock, so most people involved worked a watch system. Ruby Garrett (Sgt Brown) did so for five years in the underground HQ of Bomber Command.

I was already a typist, so after a six-week course I was able to operate a teleprinter and transmit messages to different stations, having learned the various codes and procedures. Once a month I had to sign the Secrets Act Book, as our work was of a secretive nature.

Day 1   8 a.m. to 1 p.m. and 6 p.m. to 11 p.m.
Day 2/3   1 p.m. to 6 p.m. (then PT, square bashing or FFI inspection)
Day 4   as Day 1
Day 5/6   free to 11 p.m., then on duty 11 p.m. to 8 a.m.

On the fifth day we were told to rest ready for night duty, but I'm afraid we usually went off somewhere for the day. We came off duty at 8 a.m. and could not leave until we were relieved.

Pat Pern (Wray), a coder in the Chatham Tunnel, was on the four-watch system: 2 p.m.–8 p.m.; 8 a.m.–2 p.m.; day off; 8 p.m.–8 a.m.

The night watch was deadly; we had one corned beef or Spam sandwich to see us through the night and lots of brews of strong tea. Eight Wrens sat at a bench on high stools coding and decoding all night. Awful! Then back to quarters where we had breakfast which had been cooked at 6 a.m. for those going on watch.

(Mollie Crisford also remembers the 'Tunnel' where she was a coder for a while.)

There were eight Wren coders on each of the four watches, with one Leading Wren in each watch. The Coding Office was always busy and the six-hour watches were pretty strenuous. At night there was a lot of enemy E-boat activity, which kept them frantically coding and decoding signals between attacking ships and the C-in-C. As they prepared to go on duty the Wrens would estimate the weather like a lot of old salts. 'Too windy for E-boats,

Patricia Crossley (*centre*) started as a typist and eventually transferred to Boats Crew, ending as a coxswain. Just before D-Day she became the first woman pilot of HM ships. The main duties of the boats crews were to take mail, stores, signals and liberty men to and from ships anchored in Plymouth Sound.

Wrens practising on the rifle range in December 1940.

A Wren airframe mechanic working on the fuselage of an aircraft. (Photo by Lee Miller)

Pat Machray (Moth) was at first the only WAAF flight mechanic on the flight.

Women of a mixed AA crew operating an identification telescope.

A leading aircraftwoman electrician checking the wiring of a Mosquito engine in 1945.

A WAAF sparking-plug tester cleaning and testing a Lancaster's 96 plugs.

A WAAF flight mechanic screwing up the cowling of a Bristol Beaufighter.

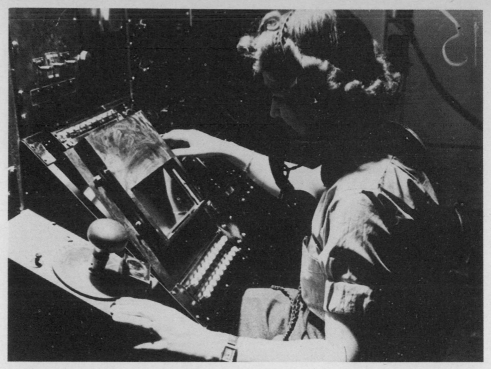

A radar operator plotting aircraft in 1945.

Bombing up. A WAAF MT driver delivering a bomb-train from the ammunition dump, 1944.

Gale Force 8 tonight' or 'Full moon tonight, perhaps we'll have some peace'.
When it was a quiet night they were allowed to 'split the watch', which
meant that four of them could go at midnight to the Moat, which was a
dormitory somewhere in the outskirts of the Tunnel, where they could sleep
on beds for three and a half hours. The second half of the watch was the more
popular for rest, as that meant sleeping until they went off duty at 0800.

The air in the Tunnel was often fetid. There was air-conditioning of a sort,
but when there was an air-raid in progress, and that was often, the air-
conditioning was switched off, to prevent the smoke-screen being sucked
down.

Frances Annett (3/0 Agar Hartley) was one of a handful of Wrens who
went to Washington to work as a coder.

We sailed from Greenock one January morning in 1942 on the RMS *Asonia*.
We were too fast for a convoy and only had air cover as far as it could be
given at both ends. We thought we were the first Wrens to work at sea
because we coders took over the daytime watches with the men.

Anti-Aircraft

If I were offered the choice of a mixed battery or a male battery, I would take
the mixed battery; the girls cannot be beaten in action. In my opinion they
are definitely better than the men on the instruments they are operating.
They are amazingly keen at going into action, and although they are not
supposed to learn to use the rifle they are as keen as anything to do so.
(Commander of first mixed battery to shoot down an enemy plane)

The first mixed AA batteries went into action in the late summer of 1941.
Two years later there were 57,000 Ats in AA Command, the equivalent of
the fighting element of the 8th Army. The women of Anti-Aircraft
Command were especially proud of their close association with the Royal
Artillery and were allowed to wear the grenade badge on their blouses as
well as the white RA lanyard. When on site privates were addressed as
'Gunner' and corporals as 'Bombardier'.

The division of labour was straightforward; the women worked out
where and when to fire and the men did the actual firing. Evelyn
Hambley, an officer who trained in mid-1941, gives an account of the
cumbersome procedure of those early days. An early form of radar known
as 'General Location', or GL, was used initially to track enemy aircraft;
two women then used a 'height-finder' to determine height and range,
which together with details of wind-speed, etc., were passed on to the   49

women operating the predictor. The combined information then went to the Plotting Officer seated in his (later her) underground control room.

The plotting-table was about four feet square with a glass top covering a map of the area, and a single light underneath indicated moving planes. Using the information supplied by the predictor and a slide rule, the PO calculated the anticipated forward position of the enemy planes, which was passed to the gun crews. Night firing was of necessity a hit-and-miss affair!

A more sophisticated combined predictor/height-finder was later introduced, which – together with improved forms of radar – increased the success rate both by day and by night.

Alice Bell started in the ranks and ended up as one of the first ATS plotting officers.

Previously there had been a minimum of three male officers on each site. This was where I replaced a man because the new complement was one ATS plotting officer and two male officers. As well as my plotting duties I had administrative charge of about 1,000 ATS girls.

One of my proudest moments was at the beginning of my time as a PO. I had to take the bearing and range given to me verbally and work out the estimated bearing, angle of sight for the guns, and work out the fuse length. We shot down a plane, and I had worked it out!

Duties were usually organised, as Hilda Mason explains, on an eight-day roster.

Day 1	Full manning, being prepared to go into action any time during twenty-four hours from 1400 to 1400.
Day 2	Fatigues, when we mounted guard during the day, men taking over for the night, swept roads, emptied bins, spud-bashing, washed, dried and ironed the men's football gear, etc. Evening pass until 2259 hours.
Day 3	Half-manning. This meant being a reserve team in case of accident or illness in the full-manning section. The day was spent drilling and attending lectures.
Day 4	For half the section a 24-hour sleeping-out pass, the other a half-pass until 2359, the morning spent doing fatigues.
Days 5–8	A repeat of 1–4 (with second half having 24-hour pass on day 8).

If you were on full manning duty, there was always the chance of a night raid. Then, as Margaret Hunt says,

we threw on our clothes, steel helmets often jammed on top of curlers, and away we rushed to the gun-pits. After a raid was over we couldn't hear for quite a while because of the noise from the guns. I can still smell the cordite in the air and remember the steaming cups of cocoa we were given before returning to a fitful sleep and what was left of the night.

Searchlights

The girls lived like men, and, alas, some of them died like men. Unarmed, they often showed great personal bravery. Like all good things they were in short supply.

GENERAL SIR FREDERICK PILE (AA C-in-C)

The other part of AA Command, the searchlight crews, would also have been in action on nights like those. Training for Ats started in April 1941, and by the end of 1942 the only all-woman searchlight regiment in the world, the 'Famous 93rd', was well established. In fact it was to the women (because of their supposedly more 'delicate touch') that the new 'Elsie' radar system was entrusted.

Freda Spowart was posted

to Bucket Wood, near Watford, a small camp with eleven crew, a cook, corporal and sergeant. I was welcomed into a grand bunch of girls, mostly from Yorkshire, and the very first night plunged into the action of an air raid. There was eleven of us, all girls, under the watchful eye of a woman sergeant. We got instructions from HQ over a field-telephone which was manned night and day. Being in the London area we was out most nights manning the searchlight, and oh! what a cheer would go up when the ack-ack managed to shoot down a plane caught in the intersection of our beams.

Kathleen Burton, of A troop, 93rd Regiment, was a 'Number 5', that is to say, the actual operator of the light and entitled to wear a sleeve badge with the letters SLO (Searchlight Operator). For the first few weeks after her unit arrived on site a male sergeant and private stayed on to show them the ropes, which included demonstrating how to use the machine-gun and rifles. But these were removed when the two men left.

The first thing we had to do was arrange for guard duties; never done any before, so our sergeant said: 'Two girls at the bottom of the field by the road!' People were surprised at seeing girls on guard and remarked on it, too. We wore battledress, brown leather gaiters and boots. What guards we were with no weapons to hold!

Freda's unit was similarly unprotected.

We had a rota for night guard duty. Two each night. We had to man the radio, and every hour one of us had to go down the field to check the generator was working and generally look around to make sure there were no prowlers. Being all girls, we weren't allowed any weapons, so we went around armed with a Tilly lamp and a big stick.

But it wasn't just prowlers who were the danger. A male crew would mount its machine-gun on a tripod ready to use against any attack from the air. Women had to use other tactics, as Freda somewhat laconically relates.

51

I got 2s 6d [12½p] a week extra as my job was supposed to be dangerous. In a way I suppose it was as the Germans would sometimes fly down the beam machine-gunning. At this we would lower the beam to ground-level and swing it round. This would temporarily blind them, coming out of the light into the dark.

But I think the *happiest* moments were when we would get a message for a 'Homer Beam'. This meant one of our gallant airmen was coming in on a wing and a prayer. We would expose the beam, swing it up and down and point it in the direction of the nearest airfield where he could safely land. The feeling of joy we felt when we got word that all was well, knowing that, although we helped to destroy, we could also save life.

Balloon Operators

In the early part of the war women factory workers helped manufacture barrage balloons and WAAF fabric workers were responsible for their repair. In 1941, when so many trades were being opened up to women, it was decided to see how the Waaf would cope with the physically demanding work of handling the balloons on site.

At first it took twenty women to replace a male crew of nine. But this was slowly reduced, first to sixteen, then to fourteen, and finally to twelve. By early 1943, Waaf formed nearly half of all personnel in Balloon Command, eventually taking over all sites.

Phyll Wood (LACW Whitman) served on a sports-ground near the Royal Chelsea Hospital and describes a normal day as starting with

breakfast at 8 a.m. unless you were on early guard duty. Tidy billet, service winch, balloon and cables, splice any ropes or wires needed. Provided all the work had been done, we could relax during the afternoon. Guard duty was done in two-hour shifts, and I used to do embroidery or knit during my evening shifts.

I didn't like night guard duty, armed with a truncheon, torch and whistle, especially when the winch had to be run up every hour in cold weather. I was always terrified to climb down from the winch in case someone had crept on to the site unobserved.

Jean Spear, based near Swansea, didn't like the two-hour night watches, either:

walking in the dark around the balloon, making sure the nose faced the wind. Especially eerie when bedded down in stormy weather it made a 'sighing' noise. We were two per guard and had a whistle and truncheon to protect us. On the 5–7 a.m. guard you had to empty the toilet-buckets and bury the contents nearby, the only times our gas-masks came in handy. Then one of us got the rest a nice cuppa.

To save time it was usual to keep the balloon afloat, but securely fastened. But if it was stormy, as Kitty Reynolds, another balloon operator, explains,

you had to tie it right down and it might take two or three of us hanging on to the tail-guy to steady it. At the back of the balloon there's an open part, near the fins, and I've heard of people going up in it.

When they phoned through to say there was an alert on we'd have to put the balloon up to MOH (maximum operating height). There were eight of us on call and we'd rush out within seconds of being put on alert. One would start up the winch and the others would remove the sandbags and blocks tethering it down. The idea was to force the enemy planes to fly so high they couldn't aim their bombs accurately, but when our own planes were due to come back we'd bring it back down again.

Handling these huge balloons, especially in high winds, was tough work indeed, and some claim to have suffered permanent injury as a result. Kitty thinks she slipped a disc because of it, and Jean believes 'that it was not a good job for females. I've suffered with back trouble ever since. Shifting 120-pound concrete blocks or three 40-pound sandbags at a time was very strenuous, and no helpful advice on the proper way to lift caused damage.'

Motor Transport

Women practically took over many branches of motor transport. They drove everything from motor-bikes to lorries, delivered anything from mail to blood plasma, picked up anyone from top brass to survivors of bombing raids. They drove in all weathers, for hours on end, often in pitch darkness with only their masked headlights to see by. Anyone who still makes jokes about 'women drivers' should read this section and think again.

Eve Sugden, WAAF (Feltwell, Norfolk, 1944): The most recent arrival at the motor pool was greeted with open arms by the last arrival, and I soon found out why. I inherited the 'honey wagon', a Kommer with a strange flat back. In the morning I drove with what must have been two airmen left over from the first war, so decrepit and tattered were they. Our first call was to all the far reaches of the airfield where plumbing was impossible to install. There the men took large clean cans and brought out the full ones. [I used to] drive around the airfield wearing a large handkerchief soaked in perfume and at the sewage plant turned down the only cup of tea in my WAAF career.

[After two months] I did some duty taking the pilots out by bus to the bombers for their nightly raid on Germany. They were gay and joking on the way out. The next morning I picked up the tired, dirty and often injured

53

men who made it back. Sometimes I drove an ambulance which had to find its way across various farm fields to pick up what was left of a couple of aircrews who did not make it through the circle or bump.

(Warmwell, Dorset 1944–5) Later I became the 'Flying Control Driver' at RAF Warmwell, a base used as an emergency landing-field by planes too damaged or with crew too badly injured to make it back to their home bases. This was a 24-hour-on-24-hour-off job and it kept me well away from the motor pool except for petrol and inspections. My vehicle was a tiny Hillman van equipped with a light on the roof that invited the pilots to 'Follow me' or 'Stop'. On the rear flap sat one of the officers from the tower equipped with two large flashlights.

On one particular night in 1944 I was told to stand by as a badly crippled Halifax bomber was coming into our field. The Flying Officer on duty that night and I got into my tiny Hillman and I started the engine. The FO was not too fond of my van, which was apt to stall at the most inconvenient times. He implored me to make sure that it did not stall on this particular night and to 'keep my foot down, no matter what'.

The flare path lit up as the roar of the bomber was heard. I drove to my assigned place, which was right in the path of the plane in order that the pilot could see the lights and be guided by me into a bay made of grass and dirt where ambulances and fire-trucks would be standing by. 'Go!' yelled the FO, following his instructions with a stream of bad language to encourage the van. His blasphemy seemed to get very high-pitched, and I felt that he was being a little more obnoxious than the job usually called for. 'Faster!' he yelled. Well, there was a limit to the speed a 15-hundredweight van would do on a grassy and bumpy airfield in the dark, but I did my best, putting on the 'Stop' light and swerving to the side of the bay as usual. There was quite a thump as the bomber hit obstructions, men in fire-fighting equipment ran and screamed, bodies alive and dead were removed from the plane. My officer, pale and sweating, said: 'All right, let's get back to the tower.' Only when we had parked the van, climbed the stairs and had a hot cup of tea, liberally laced with rum, did he tell me the truth. The Halifax had lost all braking power. Had my van slowed or stopped, we would have met a heroic but untimely death beneath its wheels. My first brush with death had been at the receiving end of a bomb dropped by a German plane. Ironic if I had been run over by 'one of ours'.

Bunty Marshall (Tailby), WRNS despatch rider: I was taking some important documents up to the C-in-C in Edinburgh and I was on the ferry going from North to South Queensferry. There was a crowd of army DRs on the boat, and I went on ahead of them and said see you on the way back. But a light armoured vehicle was overtaking a lorry on the brow of a hill and went slap bang into me. I went through his windscreen and landed up in hospital, luckily with not more than a broken nose and a few scratches, but my despatch-bag never turned up.

Betty Stanbury, ATS: I was given a 15-hundredweight truck to drive. I signed for it and was personally responsible for it. No one else could drive it unless they got permission from the CO. It had no doors, just wrap-around canvas; no windscreen, just two pieces of glass about twelve inches square for driver and front passenger. Had to wear goggles in the winter to protect my eyes.

Peggy Wells, WAAF: Compared with the ATS drivers we were badly done by. All that we had in the way of working clothes, apart from tunic and skirt, was one battle-dress, one greatcoat and – if on tractors – a leather jerkin which was miles too big, so the wind blew through the arm-holes. When it rained your battle-dress would take a day to get wet and a week to dry, so you just wore it wet and it dried on you. . . .

Being drivers, we were called upon for all types of job, such as taking the ambulances to crashes and picking up injured crews. This was sad, especially if you knew them, but you had to carry on. Also you might be called to take more fire crew out if any aircraft were on fire. This was sad, too, if it was burning too fiercely for anyone to do anything, and it could be quite dangerous if bombs were still on board.

Cara Allen (Miller), WRNS, Inverness: The drivers were all sent down to the driving pool and allocated a 3-ton lorry each. Five of us were sent with our lorries to Thornbush to drive for supply. This was a clothing and victualling store housed in an old distillery beside Kessock Ferry. Our duties were to take the Wrens to work there each morning in the back of our lorries, then we would be given our jobs which mainly consisted of going to the station yard with a working party to collect supplies and delivering them to the various stores at Thornbush.

I once drove to Rosyth Dockyard and back in a day, spending the time there driving round the dockyard being loaded and unloaded. I didn't arrive back at the barracks until the middle of the night and was told to report for duty next day, but when I woke up I couldn't open my eyes, so had to report to sick-bay instead. I think it was caused by driving all day in the snow.

In spite of all this we had a lot of fun and felt we were doing a worthwhile job. As drivers we had more freedom than many other categories, as when we were out in our lorries we were in complete charge and no one, not even an officer, could tell us what to do, only where to go.

Wendy Ferguson (Batt), WRNS driver at Newhaven: [After the Dieppe raid] there was a two-mile line of ambulances coming into Newhaven to pick up all the wounded, and I can remember waiting in my Utilicon to pick up the walking wounded; this Canadian sitting on my running-board crying his eyes out, he'd lost his best friend, all their rifles had broken, it was my first sight of troops coming off the battlefield, shut up in the boats, all lying dead all over the boats. . . . There was one young woman, very pregnant, looking out to sea, and the padre I'd run down to the dock said to me: 'I've got to tell her . . . her husband's been killed.' Then later on I took him out to the cemetery where all the chaps were being buried, and the young girls, widows of the men who had been killed, looking about eighteen, nineteen – so young.

One [senior officer] expected a Wren driver to collect him at 6.30 a.m. and drive him up to the top of the Downs to do his keep-fit exercises. He was keen on bridge, so he used to go to someone's house for dinner and bridge and keep you waiting till 1 a.m. Sometimes he'd say you could sit in the kitchen, sometimes he'd say go off and come back in two hours' time. This happened once and I had exactly enough for a half-pint of beer which I had to sit nursing all that time.

Once I had to take a ship's engine from Newhaven to Dover in the *Utilicon*, and the skipper said, 'Come down and have breakfast,' and what did he give me? A full glass of gin! I thought I was going to have bacon and eggs.

Boats Crew

There was one form of transport reserved for Wrens, as members of boats crews. This was a category introduced in 1941, and the first Wrens to work on boats usually had experience of sailing or cruising already. Eventually there were all-female crews including, as we have seen, stokers responsible for engine maintenance.

Pat Konig (Chadwick): One afternoon in 1943 when I was coxswain of a small motor-launch, I and my crew of one, Wren Barbara Kneebone, were on our way down-river to pick up some chippies from a trawler moored in the River Dart. We got alongside and were waiting for the shipwrights to collect their tools when we heard a noise that sounded like machine-gun fire. We thought it must be practice and got on with our job, but the chippies had recognised enemy planes and were lying flat on the deck of the trawler. It didn't take long for us to take the hint, which was just as well as there were six enemy planes overhead. In a few moments we felt the blast of a bomb much too close to be comfortable. We looked up and saw that a large collier lying astern was sinking, with her crew floundering in the water.

We jumped into our launch and set out to help. The crew of the collier were hanging on to anything that was still floating. Everything and everybody was black with coal dust, and you could hardly distinguish men from driftwood. There was a crane alongside the collier which was rapidly sinking, and our chief fear was that some of the men would be crushed by it. We worked furiously to help them aboard the launch, which was constructed to hold no more than eight people. In next to no time we had double that number on board. Naturally enough we shipped a lot of water and the engine got soaked and wouldn't start. Another small boat came alongside and took off the worst of the wounded. All this time the crane was slipping, and soon we had to abandon ship and climb on to a fleet minesweeper. This was herself in a pretty damaged condition; in fact we could feel her sinking as we went aboard her.

After about twenty minutes two MTBs appeared. Barbara went in one, I in the other each with over twenty survivors. Some of the men were pretty badly hurt, and we had plenty of opportunity of putting our first-aid knowledge to practical use. Eventually we got ashore. The wounded were driven off in ambulances, but we had to walk a mile back to our base. Everything had happened so quickly that we had quite forgotten about the coal dust. Barbara was a natural blonde, but there were people ashore who didn't recognise her, as by this time she had acquired the colouring of a brunette, and a pretty dark one at that.

My first duty on getting ashore was to report to the Commander that I had lost my boat. I won't repeat what he said.

Pamela Burningham, HMS Abatos, *near Southampton:* Our main duty was to take any of the Captains and other officers out to ships, to other bases or across to the Isle of Wight – this was undoubtedly our favourite trip. We used to land our passengers at Ryde or Cowes, from where they would go by car to the south of the island, leaving us to amuse ourselves for the rest of the day . . . but by no means all our days were spent in this happy lazy way. There was a lot of scraping, painting, scrubbing, polishing, etc., to be done on the boat between trips, and in the winter months with rain, snow and ice on the boat and the bow and stern lines frozen solid life could be hard.

To start with we had a male coxswain, a very nice leading hand called Nobby Clarke. He had been through some bad times, surviving being torpedoed on a Russian convoy, so he was given this easy job for a while. His mates used to call him Wren Clarke and tease him about being with the girls. But this soon stopped, and I think he quite enjoyed it in the end. We certainly respected him, and there was a good friendship between us all. He used to stick up for us if the matelots said anything against our work.

Later she was part of an all-female crew, including PO *'Jimmy' Edwards. See Barbara Smith, below.* One winter's day we had to take the LCP out into the Solent to collect an officer off a ship – a frigate if I remember correctly. The weather was awful, strong winds and the rain was blowing sideways. We ploughed out to the ship and as I was deckhand I was well wrapped up in oilskins and sou'wester as I struggled to stay upright on the foredeck and hang on with my boathook. As soon as the officer was aboard I stowed my hook and nipped down under the canvas cover as quickly as possible. The lieutenant was busily removing his wet raincoat when he suddenly saw [our dog Susan] at his feet. Turning around he next saw that the deckhand was a girl and finally – to his horror, judging by his expression – that the helmsman was a helmswoman. I swear his face turned white for a moment or two. He'd been out East since the beginning of the war, had never heard of Wren boats crews and just couldn't believe his eyes.

Barbara Smith: I was assigned to the Maintenance Yard's crew, nominally under the Engineer Commander, but our real boss was a remarkable woman, Petty Officer Leticia Edwards, known to everybody as 'Jimmy'. She held a Master's Ticket and was a fine yachtswoman and, it was rumoured, had been the only woman on a tea-boat in China! At all events, she was far more qualified than most of the men and everyone respected her. We were often rebellious and cheeky, but we did come to work hard and long hours, and because of Jimmy's expertise we were called upon to do some unusual jobs, being called out at all hours to slip craft, often tied up three abreast, from the inside and getting them halfway up the slipway before the CO realised it was happening.

Barbara Edwards (Martin) became a PO writer, then a coxswain and ended up as a Boarding Officer, taking secret orders to merchant vessels: It was hair-raising sometimes, especially when there was half a gale blowing and one had to get from the drifter's deck via rope ladder to the merchant ship, often having to more or less leap across. . . . While on board an American Liberty ship the ladder had apparently been loosened while I was with the captain, so I fell twenty-four feet to the deck of the drifter. I spent three months in a plaster jacket and then went back on duty, none the worse! While I was in hospital the Americans were incredibly kind and generous. Every ship that came into the anchorage sent one or two of their officers to see me, always laden with gifts of cigarettes, *steaks*, etc., which of course we never saw in wartime. I had a wonderful interesting job, although very hard work – sometimes we were at sea for fourteen or fifteen hours waiting for convoys to arrive.

Patricia Crossley (Turner)'s main duties as a coxswain of the Wren in 1943 were to take mail-stores-signals and liberty men to and fro from ships anchored in Plymouth Sound and the Hamoaze.

One summer's day we took the British Liaison Officer out to meet four American destroyers who had arrived in this country for the first time. As we approached the ships, a look-out in the bridge had obviously realised 'it was girls' – a second pair of binoculars appeared followed by a telescope! By the time we got alongside, the entire crews of the ships must have been in the upper decks including the cooks. After five minutes I was asked to 'lay-off' as no work was being done on board!

Clerical Various

Being a clerk (or 'writer' as it was called in the WRNS) may not have had the glamour of some of the other jobs, but it was vital work and many of the women doing it were entrusted with the most confidential information.

Jocelyn Weale (Weeks), personal stenographer to Admiral Sir Percy Noble, C-in-C Area Combined HQ, Western Approaches: Amid the routine office work I did for Admiral Noble I can remember vividly some particular episodes. One of these was a post-mortem on a badly mauled Convoy. It had suffered so much and had lost an escorting aircraft-carrier that it was decided to have all the reports from the escort-ship commanders taken down in shorthand and transcribed to be studied for future guidance. I had all the corvette captains' reports to take down: the COS and other Staff were assembled in the Conference Room and I wrote solidly all the hot afternoon. It was not a very encouraging story, and I thought that after nights and nights of attacks and under great strain the corvette commanders had done very well to get out such lucid and detailed reports.

Waaf Corporal. The last Waaf to leave the War Room. Duty typist 1943–6: The War Room was a strange place to be in. Show your pass, through corridors, down stairs, through more corridors. I started in the Registry, where all the mail and signals came in and were passed around. In this area at night the résumé of the twenty-four hours' events was run off and dispatched to all senior officers, plus Churchill's War Room.

Moving along the room was the duty officer and duty typist. Next the officers in direct communication with Bomber, Fighter and Coastal commands, with a WAAF typist alongside each, scrambler phones, etc. Then the bottom room was the Middle East and Far East.

The Duty Officer sifted through all the information from Photo Recces, U-Boat sightings, fighter and bomber raids and casualties. When all was prepared the Duty Typist had to type stencils of all gen. There were many nights when all was held up waiting for the final casualties – one hoped enough room was left and that casualties were not too bad. Then the Duty Sgt would run off the stencil on the Gestetner machine and Registry would be a hive of industry, folding and sending the envelopes to the required areas. Off-duty, up into the fresh air and breakfast back at the hostel.

Ellen Jackson (Knowles), clerk at RASC Command Supply Depot: This was where all the troops stationed in the surrounding area came to draw food rations and petrol. Food was issued on three days a week, and an NCO from each unit brought in an indent for the food required on the following issue-day. This gave the number of men in the unit, and my job was to work out their entitlement of the basic foods in accordance with the army ration scale. Initially I worked with a corporal and a private, but after a few weeks the corporal went to OCTU and the private was promoted in his place. After about a year he was posted overseas, I took his place as corporal and a private soldier took my place. We really felt we were taking the men's places so as to release them for overseas service.

Elsie Vernon (Evans), WRNS. Supply Branch: The work was mainly clerical, keeping a check and a financial record of the supplies of clothing (or 'slops') and various items which the sailors were allowed to buy four or five times a month. On these days the clothing store was open for most of the day, with long queues of sailors waiting outside to take their turn buying socks, underwear, naval jumpers, soap, etc.

We all enjoyed these 'slop days', exchanging banter with the sailors, with our POS standing by to keep the ratings in order. I can smile at it now, but I can still remember the ordeal it was for a young inexperienced Wren coming back from an early lunch and having to pass a queue of thirty or forty sailors waiting for the stores to open. They were always very free with their comments, as you can imagine.

59

On Duty

Dorothy Osbon, Waaf, MT storekeeper: Sometimes the MT people would come in for spare parts of lorries or cars, or the Motor Repair Transport section would come down for spare parts. If they were on a special job, I would walk up to their section to see what work was involved as I was responsible for getting all the spare parts. We had our own transport section, but the sergeant before I got there would dive in the stores, get the part required and put the old one in its place, so things were in a bit of a mess, piston rings all over the place. . . . so I decided to go through every spare we had. I worked every weekend except when I had to go on church parade.

I started going on convoys to collect my own spares, to other RAF stations and the various firms. I got to know the parts numbers so I could tell which vehicle they belonged to, and an instrument was bought for me so I could measure the thou of the various piston rings. Then I started keeping engines, and while I was there no one wanted a thing. I got on well with the firms, and they never let me down, even if it meant taking a spare off their own vehicles.

It was some of our vehicles that was used in August '43 for the invasion of Sicily when the Argyll and Sutherland Highlanders went in. I always remember them saying to me think about the types, they'll be landing on sand. I ordered the spares, typed out the demands over the weekend, my SL just signed them. They were a grand lot of people, they would never let you down. After the war one of the firms offered me a job. My Squadron Leader wrote a letter for me, but I couldn't take it as my mother was ill.

60

FOUR
Spit and Polish

Our quarters ranged from Nissen huts, bitterly cold in the winter, sometimes wooden huts, a little better, to the grandeur of Inverclyde Castle on the shores of the Clyde at Kilgreggan. Later, after D-Day, we were in requisitioned semi-detached houses with a proper dining-room, had a bedroom with two or three of us sharing, cooks and orderlies to look after us. Very civilised.

BETTY STANBURY, ATS driver

Not many servicewomen lived in such a variety of quarters as Betty Stanbury, but her experience gives a good idea of the range available.

Castles, it must be admitted, were rare; though Dora Sibley (whom we first met joining the WAAF as a cook) ended the war as a squadron officer running a WAAF convalescent home at Dungaven Castle, the home of the Duke of Hamilton.

It was more common to be billeted in private homes or in a hotel or other large building taken over for the duration. This seems to have been usual for Wrens, especially those posted to ports and other sea-side towns. Barbara Smith describes how a large family house might have two dozen Wrens packed in, which meant that 'the amenities became very stretched. In the evenings when one was off duty, because the hot water was critical, there would be two in the bath, one on the loo, and another washing at the sink – there was simply no privacy if we had to keep our "dates" and be clean.'

At the very start of the war, however, private accommodation was not immediately available, which explains why the first Wrens were usually 'immobile' (that is, living at home and serving within easy travelling distance). This was the case of Barbara Edwards, mobilised in December 1939. According to her, 'there were no WRNS quarters then, so unless one lived where there was a base there was no hope of joining up.'

Such solutions were not possible in camps situated away from towns. The 700 or so Wrens stationed on the island of Hoy, in the Orkneys, slept 'thirty-two to a cabin', Nancy Hammond (PO Drew) tells us: 'all on various watches. Always being woken up, or beds pushed around by Wren cleaners while we were sleeping during the daytime.'

These living conditions, though relatively rare in the case of Wrens, 61 were common in the two other women's services. Most lived in the sort of huts which they had first encountered during training. Paula Irwin, a WAAF accounts clerk, describes the one to which she was assigned on her first posting as

> an exact replica of the one [at initial training camp] except that at Weeton, being permanent staff and not rookies, we now had a tall green metal locker each. In there we could hang our uniforms and keep all our kit. Underneath each bed we also had a 'bomb-box', a large, heavy, lidded wooden case with rope handles at each end. In these we kept our bulky extra kit such as gasmask, tin hat and rolled-up oilskin gas-cape and ground sheet.

Women often tried to make their living-quarters a bit less bleak. Eileen Cavey, a WAAF clerk in the Master Provision Office at Stafford, says that

> it was only the girls I shared the hut with that made life worth living. There were thirty-two of us. At first we had bunk beds and the place was a mess. We managed to make things cleaner after a lot of hard work, but the walls and paint were awful. Then someone had the bright idea to redecorate the hut, so we all put two shillings [10p] into a kitty, I think it was. We painted the walls a nice cream; the doors and windows were an awful green, so we painted them a milk-chocolate brown and it looked great. . . . Hut 52 was mud in the rest of the camp as the CO got to hear of what we had done and issued paint to all the huts and they had to paint their own huts. But we never got reimbursed for what we had paid out.

It was possible to brighten up the huts, but there was not much they could do about the intense cold. Eileen, a Roman Catholic, would hide two buckets on her way to mass on Sundays, then fill them up with coal from the coalhouse. 'We used to have a gorgeous fire on Sundays,' she says. 'I did that for months and months! I told the priest, "I'm a thief," and he said – he was a lovely Irishman – he said: "Good for you. I hope you fill the buckets right to the top!" He really didn't blame me as the winters were so cold.'

Indeed they were; that of 1939–40 being the coldest for some fifty years. A Wren writer stationed at the former Butlin's camp at Skegness in that winter remembers 'trying to type with woollen jumpers and woollen jacket over that and then a greatcoat, all wrapped up with blankets. And it's the first time I ever tried to type with gloves on.'

Babs Howard was one of twenty-five Waaf to a hut at No. 16 MU, Stafford: 'We weren't allowed to light a fire until 5 p.m., with the result that we used to go to bed early if we weren't going out, tie our scarves round our heads, wear our gloves, have our greatcoats draped over our beds.'

The Ats were no better off. Shirley Aston remembers that the stove in her hut was only allowed to be lit so many times a week and we had bare lino floors over concrete, and when we woke up in the morning our face-washers would be frozen solid. If we could get round the cook, he would fill our hot-water bottles, but the MO said we would all suffer from rheumatism when we got older (I do). These same huts were condemned as unfit for human habitation when squatters moved in after the war.

Washing and lavatory facilities were rarely satisfactory. It was all right, Alice Bell tells us, if you were in a 'Spider' hut, that is, if there was a central 'ablutions' unit linked to the surrounding huts by covered passages. But that was rare. Alice's hut at the army camp at Weybourne

had a door at one end only; at the other end there was just a space where a door should have been fixed. The huts were not properly finished. I leave you to imagine how cold it was. When we got up we had to go out into the cold to go to the ablutions hut to get dressed (i.e., we had to undress again to wash and get dressed again).

'We had to go out into the open in all weathers to the ablutions, which wasn't funny,' Ruby Garrett (Sergeant Brown) tells us. 'Invariably the blockwould become flooded through blocked drains, or plugs were missing from basins. I learned to carry my own plug with me.'

But for those posted to camps just being set up the facilities were even more primitive. Molly Gale remembers that on arriving at Burrow Head, the 2nd HAA Practice Camp, 'I was taken to my billet, a bell tent (lucky I'd been a girl guide); contents, duck board, bed and soldier's box. We were under canvas from May until the October, the men in huts. The worst horror was the canvas latrines.'

These left a strong impression on Betty Stanbury, who explains that

Burrow Head was a camp for male troops only. We Ats had no facilities for washing or toilets. Eventually we got enamel bowls for washing ourselves and makeshift toilets – pails with a seat on top and canvas staked out all round them; all right until the sun shone, then anyone using them was silhouetted against the background, so they had to paint the canvas black.

Grace Houghton writes that facilities were just as primitive at Marchwood 128 AA Battery.

After many weeks we moved into huts but still had to wash outside in a wash-house in really cold weather. Toilets were four posts with sacking. When the sun shone your shadow could be seen, and one morning the wind was so rough a post fell down and left one of the Ats sat on the throne. What a cheer went up from the gunners!

According to officers and NCOs from whom we have heard some women had to be persuaded to use the facilities at all. Evelyn Hambley, an ATS subaltern, says that

Hygiene was often a problem and the lack of a plug the excuse for not bathing. At one time it was mandatory for weekly head and foot inspections to be carried out, and this I found invaluable, plus compulsory baths and showers which ensured that the water-shy maintained a decent standard.

Another mandatory weekly event, at least in the WAAF and ATS, was when the whole hut had to stay in and spend the evening cleaning and mending; something referred to in the WAAF as 'domestic night'. In the case of Ivy Roberts (Sergeant Johnston) it was on a Monday

> when the hut had to be cleaned from top to bottom and we would be inspected. We all had our own little domestic jobs to do; I think the biggest problem really was getting enough hot water for bathing, washing clothes and getting them dry; and about our ironing, never an iron, and we weren't allowed to bring one from home.

'We had our cleaning night of a Thursday,' says Dorothy Osbon. 'Our floors polished and the kitchen tiles washed, the table scrubbed. We found the best way to do this was to take off our clothes but keep on our vests and pants. The station officer was French. I don't know what she thought of it when she came round on inspection.'

Lilian Shattock confirms that in the warm weather in every hut you could see 'girls in their undies (not glamorous) polishing floors, windows, black-leading combustion stove, whitening hearth. This was done on inspection nights once a week. Hut didn't pass satisfactory it meant no weekend passes.'

Dorothy Hobson still can't understand why they had domestic night and the airmen didn't, an opinion shared by former ack-ack signaller and fellow-Australian Shirley Aston:

> One of our problems when stationed in Bath was that we had to spend one night a week doing mending, etc. One of our precious nights off wasted – as if women needed time off for that, they'd be much more efficient at looking after their uniform than men (no doubt another idea of some female officer – they certainly knew how to pick them).

It seems clear that women, however demanding and tiring their duties, were expected to spend more time generally on 'housework' than men. Marjorie Nott recalls with evident annoyance that 'the polished floors had to be bumpered [polished] every morning after a night bind [night duty]. The bumpering was always done by the Waafs, and these bumpers were quite heavy when we felt tired.'

And one can imagine what the women thought of the extravaganzas of 'bull' demanded when the camp was to receive a visit from a VIP. On one occasion Shirley Aston and her mates

> were confined to our Nissen hut for a week on a splurge of cleaning and polishing as the Princess Royal was making a visit to our camp. We were furious as our spare time was limited, owing to our 24-hour shift-work. We had to paint jam-tins, rocks, etc., and were tickled pink when a lady-in-

waiting to HRH picked up one of the jam-tins and became covered in red paint. We heard from various sources that the Princess was appalled at our living conditions, especially the state of the kitchen.

One wonders if the visit led to any changes in what went on in the kitchen, since it is rare to find much in the way of praise for the food they had to eat in the services. Mary Palmer says that the food served in the WAAF was 'indescribable'.

There was plenty of it, but the cooking and the way it was served up was awful. Eggs were fried on the top of the huge black-leaded stoves so they had hard black bottoms and hard yolks. Everything was oozing in grease. The broad beans were cooked in their pods, dirt and all. We almost lived on bread and margarine and jam at teatime with the inevitable fruit-cake and Swiss roll. On entering the cook-house the smell put us off before we got to the food. The duty officer used to come round and see if there were any complaints, but we soon gave up complaining. The bins for pig-swill were chock-a-block with our leftovers. There must have been the fattest pigs in being around our camp.

Babs Howard got short shrift when she complained about the food.

I was the only Waaf in the squadron orderly room at Stafford and next door was the Squadron Officer i/c. I cannot remember her name, but she had been a cook. We had a separate cook-house for Waaf and apparently there had been much wastage of food, particularly bread, so she ordered that we have 'tact' biscuits instead. The following morning I was moaning to the Flight Sergeant, Corporal and Warrant Officer, and they egged me on to go and knock on the Squadron Officer's door. Without thinking I went and knocked; she called 'Come in', 'Yes, Howard, what is it?' I said it was about having no bread for tea the previous evening and how hungry everyone had been. To this she replied: 'I am very glad you were hungry, as there are thousands starving in Europe.'

Complaints, as well as rarely being of use, could get the complainant into trouble, as Mary Winter explains.

The food continued to be appalling, the cooks seemed to ruin what we did have. One day one girl, braver than the rest, answered back when the WAAF officer came round and asked if there were 'Any complaints?' 'Ask the fish, ma'am,' said Biddy. 'It speaks for itself.' Needless to say she got jankers, too. There wasn't much you could do about stoking up with food elsewhere; there was the Naafi, of course, where you could get tea in your mug and a slab of Sorbo gingerbread, but not much else unless you had the money to pay for it.

But it sometimes worked. Dorothy Osbon writes that at one camp in South Wales

when we first went there the food was not all that good; then one very hot day they dished up mince [and] the men decided not to eat it, so the next day it was dished up again. There was nearly a riot, but it got thrashed out and things improved so much in the later years some men went up for second lunches.

There are one or two references to very good food, prepared by professional cooks, but the best that can normally be expected is a sort of back-handed praise. Ruby Garrett describes the food at Bomber Command HQ as

quite good considering, but we lived mainly on baked beans for night duty or tinned herring or cheese, with tins of sometimes rancid butter to spread on the bread. Often we would come off nights after having beans during the night and find it was on the menu for breakfast. Still, on the whole we couldn't grumble; we were better off than some others.

Service personnel have always grumbled about food and probably always will. But many of the cooks from whom we have heard had their complaints as well. Some, like so many women, were just plunged into their duties at the beginning. Brenda Stirling, a Fany/Ats, was called up the day before war broke out. 'Imagine my feelings,' she says, 'arriving a young nineteen-year-old, with a petrol cooker to cook on and nobody to tell me how many there would be for lunch and no sink to wash in!' According to Grace Houghton, conditions were much the same well into the following year.

Our day began at 6.30 till eight or nine at night. This was in 1939 and late 1940; as more ATS came in the hours were cut down. We had a large old black range and four boilers outside for veg and tea. We used to hate dinner-time, for the officer and sergeant on duty used to ask for any complaints; always someone stood up, and the officer used to taste, and if he didn't like it we were in trouble, and as we were learners this often happened, but in the end we won over. Until the cook-house was built we made do with field-cooking, very large boilers for veg and stew, then clean them out to make tea in.

Things could be just as bad in the WAAF, as Gabrielle Reilly says.

We would wear clogs in the kitchen because of having to wash the floor down all the time, and thick white overalls and white turbans round our heads. The old range was a devil to light in the chill of the early morning, and there was a horrid coke-fired copper, and at the end of the day shelves and tables to scrub clean and brush the cockroaches out of the way; the kitchen, one way or another, was more like a battlefield, really.

We have heard from former Wrens, too, who were unhappy with their food and eating conditions. But their complaints were probably less justified than those from Ats and Waaf, as we can see from accounts by Wrens who experienced at first hand life in the other services. Mollie Crisford, during her time with the WAAF, was surprised to be

issued with a mug, knife, spoon and fork and taken into the mess for the midday meal. The mess was a great contrast to the one at Pembroke House.

Bare trestle tables and benches, and by the serving-tables two buckets, one for left-overs (as the cooking was poor, this was quickly filled) and one filled with water to rinse one's cutlery in before taking them to the washroom for a better cleaning.

When she rejoined the WRNS it was 'a joy to have white table cloths again, laid with clean cutlery and *tumblers* to drink from. The supper was well cooked and tasty.'

Heather Gibling was seconded both to the WAAF and to the ATS, and was equally thankful to get back to the WRNS, as these extracts from her wartime diary show.

To Yatesbury for radar training with the RAF . . . [later] . . . Grand to be back with the Navy again. Wren quarters are all up on the hill behind the town, in lovely big houses with gas fires in the rooms, chests of drawers, soft blankets. Talk about lap of luxury (as compared with the RAF!). Waited on at meals, flowers on table, new bread, officers very kind and everyone friendly. . . .

Went over to ATS OCTU and froze! No heating, no fires, trekking between blocks in the rain, vast dingy mess, no service. Thankful to get back to Framewood.

So conditions did vary between the different women's services. What all three had in common, however, was a life governed by rules and regulations. And though the need for discipline was generally accepted – theirs was a generation brought up to do as they were told, after all – there was much to surprise and annoy the servicewomen of wartime Britain.

Discipline

The trivialities of discipline were very exasperating. The rule 'Hats must be worn at all times except when going to the mess' was particularly maddening in summer. The radar-manning hut was just outside the main camp, across the lane in fact. One beautiful evening my friend and I were returning to the hut for duty and we took a chance carrying our hats in hand. As luck would have it, the RSM came along. He, of course, did not close his eyes to such a cardinal sin and we duly received seven days' extra duties. Extra duties, indeed, when our days were fully occupied from reveille to lights out!

SADIE NIAS, ATS

Sadie Nias's attitude is typical of many, particularly those who served as 'other ranks'; in other words who had no authority over fellow-service-women. They were proud to be serving their country and were prepared to work long arduous hours, to face danger if necessary (Sadie was radar operator on an ack-ack battery after all), but they resented what she calls the 'trivialities' of discipline; above all, when they felt they were not in the wrong or when a superior pulled rank in an unreasonable manner.

Wendy Ferguson used to get 'a bit bolshie' about silly little things, such as when she was walking with a bundle of parcels and a Wren officer accused her of not saluting. So she dropped the parcels and saluted. 'That's the sort of thing that annoyed me,' she says. 'Some women made marvellous officers, but others thought they were the Queen!'

Some officers, indeed, would have put her on a charge for failing to salute; which is what happened to Connie Poolman when she had only been in the ATS for a month or so.

> One day I was walking to the YMCA when a voice called me to stop. It was an ATS officer and she told me I had failed to salute her (I explained that I had not seen her, but that was no excuse), that my skirt was too long and my hat was not on straight. I thought my hat looked better on one side but knew better than to say that.
>
> Next day a sergeant came and told me to put on my hat and come to an office. There was an officer there and two other girls. One of these two stood in front of me and one behind me. Then the officer said: 'Prisoner, remove your hat.' I did nothing, and the officer repeated the command. When again I did nothing I was told I must remove my hat. Then I realised *I* was a prisoner. I was very alarmed. What was going to happen? I had been told nothing before about the possibility of being taken prisoner. Would I go to prison? The officer read out the charge, that I had failed to salute an officer and been improperly dressed. To my relief I was not sent to prison, but sentenced to three hours' extra duty for a week. This meant peeling a great many potatoes.

The chance of getting 'jankers', as this kind of punishment was called, was greater if you served on a big station. Mary Palmer recalls that when she was at Cranwell, an officer training unit then as now, they had more than their fair share of saluting to do 'as no matter where we went on the camp we would always see officers'. Florence Richter, stationed at Medmenham, agrees that 'on a big camp there were always problems. Discipline was strict as security was so important. There were more officers and NCOs than other ranks and there was always someone on a charge, mainly for minor offences.'

On smaller stations things tended to be more relaxed. Kathleen Burton, of the Famous 93rd, says that she 'would not have liked to be on a large camp with all the discipline and saluting . . . but on site we were on our own and only saw our officer on pay-day.'

The more officers and NCOs there were around, the greater the chances were of being pulled up for something to do with personal appearance. Hair had to be well off the collar, make-up had to be discreet, jewellery

The Princess Royal inspecting a barracks in 1943.

Kit inspection at the 7th heavy AA Training School, Oswestry, October 1941.

Eileen Scott-Martin (then Sgt Flynn of the ATS Provost Corps) (*left*) with a colleague and two US Army MPS.

An ATS provost sergeant adjusts the armlet of a corporal at the South Eastern Command Training Centre in September 1941.

Eileen Scott-Martin (before she joined the Provost Corps) cooking porridge in an Army field kitchen early in the war.

WAAF cooks with part of the morning's work ready for dispatch from a central food factory.

limited to engagement or wedding rings, clothing to be neat and clean, buttons and badges polished daily. (On Margaret Hunt's camp they were expected to clean and polish their boots and shoes underneath as well as on top.) The experiences described by Claire Lowry (Turner) were fairly typical.

> Throughout my time in the Wrens I was constantly in mild trouble with the officers. I wore my hair in a wavy bob, but it didn't matter how I tried, my troublesome hair always seemed to be a half-inch off my uniform collar. Occasionally I wore pink nail-polish and felt like making up with brilliant lipstick. These excesses were against the rules, and sure enough a PO Wren would spot me and report me to the Wren office. Called to the office, I would stand on the square of carpet, to be thoroughly told off and perhaps lose a few privileges.

Women had to spend a lot of their spare time looking after their uniform and the rest of their kit. It was difficult to get things dried and ironed, while the stiff starched collars were a particular problem. According to Jean Spear:

> if you really wanted your clothes cleaned and dried properly, some of the time you took them to the Chinese laundry – there was always one in the nearest town. I only got – what was it? – 7 or 14 shillings a week, and you had to pay for that yourself. That never came out of the Air Force funds at all.

Sometimes clothing and other kit went missing, and that was considered a particularly serious offence. As Ivy Roberts says:

> To lose equipment was something you never allowed to happen and, as for ruining it, you might as well shoot yourself first. I remember one time I had been on sick leave and when I had gone some of my laundry had not come back, so I asked the girl in the next bunk, my friend, to keep an eye on it until I got back. When I did it was missing; she didn't know where it was. I was furious; I would have to pay for it for starters, so I made the whole hut turn their kit out – by this time I was a corporal and felt I could do this – and my friend had most of my things and the girl opposite the rest. It didn't happen again.

Such petty theft appears to have been far from uncommon (though it was very rare to find a friend involved), but to have had an item of kit stolen was no excuse. You were held personally responsible for everything issued to you and had to make it good if it went missing, whatever the reason.

Freda Spowart was dismayed to discover, when about to leave the local pub one evening, that her greatcoat had gone.

> I was going on leave the next day, but that was cancelled after the sergeant had reported it and I was told if it wasn't found within twenty-four hours I'd be put on a charge. Thankfully the landlord came up with it the following

71

day, saying an American had taken it for his girl to go home in because she was cold! So I was able to go on leave, but it was a mad rush to get my buttons and badges cleaned or I would have been on another charge if an MP had seen them dirty.

Another At, Grace Houghton, describes how her hat was stolen at a dance.

I came back to camp on a bus and a redcap [military police] Ats made me put on my tin hat as she said I was not dressed right; I caused a great laugh on the bus, but I felt such a fool and I had my pay stopped for losing part of my uniform.

On camp it was the newcomers who usually lost items of equipment before they learned better, as Mary Winter discovered.

I had finished breakfast, gone into the ablutions to rinse my mug and irons in clean water and left them on the side of the basin while I spent a penny. When I came out they had gone. Not wishing to starve, I reported the theft and to my horror was put on a charge (known as a 'fizzer'). The next day I appeared before the WAAF officer, was marched in, cap off, escorted by two of my peers. One would have thought I was on a capital charge! The warrant officer said, 'ACW Boxer, you are charged that on the such and such day 1942 you did lose one knife value 4½*d* [2p], one fork value 3*d* [1½p] and one spoon value 3½*d* [1½p], etc.,' at which point I unwisely allowed myself to smile, and was sharply reprimanded by the officer who said, 'Does it amuse you, Boxer?' to which I hastily replied, 'No, ma'am,' but of course it did, the utter triviality of it all; not only that, the wrong-headedness of it, for it was the thief who should have been charged, not me!

'You had to look after kit and keep an eye on it,' Lilian Shattock confirms, 'but most girls were honest; that's part of comradeship. I had many a dream once demobbed about losing my uniform, even in later years.'

Perhaps the most common reason for being put on a charge was for returning late from an evening out or from leave. Liz Sealey (Tyson-Potts), after a night out in Brighton, was once 'actually marched up the road, under naval escort, from our Wrennery about half a mile away to see the Captain (a most awesome individual) up at his office at Roedean. I received a blistering dressing-down and was confined to barracks for a couple of weeks.'

It was absolutely no excuse to claim that a late arrival was due to circumstances beyond your control, and ex-Wren Beatrice Arlidge (White) remembers feeling rather resentful at being regarded as a 'defaulter' and losing a week's passes on account of her train being late.

To be absent without leave (AWOL) was considered an extremely serious offence, a fact which some at first didn't realise. Edna Smith had only been in the ATS a couple of weeks when she received an invitation to a party, so she went and asked if she could have a weekend leave.

RED CROSS & St JOHN
needs your help
[SEND YOUR GIFT TO St JAMES'S PALACE, LONDON, S.W.1]

AFS
ARP
LCC

WOMEN REQUIRED
FOR MOTOR DRIVING
& TELEPHONIST DUTIES
APPLY ANY FIRE STATION

CARRY THE MESSAGES

The motor cyclist messenger, roaring across country from
Headquarters to scattered units is now an ATS girl

Join **NAAFI**
Serve the Services

Vacancies waiting for COOKS
COUNTER ASSISTANTS
MANAGERESSES
(to live in)
ALSO NEEDED—PART-TIME WORKERS
FOR A FEW HOURS DAILY IN LOCAL CANTEENS

FULL PARTICULARS FROM ANY EMPLOYMENT EXCHANGE OR FROM
NAAFI IMPERIAL COURT, KENNINGTON LANE, LONDON, S.E.11.

It was refused because of the short time I had been in the Army. I said to my friend, 'They can't stop me; I'm going,' so off we went. We got back on the Monday, and everyone looked at us as if we were criminals. We were marched into an ATS officer room and were reminded that we were in the Army. So that was my first seven days' jankers – not allowed in the Naafi, every night in the cook-house with the big pans getting them to shine. I didn't realise how important the job was I had signed up for. I never done it again.

But some women did deliberately overstay their leave or go absent without leave, fully aware of the consequences. Some did so for a lark, others because a husband, fiancé or boyfriend was about to be sent abroad and there was no other way of seeing them, yet others because they had just had enough. Actual desertion seems to have been fairly rare. It was certainly more common among conscripts than among volunteers. And those on operational duties seemed (from what we have been told) to be less tempted to go AWOL than non-operational staff such as cooks or those who worked in the officers' mess.

Those who did go on the run usually headed for the big cities, where they could hope to pass unnoticed. But this was difficult, according to Alma Seal (Hann) and Eileen Scott-Martin, both sergeant 'redcaps' in the ATS provost corps. As Alma explained:

Most would get picked up because they looked so scruffy and dirty. It wasn't easy for them to get a change of clothes because of the rationing, and of course the Ats only had a few coupons for handkerchiefs and things like that. We used to stop them in the street and check their cards and passes. We only had occasional trouble arresting them. Once in Oxford Street I came across three women who were on the run; we'd had descriptions of them, and two got away but I held on to the third. We used to take them back to our HQ in Buckingham Palace Road, then inform their unit. They used to send an escort for them, usually an NCO and a private.

The ATS sent some of the more persistent offenders to a special camp called Luxford Reinforcement Unit, to which Mae Cassidy (Wilson) heard one day she was to be posted as a corporal.

We became a bit apprehensive, and officers kept coming in to see us and appeared to be sorry for us, but no one would say why. But we soon found out. This was a camp for bad girls, or, as we called them, the 'Ladies and the Tarts'. The tarts went with anyone, the ladies were more choosy. They knew where to get jobs when on the run without having any cards, mostly in Glasgow, Liverpool, Manchester and London. Some were very tough, and fights were not uncommon. We were the only camp allowed to lock up girls in the guardroom, but some even managed to break out of that. I remember one time, when a girl escaped over the fields only dressed in pyjamas and denims, we chased her with the local police, with me standing on the running-board; it was like something out of a cops-and-robbers movie.

VIPs also paid us a visit. I well remember when the Princess Royal came. We had asked the girls to show some respect, but no, as we called them to stand they remained seated and started singing rude songs. Another time the entire camp was lined up for the OC Northern Command to inspect us. He came round the corner of the buildings with his entourage, resplendent in his tartan trews, one wolf-whistle from the girls and he disappeared again.

I actually remember waking with a girl standing over me with an axe. Luckily it wasn't me she was after.

We do not have any accounts from Waaf so closely involved with deserters or persistent offenders, but it can be assumed that there was a similar proportion of women who refused to toe the line. The numbers of women in both services were more or less equal, and both were open to conscripts at the same time. It is probably fair to say about both the ATS and the WAAF what Shelford Bidwell wrote about the former service in his history of the WAAC:

> The solid evidence of history is that the Ats *were* extraordinarily well-behaved . . . but it would be foolish to pretend that the auxiliaries were all angels, and mealy-mouthed to conceal that an appreciable number of hard cases passed through its ranks, capable of regularly breaking out of confinement, assaulting their superior officers and guilty of theft and prostitution.

In the early part of the war there was nothing to stop women leaving the services if they wished, and punishments were limited to fatigues and minor loss of privileges. Katherine Beauman points out that 'desertions' from the WAAF in the first eighteen months of the war were particularly serious, not by reason of the numbers involved but because of the loss of highly trained personnel (some of whom – plotters and radar ops, for example – were in possession of classified information). It was only after the Defence (Women's Forces) Regulations became law in mid-1941 that Waaf and Ats became subject to full military discipline. Thereafter they could be subject to stoppages of pay, and absentees could be brought back under arrest.

The WRNS was somewhat different. Being basically an organisation of volunteers, it could not impose military discipline in the same way as the other two forces. Jean Donaghy (Fennemore), a Wren welfare worker, tells us that 'few disciplinary problems seemed to arise, and as there were no repercussions for deserters the occasional miscreant's card was tersely marked "RUN" with the date. There were very few runners in the WRNS!'

It can be contended that there were surprisingly few 'runners' or other offenders in any of the women's services. We have seen how the ATS, WAAF and WRNS started from nothing, almost as an afterthought, when the shadow of war was already falling on Britain. The first volunteers found themselves commanded and trained by officers and NCOs who were themselves often sorely in need of training. Volunteers and conscripts alike exchanged their familiar surroundings for the indignities of communal life. They became surnames and numbers, were told what to wear, when to wake up, when to sleep and what to do in between. If they slept with men to whom they were not married, they risked censure; if they married servicemen with whom they wanted to sleep, they would be posted apart.

In view of all this it is admirable that so many women stuck to their posts with humour and fortitude. And if some didn't, then it can be understood.

FIVE

On the Land

My friend Nora and I decided we would volunteer for the WLA after seeing the posters of a rosy-cheeked girl in breeches and sweater feeding a calf from a bucket. Very far removed, as we were to discover, from reality.

MARJORIE VINE

Women in the forces came to replace or work alongside men in many areas, but they were for the most part viewed as adjuncts to men. In the case of the Air Force, for example, women could service the planes, plot their paths and talk them down in case of emergency; but the aircrew could only be male.

For members of the Women's Land Army, on the other hand, there were no such limits. According to Anne Fountain (Hall), who worked as a trainer at a Farm Institute, 'a lot of girls had come quite unprepared for the nature of the work expected of girls, not realising we were to replace men and so were expected to do a man's job. Quite a number did not outlast their first week.'

This was halfway through the war, when many of the women entering the WLA were recruits, not all of them attracted to a life on the land. The core of the WLA consisted of volunteers, however. And, though many of them were surprised, even shocked, when they discovered what was demanded of them, the great majority stuck it out.

The need for land-girls (as they were called) was very great. Within a few months of the outbreak of war some 50,000 men had left the land. A good half of these were Territorials who had been called up; the rest had been lured to the towns where unskilled factory jobs could pay them double the 37*s* 6*d* (£1.88) that was the normal weekly wage of a farm labourer. So women would have been needed just to make up the shortfall in numbers caused by the exodus of men. But as the war went on, as our traditional sources of food from overseas fell into enemy hands and the U-boats took their toll of shipping, the demand for home-produced food increased rapidly. Farmers had to plough up their under-used grasslands and plant crops, derelict land was reclaimed for agriculture, while fen and marshland were drained and opened up to farming for the first time in history.

76   The figures show to what extent women took part in this process of

expansion. In the five years from June 1939 (when the WLA was re-formed) the number of full-time male agricultural workers actually fell from 546,000 to 522,000; the figures for women, meanwhile, soared from some 55,000 to over 200,000. Women, then, from being less than a tenth of the labour force rose to well over a quarter.

Of these, between 80,000 and 90,000 belonged to the WLA. (The rest, for the most part, were countrywomen, perhaps fearful of being directed to factory work, who made private arrangements with farmers.)

Some two-thirds of land-girls were from the country or small towns; the remainder from London or other industrial cities. Many, like Marjorie Vine and her friend Nora from Tyneside, had a romantic view of the country, which the recruiting posters did nothing to dispel. Marjorie's father, in fact, had worked on the land and, as she says, 'was surprised at my choice and was convinced I'd hate it and beg him to come and take me home'. Other parents had different worries for their young daughters. Beryl Harrison (Bagley) was a sixteen-year-old junior clerk when, with her seventeen-year-old friend May, she decided to join the WLA.

> We thought it would be fun and exciting to work away from home. We walked the two and a half miles to Leamington Spa and were told at the War Ag. Office we had to be seventeen, so I said I was! Through the week preceding my departure my father gave me a lecture on what would happen if I 'brought trouble to the family' and threatened me 'with service' if I did.

The 'War Ags' were the 'County War Agricultural Executive Committees', set up by the Government to see that official policy was carried out. They had wide-ranging powers and could, if necessary, take over the land of farmers who refused to carry out their instructions. Most members were farmers themselves, and each committee included a trade union representative and an official of the WLA.

By the outbreak of war the system for interviewing, training and posting land-girls appeared to be efficiently organised. According to *The Farmer's Home* (supplement to *The Farmer and Stock-Breeder*) for 5 September 1939:

> Recruiting for the Women's Land Army has been greatly intensified by the crisis through which this country has been passing. . . . The experience of the last war showed that the securing of the nation's food supply is in its way as vital as the front-line fighting itself. . . . When the WLA is at full strength it is hoped that it will number about 50,000. About a third of that number have already volunteered, and hundreds of applicants are being interviewed daily.
>
> Under war conditions, those who have no experience of land work take a month's intensive training course, if possible at a farm in their district. Some town girls have already taken peace-time training, and farmers have found them very ready to learn.

Most land-girls did indeed receive a form of training. But many,   77 particularly in the early part of the war, were simply set to work on their first day. Freda Botham (Hobson) recalls arriving at her first farm and next morning being 'thrown straight into work; breakfast and out to the cow-shed at 6.30. Taught to hand-milk a cow as the cowman was leaving in two weeks.' Norah Turner (Boss) started work in a threshing gang with 'no training whatsoever – straight in the deep end'; while Clare Wallis simply exchanged the life of a London art student for that of a poultrywoman.

But it was not just the farm duties which came as a shock to some recruits in their first days. Many had to face living conditions for which they were ill prepared.

Beryl Harrison, the sixteen-year-old, was sad to learn that she was to be separated from her friend May, who was assigned to a private farm near Rugby. Beryl, like something over a third of recruits, was sent to a hostel with other land-girls. It was only a few miles from her home, but she had never travelled more than the two and a half miles to Leamington Spa before, so her mother went with her. When they reached the hostel they found it was

> a Nissen hut with coke-burners along the middle – bunk beds and stone floors! My mother cried and said, 'You're not staying here,' and pleaded with the warden to look after me. I don't remember much about the first few weeks, only that I was very frightened but put on a big act to prove I was grown up.

A lot of the hostels were pretty bleak. According to Bronwen Cook, hers 'was built for Italian POWs, but wasn't passed fit for POWs to live in, but was good enough for the WLA'.

Whatever the conditions, at least those assigned to a hostel had the company of others and the chance to relax together at the end of a long working day. Those billeted on private farms, usually alone, faced a considerably more lonely existence.

The lucky ones were made to feel part of the family. Clare Wallis's eyes still light up when she talks of her first posting.

> I took the train from Paddington and was met at Chippenham by Mr Cook, a very dapper-looking gentleman farmer, beautifully tailored breeches and leather leggings, hacking-jacket and trilby hat. We drove back to the farm where I was greeted by Mrs Cook, a charming woman with seven children, and I can remember the wonderful heady smell of the wood-fire; they made me so welcome.

Quite a few accounts refer with gratitude to the farmers, their wives and the other farmworkers, many of whom provided help and encouragement in the early days when things were new and difficult. Rosamond Rampley (Brookes) has fond memories of one of the local men who 'was seventy years old and had worked at Tatton Hall since he was thirteen.

He wore a leather corset for back trouble, and creaked every time he moved. But he was a mine of information on all growing things, and taught us a lot.' In fact when Rosamond married her RAF flight sergeant the old man made her 'a beautiful bouquet of red roses and carnations grown in the gardens' and all the workers attended the wedding.

Bronwen Cook, who went straight to Manor Farm, High Beech, and learned as she went along, writes that 'the men were very helpful and had some funny sayings; for instance, when I couldn't reach some harness one of them said: "Here's a fag-paper to stand on" '; while Bettie Baird (McDonald) 'got on very well with the farming community. I think they appreciated us, although we continually had to prove that we were strong enough to carry the heavy bags of potatoes.'

But not all contacts were so pleasant. The second family Clare Wallis worked for was 'like something out of Stella Gibbons'. At breakfast on the first morning they

all had to get down on bended knees while the master raised his voice in extempore prayer, with my stomach rumbling and me wondering when the damn things would end (after all, I'd already put in over an hour's work). Then after what seemed like a good five minutes they all fell on the food, virtually eating with their hands! Revolting!

Even when the people were friendly it was unlikely that conditions would be anything but primitive. At the start of the war farming was much as Thomas Hardy described it: brute strength, horses and a few old steam-driven machines. Tractors were far from universal, and the combine harvester was only just starting to put in an appearance. As late as 1943 under a half of farms had piped water, while fewer than a quarter had electricity.

But when primitive conditions combined with unpleasant work and uncongenial company, then things could become unbearable. According to Grace Wallace (Jackson), who lived in a hostel:

when we had a bath after working on the thresher all day you could not stay in for long, as the top of the water was a floating mass of hay lice, so we always had to finish off with a shower. Of course all the girls were not so lucky. If they lived on a farm, they had to be satisfied with a wash-down in the farm kitchen. There was no privacy from the prying eyes of some lusty farmer who thought you was there to satisfy their needs which they were not getting from their wives.

Many former land-girls feel that they were exploited by the farmers. 'We used to pray for rain to have a day off in the hostel,' writes Doreen Douglas (Brown). 'The farmers would say: "Come on, it's only Scotch Mist." I think we were cheap labour. The farmers made a bomb out of us. They would have had to pay a man much more.'

The more prosperous farmers, and their wives, come in for severe   79 criticism. Beryl Harrison says: 'We were better-treated on poorer farms than on "gentleman farmer" estates, where they treated us like scum and made it quite clear we were there on sufferance.'

Grace Wallace agrees.

> Some of the farmers thought we were there just to do all the dirty jobs that no one else would do. I remember going to one place with another girl. The Lady of the Manor took us to a field about one and a half acres. It was covered in weeds and thistles almost as tall as ourselves, and we were told to clear it. We had no gloves to wear, so you can imagine what our hands were like by the end of the day; even our faces were scratched and stung. She used to sit in her car at the far end of the field to watch us. If it rained and we went to shelter under a tree, she would come round and make us go back. Some girls lived on farms, and it was thought that they lived a good happy family life, but this was not always so. Some had nowhere proper to sleep and were treated like skivvies by the farmers' wives, having to do housework as well as farmwork. It took a long time for the farmers to realise we were quite capable of doing a man's job when we had to.

This was most galling of all, to be treated as a servant when they had signed up for skilled farmwork. Anne Fountain writes of one particular farm where she and her sister Cara 'were used as skivvies. We slept on lumpy beds in the attic, and I had to do the washing-up and domestic chores – not land-girl jobs! At five foot tall, it seems I was not considered tough enough for farmwork, other than to help with the cows.'

Anne eventually complained to the local WLA representative and was allowed to transfer, an option also taken by other women. This rumbling of discontent may well have prompted the following letter, written in October 1940 by Lady Denman (Honorary Director of the WLA) to *Home and Country*, the magazine of the National Federation of Women's Institutes, of which she was chairman.

> I should like to appeal to Institute members who are farmers' wives . . . to consider how best the labour problem can be met by the employment of members of the Women's Land Army. . . .
>
> The prejudice against a woman attempting to do a man's work dies hard but the progress of the Land Army in the last year shows that it can be done. . . . With amazing adaptability ex-secretaries, shop girls and factory hands have become country women, if not for life at least for the duration.
>
> All the preliminary instruction they get is four weeks' free training at a Farm Institute or College or on the farm or garden where they will be employed subsequently, but, as one farmer put it 'The average Land Girl picks up the work extraordinarily well, and it is thanks to them and to the local women who have taken on men's jobs that we have got our work up to date today.' . . .
>
> Tributes like this are not uncommon, as Women's Land Army Secretaries in the counties will testify. Of course there are some misfits and failures. This is inevitable in any organisation, but the percentage is not great. . . .

Women's Institute members can help to overcome any prejudice which may still exist in their district against the idea of women working on the land. They can not only encourage the employment of the Land Army, but they can do much to see that when the newcomer arrives she is welcomed and made to feel that she is among friends. . . .

Individual members have broken down the loneliness of new surroundings by inviting the girls to their homes and, in some cases, giving them the use of a bath if one is not available at their billet. Such acts have not passed unappreciated. On their side, volunteers write in glowing terms of their life and the kindness with which they have been treated. They are conscious of belonging to a force which . . . is a growing factor in helping to keep the nation's larder filled.

This letter mentions some of the problems that land-girls had to contend with: prejudice against their taking on men's work, problems of adapting to new surroundings and demands, and the loneliness suffered by many of them billeted out. It does not refer to cases of exploitation, nor does it mention one other cause of resentment: the growing disparity between the income of farmers and of their land-girl employees.

According to an appendix printed in V. Sackville-West's *The Women's Land Army* (1944), land-girls were

employed on the basis of a guaranteed weekly wage covering a working week of not more than 48 hours in winter and 50 in summer. A worker of 18 and over in no case receives a cash wage of less than 22/6 [£1.12] after a deduction has been made to cover board and lodgings. . . . Additional payment must be made for [excess] hours worked at statutory overtime rates.

They were also entitled to a week's paid holiday per year, all public holidays, a weekly half-holiday, an occasional long weekend and as many Sundays off as possible. In reality they often – especially in the summer – went for weeks on end without a break, and it was not uncommon for them to have to argue with farmers about their entitlement to overtime payments. But even when they received their due they often felt themselves to be both undervalued and underpaid. We hear of land-girls gratefully accepting tips from farmers, since this helped to pay for their train fares home (unlike the forces they received no travel warrants, nor were they entitled to reduced fares as was the case with factory workers). And they never seemed to have enough to eat. Some, very few, lived off the fat of the land. More typical was what happened at Grace Wallace's hostel where they were given 'four slices of bread with some kind of paste on them', which had to keep them going from 7 a.m. to 6 p.m. or 7 p.m.

Meanwhile the incomes of farmers had been rising steadily and dramatically – by 207 per cent in the period 1938–42, compared with an average national increase of 35 per cent. It is not surprising that the land-girls, putting in between fifty and eighty hours of hard physical labour per week, should feel a certain amount of resentment.

But what did they do during this long working week? No job, it seems, was considered beyond them, from milking to threshing, from stooking to rat-catching. Simple strength was often needed, but so, too, was the ability to handle machinery, from the newly fashionable milking-machines and tractors to huge excavators for carving out drainage-ditches in fen and marshland. They had to learn ancient country arts, many long since vanished, but also adapt to an era of rapid technological change.

Their daily routine depended on a variety of factors. Some worked on a single farm, which could specialise in anything from dairy produce to cider or, indeed, have everything from poultry to pigs, with a few fields of barley and oats on the side. Some were in horticulture. Others could be based at a hostel and travel to different jobs each day depending on the rhythm of the seasons. Four or five thousand of them, belonging to the Women's Timber Corps, could live for months with only the forest for company. Others, finally, were the travellers, applying their skill wherever needed. Here are a few accounts to give an idea of what these women had to do.

A Routine Day during Hay-Making: Up at 5 a.m. wash, dress, quick cup of cocoa, cycle to farm; 5.30 a.m. get the thirty-eight cows in from field, chain them up in their stalls, feed them their ration of bran, etc., wash and dry their udders ready for milking, two men and myself milk them between us, turn cows out to grass, put milk through cooler and cleansing machine, muck out cowsheds, in to breakfast at 8 a.m., back out again at 8.30; bottle up milk, harness up horse, load milk-cart and off on my milk round, usually back to farm 12.30; unload crates of dirty bottles, unharness horse and put him out to grass, cycle home for dinner, back about 1.45 to wash and sterilise bottles and milk-churns, help to muck out stables and pig-sties, maybe whitewash inside of cow-sheds, clean harness, horse brasses, etc.; about 3.30 p.m. bring in cows from fields, milking from 4 to 5, then while cowman mucks out sheds harness up one of the shire horses, collect sandwiches and a two-gallon churn of tea from the farmer's wife and take it out to the men in the hay-field (riding on horse's back with the churn hanging from his collar); work in the hay-field till almost dark (driving the hay-rake or the swath-turner, sometimes helping to build the rick); return horses to the farm about 10 p.m. (double summertime, remember!), feed and water them before turning them out for the night, then cycle home fit only for bed. (Bronwen Cook)

Driving the Tractor: Poor Ted Ashford, who had to teach me. I often wondered what his thoughts were – a woman driving a tractor! I learned to drive or an International, can't remember the horsepower, it was so huge it seemed to me. Big tyres at the rear and iron wheels up front. The steering-wheel was similar to the steam-rollers; one had to steer by a wooden handle

Annice Gibbs (Connett) was a
member of the Women's
Timber Corps, as the crossed
axes and FORESTRY flash show.

Grace Wallace (Jackson).
Grace worked for a long while
as part of a five-woman
threshing team, travelling
from farm to farm.

Bettie Baird (McDonald) e
up as an expert mole- and
catcher.

Trainee member of the Women's Timber
Corps during her one-month forestry
training course.

Hilda Flower (Shurlock) ended up as a
trainer and is one of the few people to have
been fined for having an unlit cow on the
public highway. Hilda milking Dinah.

Stella Hewlett (*fourth from left*) having a break from picking tomatoes.

Johnnie Luxton (Johnson) working on a binder.

Winifred Spanier (Lyons) standing (*left*) in front of her excavator used for clearing out dykes all over Suffolk.

Draining newly ploughed acres. A twenty-one-year-old girl hauling a single furrow plough on a tractor, March 1942.

Land-girls pause to watch a squadron of fighters returning from a sweep over enemy-occupied territory.

A team of land-girls harvesting Britain's largest wheat field. Sussex Downs, August 1941.

attached to the wheel, and turning was difficult at first. I had to turn the handle around so fast. The throttle was on the steering-column. I mastered it quickly, so I thought, but the difficulty was in reversing. Then it was the old Fordson, so much easier as it was smaller, with just three gears, and throttle up front pulled out notch by notch – full out very fast, almost closed very slow. It had rear iron spiked wheels and iron front ones, so could dig in and pull heavy loads. Both tractors had to be started by swinging a handle in front, and that was an art in itself. (Midge Matthew, née Hoare)

Rick-Making: In the barton, or rickyard, we had an elevator, where someone on the wagon of hay unloaded into the machine which took it up into the rick where another two men 'made' the rick. Sometimes it was square, sometimes oblonger when working near Bristol-round, which were called 'windmows'. If we had a wet season, it was hard work to 'catch it' right to dry and dry again, which made bad hay. When this was cut out and used in the winter it was slightly mouldy, or 'fausty' as they called it. If not too dry a huge 'liner' (a big bundle of straw) was placed in two or three places in the hay rick, like a funnel gradually drawn up as the rick grew higher, which created air to breathe. If horses were used carting hay they were tied up each time by the rick, when the wagons were being unloaded, and had water and hay. It was a lovely contented and munchy sound, which I can hear now. (Midge Matthew)

Market-Gardening: I was drafted to Tatton Hall, a beautiful stately home, where we grew vegetables and fruit, including vines, figs, peaches and nectarines. There were seven girls in the market-garden, three men past recruiting age and several COs. . . . There were about ten glasshouses in the gardens, all heated in the winter from boilers which ate anthracite greedily. We had to load the cellars every week, which meant filling an old four-wheeled truck to the brim, then pulling it to the cellars, repeating the whole operation several times. We all thought we should be issued with shafts as we were working like horses. (Rosamond Rampley)

Milking: We would light the oil-lamps and hang them round the cow-stall, then give the cows some feed to keep them happy while we washed their udders. This completed, we donned white cap and overalls, picked up our bucket and three-legged stool and started to milk. We whistled, sang or chatted depending on the weather and our temper, but if we were quiet all that could be heard was the sharp *ping ping* as the first milk hit the bucket, followed later by the *slush slush* as the milk rose higher. (Dorothy French, née Tattershall)

Rat-Catching: Sometimes the men and myself would have a rat-catching session – tuppence a tail was not to be sneezed at in those days, specially as I only had 17s 6d [88p] a week, plus my keep. Unfortunately, by the time we had the barn doors open and the dogs let out of the granary, the rats had usually disappeared. (Mary Bigwood)

Muck-Spreading: One particular farm I was dispatched to was owned by a very unfriendly farmer and his family. I was dispatched to a field miles from the farmhouse and told to spread the muck dumped in heaps over this very large field. I was there on my own for eight hours spreading muck until the farmer blew a bugle to signal me to finish work as the lorry had come for me. (Beryl Harrison)

Typical Day Based at Hostel: You would begin by preparing your own sandwiches (cheese or beetroot), pile into the lorry at 7.30 and off to the different farms. In the early winter the work was mainly potato-picking and snagging turnips. Your hands were always wet and cold, and the frozen ground made turnip removal difficult. At 10 a.m. we stopped for a cup of tea, then at 12 noon opened our 'bait-boxes' and ate our 'bait', as we called the sandwiches. If we were very lucky, we might be working on a farm where the farmer's wife was a good cook and we were offered beautiful home-made soups. We would leave the farm at dusk. (Bettie Baird)

Ditching: I joined two other LGs and we lived in a wooden caravan sharing the cooking and housekeeping duties. We could be at a farm anything from a week or two to several months depending on how many ditches were to be cleaned out. We did a wide variety of tasks, including levelling moorland which had been severely ploughed up by tanks during training. The excavator was transported on a Scammel, and they were very exciting days going to our next farm, wondering what the farmers and their families would be like. (Eleanor Appleby)

Trainer: Our herd consisted of five or six 'nurse' cows on which the girls learned to milk. One of them we called Poley. She was a dehorned Shorthorn and a right soft thing. She had a calf, and on the third day after calving we let her out into the field with the other cows for a few hours after milking, with the intention of getting her in before it got dark so that she could suckle her baby. I took two of the girls with me because we had to get Poley across the main road. Not a lot of traffic about because there was not the petrol, and cars only had a small slit in the headlamps, so people did not go out much. Poley did not really want to leave her friends, and we had to keep cajoling her. Finally we got her out of the field and on to the road, but by now it was dusk. We still had quite a way to go along the main road before we were back at the cowshed, and she was in no hurry. Then we realised that a car was coming, and there we were, stuck in the middle of the road. The girls waved their arms and hollered, but at the last minute we all had to jump for safety. It was a baby Austin, fortunately not travelling too fast, but it hit Poley broadside. All she suffered was a slightly swollen bag the next day – but you should have seen the car! Radiator stove in, petrol running out, headlamps broken. Well, the upshot was we received a summons and had to attend the Petty Sessions. I went with the farm manager and a member of the War Ag. Committee. The man from the War Ag. pleaded ignorance on my part. I had not known I should have had a light on the road when escorting a cow. So the magistrates fined me £1 and told the War Ag. to pay it. I always tell folk I have a criminal record for having a cow on the road without a light. (Hilda Flower, née Shurlock)

Collecting Pig-Swill: Bins for potato peelings, cabbage and any waste food were placed in the streets, and housewives would put their scraps in. We also collected from hotels and British Restaurants. Before we left the farm we would fill the steam-boiler with water, light the fire and on our return the steam would be up ready to cook the swill. It was steamed for an hour and sometimes smelled quite appetising. The bins could be quite heavy, and we soon had a knack of lifting them between us. During the hot weather the swill was often full of maggots, and we often had them down our necks or in our pockets. We reared the pigs to ten to twelve weeks old, when they would be sold off to local pig clubs. (Mary Hood, Blackburn)

Working with Horses: I had a prize Suffolk Punch called Jock and had to stand on an upturned bucket to put his collar on. Working with two huge Suffolk Punches, one in front of the other, carting sugar-beet with the field churned up, mud well past my ankles and being pulled along by the horses – it makes me come out in a sweat thinking about it! (Betty Spridgeon)

Threshing: A huge belt connected to the thresher set the wheels in motion. The sheaves were fed into the top, then there were three exits, the straw travelled up to a chute to be gathered and formed into a rick; the chaff and waste, called 'cavings', came out of the bottom, which had to be constantly cleared so as not to block up the works, and the grain was funnelled into hundredweight sacks, which had to be moved when full. One girl had to make the rick, one to clear the cavings, one on top feeding the machine, and one tossing the sheaves to the bond-cutter or feeder, the full sacks to be moved by anyone with a free arm.

It was filthy work, dust everywhere, especially as some of the corn was so old. In a barn the work was worse as there was nowhere for the dust to escape, except the lungs. Before the war it was mainly done by casual labour, mostly gypsies and vagrants, but even they didn't do it every day. It's a lousy job. 'Reckon you girls be daft to do this every day,' said one farmer. 'Once a year be good enough for me.' 'We haven't any choice but to stick it,' I said. And stick it we did, for five gruelling months, travelling from farm to farm, till 'all was safely gathered in'. (Joyce Tomsett, née Arber)

Gang Work: We did nothing but pick sprouts for weeks on end or cut and pack lettuce or cabbage. I can remember weeding carrots, carrots as far as the eye could see. Carrots! No wonder I don't like them even now. (Stella Hewlett)

Clearing Out Dykes: After a year of farm-work we went to Hull to learn to drive a Cub excavator used for cleaning out dikes all over Suffolk. We became very attached to our Cub and at that time were the only women drivers. As 'digs' were a problem we first rented and then bought a gipsy caravan. The nights in the caravan were very cosy, with a coal fire, a cup of hot tea from the farmer's wife on our arrival home and 'Much Binding in the Marsh' if the wireless would work. In the mornings we would find the bedding frozen to the sides of the caravan. We had to work in all weather except snow, and there were some very bleak days indeed. But if we could round up some wood we would have a fire at 'dooky' time, and roast potatoes or onions, if there were any in the fields nearby. (Winifred Spanier, née Lyons)

Mole- and Rat-Catcher: It was not unusual to find oneself in a barn surrounded by fifty or so rats crawling around in the bin of oats. I was never attacked as I felt no fear. The farmers were rather surprised when I arrived, as I was only five foot and under seven stone at the age of eighteen. (Bettie Baird)

Women's Timber Corps: We camped in Nissen huts, twelve women to each hut. The floors were rough concrete, and in the centre a slow combustion boiler which did not give out a great deal of heat. It was cold and dreary. I well remember our first day in the woods, wearing thick heavy boots, gaiters and dungarees, and lifting the heavy pit-props on to trailers. At first we were allowed to shelter from the rain, but eventually we were issued with oilskins because of the time-wasting in sheltering, and with such an important war product it was vital to keep at it.

The softwoods, such as the pines, were used for the pit-props, and large quantities were cut by us. There were no mechanical devices used then, and every pit-prop was cut by hand, either with the crosscut or the bushman saw. We soon got used to the heavy work, such as lifting the pit-props and cutting them into various lengths for the mines, and we learned how to keep the weight away from our backs and stomachs, which was far less tiring. (Annice Gibbs née Connett)

We had great big fires, and we had to cover all the ashes at night so they did not glow. . . . It was very peaty ground and sometimes if it was hot and dry – although everyone covered their fires very well and dug a trench all round them – a fire still ran along under the peat and broke out in several places. When this happened everyone was called off what they were doing and spent all day chasing the fires and digging to cover them. (Stella Banfield née Keeler)

My first two years were spent in the New Forest in charge of sawmills, a few saws run off a steam engine. We measured the timber as it was hauled in, the hauliers being paid on the volume carted, either by horse and wagon or later by tractor and trailer. . . . In 1942 six girls were wanted as Census Measurers. It was vital to know where there were supplies of the right sort of timber for pit-props, ash for aeroplane wings, poplar for matches, etc. So we had to ask permission from the owners to go into every wood over an acre, and if they said 'No' persuade them to change their minds. (Jean Baxter née Stuart)

Working in a Sawmill: We sawed timber for well over a year which no one knew what it was for. It was eleven inches square, eleven feet long. D-Day arrived and we received a letter from the Ministry thanking us for our effort and telling us that the timber we had been sawing all those months was for a new emergency bridge used in the invasion, the Bailey Bridge. It was some time before we realised its importance. (Joan Smith)

Some women were put in charge of gangs of workers. Annice Gibbs, of the WTC, recalls being sent to a large estate near Bath where a beautiful avenue of hardwoods had to be felled.

90   I was forewoman, with several girls under me, and we were detailed to pick

up all the remaining bits of brushwood, etc. It was all on the grassland, mostly the size of a match, and the owner insisted every scrap must be picked up. It was a tremendous and most tedious effort and I looked aghast at the job in front of us. My girls worked like beavers and, as was to be expected after days and days of this tedious job, they just wanted to stop, but I kept them going by continually working with them. One of the girls went hysterical, and I thought: What a waste of valuable time and energy.

But some ex-forewomen have memories of more pleasant encounters. Anne Fountain was in charge of a gang of sixty who on one occasion were asked to pick potatoes on the Badminton Estate.

Imagine the excitement when we saw Queen Mary emerge from a nearby wood where she had been sawing logs for the house fires. Queen Mary talked to the girls, and when she asked who was in charge I was brought forward to be introduced, wearing a sack round my shoulders and round my waist. While she was talking to my deputy I managed to pass around the word to take a respectful step back from the Queen before scampering back to work; I set off backwards, only to fall over a log! The Queen hid her amusement with difficulty as I must have been a comic enough figure in my sacks, but the girls were so overcome by awe they didn't even smile at an incident they would normally have greatly enjoyed!

In fact the sight of royals rolling up their sleeves and pitching in at Badminton was not particularly rare. Queen Mary, then Queen Mother, spent much of the war on the estate, which belonged to her kinsman the Duke of Beaufort, and when her relatives visited they often joined in with the farmwork. This information comes from Clare Wallis who, after leaving the Cold Comfort farmers, eventually found herself as personal land-girl to the Duchess. Members of the royal family would occasionally help out ('Princess Alexandra used to help me clean out the goats,' says Clare. 'She was a sweet, charming child'); but none was as indefatigable as Her Grace.

The farm was the Duchess of Beaufort's hobby. Aboriginal cows called Old Gloucesters, great big animals, fifteen hands high. They had names like Badminton Diana, Chichester Apotheosis – none of your Bluebells and Buttercups. My job was to bring them in at night, and because they were black and you couldn't use a torch on account of the blackout you couldn't see them unless you actually tripped over them. Invariably when I eventually arrived the Duchess would say to me in her high-pitched voice: 'You're late! You're sacked!' Of course she'd always reinstate me the next day.

But the Duchess didn't just stand around issuing orders. She would shut up the goats every evening, in her usual garb of overalls and boots, with a black beret jammed any old how over her curlers. And she always recognised, and deferred to, superior expertise. Clare recalls one occasion when a cow was having difficulty calving.

The cowman was called Oliver, the Duchess was first assistant and I was   91 second assistant. Now, sometimes when a cow was calving you would have to reach right into the cow's vagina, attach a rope to the calf's legs and pull when the contractions came. Now, on one occasion Oliver was in command, steadying the cow's head, while the Duchess and I were at the other end, and his instructions were 'When 'er do 'eave, pull, yer Grace!'

The Duchess said to me one day: 'How do people think duchesses spend their time? Are we supposed to lie around on a chaise-longue all day, like Madame Récamier?'

Clare was lucky. She spent the last part of the war in congenial surroundings, with a pleasant employer, far from reminders of the harsher realities of war. And it is true that most land-girls, however hard their lives, were at least spared the dangers faced by those in the blitzed cities.

But even the remotest of rural areas were never completely safe. Mary Bigwood, working on a farm deep in Warwickshire, reports that:

> One night we had two bombs drop in the field at the bottom of the garden which blew out the front windows of the house and blew us out of bed. When the farmer went to investigate to see whether the cows were injured, he found them all standing around the crater rim, contemplating their disturbed field and chewing the cud.

Not all farms were in the depths of the country, however. Some were just a few miles from city centres, while others – especially in the South-East – were maybe a field away from an RAF station, prime targets in the summer of 1940. Mary Hood, for example, collected her pig-food from the streets of Harrow, spending her nights in an Anderson shelter rather than under thatched eaves. And Elizabeth Tuck, market-gardening within sight of RAF Biggin Hill, has stories of shattered glass-houses and of being blown off her bicycle by bomb blast.

Quiet country skies would suddenly fill with reminders of war. Sometimes land-girls would stop their work and watch a dog-fight between a pair of planes cut off from the main pack, cheering if the RAF seemed to be getting the better of it. But one such fight ended in the most stupid of tragedies, with two Spitfires doing a victory roll and colliding over the farm where Marjorie Vine was billeted. 'One crashed in our pond,' she says. 'Neither pilot stood a chance.'

Many report moments when the field in which they were working became the front line. In Grace Wallace's case it was a potato-field on a hot summer's day.

> It was very warm work bending over, so we removed our shirts. We saw a lone plane coming towards us. At first we thought it was some cheeky RAF pilot coming to take a closer look, so we clutched our shirts to us then looked up to give him a wave. Almost at the last moment one of the girls noticed something odd about the markings, shouted out a warning and we set off in all directions, running for our lives, with machine-gun bullets all round us.

I don't think I've ever run so fast or cleared a hedge so quickly. Luckily no one was hurt, but we never felt quite the same working in the open after that.

Being strafed by German planes was frightening, of course, but the average land-girl was much more likely to suffer as a result of normal farm-work than of enemy action. A horrifying number of accounts refer to illness or injury, and here is just a small selection.

One day while leading my horse through the stable I was kicked in the back by a colt and knocked unconscious. When I came to I was lying on my back on a corn-bin with a dozen men and boys gathered anxiously round me. One week off and back to work again. (Mrs Elsie Thompson née Trudgill, who left the WLA with septic dermatitis)

After appalling work taking out trees with grubbing axes during that very severe winter of 1940 in thick snow with no shelter of any sort I strained my heart and was ordered by the doctor to leave, but I applied for a transfer. (Phyl Batty)

I was terrified when I saw those circular saws, but I was put in the mill. I was told later that they put the terrified ones there as they thought they wouldn't take so many risks. I worked with a foreman who in spite of having lost his fingers on the saw was the best teacher you could wish for. There was quite a few accidents, but I was lucky. (Joan Smith)

The bond-cutting could be dangerous. One slip or lack of concentration and fingers, arms, even legs came out the thresher as mincemeat. It was not unheard of for land-girls to suffer amputations that way. (Joyce Tomsett, who caught pneumonia as a result of five months' breathing in dust from threshing)

I damaged my shoulder carrying yokes and handling milk-churns and had dreadful sores on my hands from the disinfectant we had to use between cows. My sister Barbara fell off the haycart once, and the farmer said she should wait until lunch-time. Her arm was all swollen up by the time she got to the doctor. (Elizabeth Tuck)

The WLA was very much aware of what was going on and set up its own Benevolent Fund to supplement the pitifully inadequate compensation available from the State. (Vita Sackville-West gave the royalties from her book to the Fund.) But they can hardly have realised the extent to which – nearly half a century on – many women would still be suffering as a result of their war work. Betty Spridgeon, who organises an annual land-girl reunion, tells us that they *all* 'suffer with bad backs, due to moving eight-stone sacks of spuds, etc.'.

So the members of the WLA and the WTC had as tough a war as anybody. Most of their accounts contain examples of hardship, of shortages and of exploitation. But little sense of bitterness is felt, and what there is centres around the fact that their contribution was – and in the opinion of 93 many still *is* – undervalued. The WLA was called an army, but they did not have the privileges accorded to the members of the armed services. Access to the Naafi was denied to them, for example; nor – despite a campaign on their behalf by Lady Denman – were they entitled to a gratuity at the end of their service. As Bronwen Cook remembers it: 'For my four and a half hard years of sweat and work I ended up with two weeks' pay, thirty-six clothing coupons, and we were allowed to keep our overcoats and two skirts; no medals or gratuities.'

Several use the words 'forgotten', 'undervalued' or 'unknown'. Former members of the Women's Timber Corps are particularly sad that their contribution has gone practically unrecorded. Susan Banfield, for example, has never seen it mentioned in print; while Annice Gibbs recalls, with a slightly wry smile, the time when she was in full uniform, with Forestry shoulder-flash and cross-axes badge, only to be asked by a woman: 'Do you milk cows?'

For Norah Turner the moment when it was brought home to her that they were 'a forgotten army' was

on the occasion of a War Effort March through Tunbridge Wells. Every available branch of the fighting services took part, plus the Merchant Navy, NAAFI, WVS, Home Guard, ARP wardens, Fire Service, police and nurses, while several bands interspersed the marching columns. At the very last moment someone, probably as a joke, decided to include the WLA. Being scattered over a wide variety of farms, we had no opportunity to arrange a meeting or practise marching, so we arrived on the scene, mostly unacquainted with each other. As we were an afterthought, our obvious position in the column was the tail end. The uniform was never intended to be other than functional, and we looked far from glamorous as we marched in faded green jumpers, baggy breeches, misshapen hats and heavy clomping shoes. To add to the pantomime impression we were all shapes and sizes and no one could keep in step. I still blush when I remember how the respectful crowd were suddenly reduced to hysterical laughter as we hove into view, and we had to strive hard to ignore the catcalls and *moos* that came at us from all sides.

Yes, indeed, it must have been a galling moment. But this was perhaps an isolated incident. Joan Bowman had a rather different experience.

I was very proud when our small contingent of girls at the back of a big parade of the Armed Forces, etc., got a huge cheer from the crowds lining the main street in Stratford. From feeling the Cinderella service we felt very proud.

And later in her letter she mentions that, although they weren't recognised as one of the forces, 'if you go to Salisbury Cathedral there is a stained-glass window with an ATS girl in it, a Waaf, Wren and, yes, a *Land Girl*!'

As is the case with so many ex-servicewomen, there is a mixture of pride in achievement and of nostalgia for a period when women worked

94

together for a common cause. Clare Wallis looks back on her Land Army life as very happy, even though she was missing out on the parties and things that most young girls expect. 'I stayed on that farm a good two years and became a very efficient farm-worker,' she says. 'The hay-making I took in my stride. I mean, I could work as well as any man, I was so strong! I was quite skilled in my crafts. I could do all the jobs without having to be told. And I took a pride in it. The joy of being allowed to use a tractor!'

A similar feeling of pride is recalled by Jess Clayton (Sadler), who 'overheard a farmer discussing the help needed for next day and saying "Now we'll be two men short, so you'd best bring an extra land-girl". We couldn't wait to get back to tell our forewoman *one* land-girl equals *two* men!'

But together with this is an abiding love of the countryside, which caused some women to settle down there after the war, and others to make frequent pilgrimages back. 'I always remember cycling from the hostel in the spring, the lovely scent of violets and the pretty webs on the hedge,' writes Doreen Douglas. 'When I used to go and feed animals on a misty morning I used to imagine I was in a film. . . . The life done me good as I keep fit and healthy. Some I know suffer from arthritis. But not me!'

In some cases it takes little for the years to roll away and memories to be instantly evoked. Marjorie Vine says: 'even after so many years I find great nostalgic waves going over me when I smell paraffin or watch a tractor making a lovely pattern'.

Peggy Bardwell (Sawyer) sums it up, perhaps, for all of them:

In spite of war they were golden years. We were five land-girls, all kindred spirits, and the friendship is still with us. Looking back, I thought how little we needed to make us happy. On a bitter winter day, knee-deep in mud, we would say: 'When the war is over we'll sit by a fire and eat chocolate biscuits.'

I saw so much beauty, the changing seasons . . . and in a time of destruction was able to create.

SIX

In the Towns

Civil Defence is an affair of streets and neighbourhoods, mostly on a small scale of movement.

Front Line (Government publication)

Many women volunteered their services for Air-Raid Precautions at the outset of war, and found their offers rejected. But by June 1940, after France had fallen and when invasion seemed imminent, the Manpower Requirements Committee, headed by William Beveridge, estimated that some three-quarters of a million more men and 84,000 women would be required for ARP within the year. In fact so urgent was the need during the Blitz that followed that by March 1941 even 'grannies' born after 1893 were being enlisted. The original title, Air-Raid Precautions, had now been changed officially to Civil Defence, with full-time wages for a man at £3 5s [£3.25] while women received the smaller sum of £2 3s 6d [£2.18].

Eventually, in 1943, nearly a quarter of the 1½ million Civil Defence workers were women. Though most of these were unpaid voluntary part-time members, about 10,000 women were full-timers, and in a position to demand equal pay and compensation for injuries on a level with men.

Civil Defence was set up in such a way as to distribute the services – warden's posts, fire stations, first-aid centres and rescue stations – evenly over a given area. Street wardens made up over half the Civil Defence, one in every six being a woman. In cities there were normally six wardens to a post, and one post to every 500 people. Wardens had to learn their district and gain their people's confidence so that they could be relied upon in the middle of chaos. During the Blitz, the warden's duty was to assess the situation and report such incidents as falling bombs, dangerous fires, gas-leaks, a blocked road, etc., to the police or to the Control Centre. On returning to the incident, they were to direct people in the streets to the nearest shelter, allay panic and generally give assistance, which might mean helping those who had been 'bombed out' to Rest Centres. Those working in 'Control' relied totally on the warden's accuracy.

Peggy Leppard (Chapman) volunteered at sixteen to be 'Report and Control' for Leyton and Leytonstone, with eight other girls from their

Women's Junior Air Corps, and she explained that

> When on a 'raid', all ARP posts had to telephone through any bomb damage, and us R & C phoned through for fire engines, ambulances, etc., to the nearest station to that incident. Our job as messengers was to run round our dugout 'Ops' room with messages from one operator to the next. In the Leyton Town Hall was a duplicate layout in case the main one was bombed. Our Centre was manned by two people. We had to be on duty every fourth night from 7 p.m. to 8 a.m. – or, if there was a raid, until the 'All Clear'. For this we were paid 3*s* 6*d* [18p] per night, issued with helmet, gas-mask and coat – some of these nearly touched our ankles on issue, so we had to get them altered. Two girls were on every night and we slept on camp beds in the boiler room with the boiler switching on and off. This was as well as being an 'Office Girl' in the day.

If the telephones failed, they were backed up by a system of messengers on foot, cycle and motor-bike working between the Control Centre and the hundreds of incidents, whether a UXB (unexploded bomb) or fire incendiary, etc. Kathy Gibbons (Shearwood), a messenger in the East End of London, said that she

> used to go to the warden's post with me dad of a night, so I decided to join it myself. So I did. You had to do about six hours a week at the post. Take turns in answering the phone or take messages and send them. I ran mine, and if there was an incident . . . we used to go and help dig people out, which wasn't very nice – at seventeen.

Once the air-raid sounded, Civil Defence were 'officially' the only people above ground. Many preferred to be helping above rather than down in the claustrophobic conditions of the shelters (the largest of which became the home of one Londoner in every twenty-five during the Blitz). Kathy said at that time she was never in the shelters: 'I used to roam the streets later seeing what I could do.' Dame Idina Probyn of Australia was of the same attitude. She had joined the London County Council Ambulance Service as a driver, working throughout West London. 'I was out in every raid and wouldn't have missed it for the world. I always helped other stations when I had finished my work at ours.'

Most ambulance drivers were women – 36,000 of them – and after the Heavy Rescue squad (always men) had released trapped casualties the ambulances would drive the injured to the First-Aid Posts or to hospital. Getting there was a business – avoiding fires, riding over debris, around craters, over trailing wires and hoses. Margie Bruce (Griffin) became an ambulance driver at twenty-two. She was working as a physio at the modern Finsbury Health Centre when this was transformed into a First-Aid Post and reception area to take in air-raid victims. The unit consisted of three doctors and an extra emergency doctor they could call in. The three in the physio department included herself, an untrained volunteer – a mezzo-soprano from Sadler's Wells – and Father Langton from 'The Holy Redeemer', 'a lovely man who was a great help when people were "shattered" '. Their team had to assess the patients from Heavy Rescue or ones they fetched themselves. The serious cases they sent on to Bart's Hospital in ambulances. There was no time off.

> During the Blitz you were on for twenty-four hours a day. You had to be; they were so short of people. If there was a raid on, you didn't sleep because there wasn't enough of us. When there wasn't a raid on you slept. I had just married. My husband was on fire duty every night at Somerset House and I was on duty every night at the Health Unit. We could meet only occasionally at a café to have a snack.

The First-Aid Posts were 'fixed' posts, but there were also First-Aid Mobile Units. Margie helped to set one up. It consisted of 'a rather long Green Line bus the inside of which had been cleared of all seats and fitted up with medical equipment including a primus stove'. Margie was the only one available to drive it; but, having only driven a baby Austin before, she felt that she ought to have

> a bit of a practice first. So out I came wearing my 'Sister Dora' – a great white sort of sister's headcap – and started off down Shaftesbury Avenue, round Piccadilly Circus and back again, changing gear with enormous movements. People saw this Green Line bus with apparently a Sister driving it and started waving their hands and shouting 'Hello, nursie! Hello, nursie!' Then I had to study the roads in the area very carefully. I went round on a bicycle beforehand. I knew I would be driving with the lights blacked out and you only had something the size of a shilling allowed in the way of headlights.

For a 'call out', whoever was available went to meet whatever emergency, and if the inside of the bus was inadequate to cope the team were given powers to commandeer a building to set up an emergency first-aid post. There was always one doctor on duty to accompany them – though back in 1939 when things were less organised there was one call to deliver a baby and no doctor around. 'I had to go,' said Margie.

> Our training for ARP only taught us how to cope with cuts, bruises, first stage of fractures, burns, etc. I was very innocent in those days. You knew where a baby came from . . . but that was all. The emergency doctor was called for . . . but the baby arrived first. I delivered it and got it breathing . . . then looked at the yards of cord and thought: What the hell do you do about THAT? Luckily it was the woman's seventh child, and she was a great help. Then the doctor arrived and dealt with the cord. I excused myself, went back, went to the loo and was incredibly sick from the shock of it all. After, I said to our doctor: 'Well, look, in the stress of air raids this could happen. I think we should learn how to cope.' So we were taught such problems.

Looking back, Margie remembers the incredible selflessness of the patients; the courage of the cockneys – especially the Heavy Rescue – the enormous generosity of the people, and the rôle she had to play in it all. . . .

> You see, you were wearing a uniform, therefore you had to present an image of calm and authority in that people would think you knew what you were doing. You had to behave in a certain way. You would have to cope. You had to shove your own emotions into the background on duty. It was almost a gift to you that you were allowed to help; one was only too glad to be able to do it.

And Kathy Gibbons admits: 'I preferred the war days to the days now. It's a wicked thing to say, because people was getting killed. But I enjoyed the atmosphere and the friendliness of people in those days.'

Fire

From August 1942, women who had already volunteered for Civil Defence could be compelled to do fire-watching duty for a minimum of forty-eight hours a month, in addition to their usual work.

Many women had already volunteered to work part-time for the National Fire Service in fact. There were 47,000 such part-timers during the war, plus 2,000 who worked full-time, earning £2 5s (£2.25) per week to the men's £3. They were not actually allowed to fight fires, but some drove engines and others manned the emergency telephones. The majority, however, took care of the men, making tea and snacks and generally cleaning up.

Pat Newman (Musson), a part-time telephonist/admin. worker stationed in Southampton Row, joined the Auxiliary Fire Service in 1938. 'There were so few lady volunteers then that we always went by back roads to the fire station to avoid being cat-called by children.' Her hours varied from one night a week on duty, one on emergency standby, to working two days on, one day off.

At not quite eighteen, Kathleen Clayden (Cracknell) was the youngest woman to join full-time in 1938. She 'fell in love with the uniform – a blue overall with AFS badge on the pocket'. Later, when the AFS became the NFS in August 1941, recruits were issued with a neat navy-blue suit with navy and red piped hat. But they were expected to supply the rest of the outfit themselves, and Mary Palmer (Matthew), a full timer at Henleaze, Bristol, said:

> clothes were on coupons and I had none left. So the shirt was an old one of my father's, very voluminous, which I managed to tuck into the skirt-band. The tie was one of his 'funeral' ties. I had no black shoes, so I dyed a pair of old light ones. These looked excellent . . . but the black dye smelled somewhat

99

like 'cats'. Unfortunately this didn't wear off with time and got worse when my feet got hot! Nevertheless, I felt very smart in uniform.

Training was normally for two weeks. For Pat Newman at the Woolwich fire station it consisted of

lectures on fire alarm calls, fire reports, topography, workings of the LFB, etc., from Station level to HQ level at Lambeth. Then we took part in the review by the then Duke and Duchess of Kent in Hyde Park, and obtained the AFS badge. We were told to report if war broke. On 1 Sept we were duly called up and told to bring gas-masks, toiletries and one blanket (not more) to 42Z Sub-Station, which turned out to be a warehouse on the banks of the River Thames at Woolwich. We were horrified to find that 42Z Sub-Station was the funeral department depot. The girls had to sleep in an upstairs room on bare boards with gas-masks as pillows, and the men slept in the coffin department; some of them utilised empty coffins as beds, until eventually we were moved to Wood Street School nearby.

Uncomfortable lodgings could be endured more easily than hostility from the men of the LFB who outnumbered the females by fifty or sixty to eight. Pat found them very much of the opinion that 'women weren't necessary in service life. We always came a poor second with issues of new uniforms, etc.' Other girls met with a fatherly approach. Rosemary Joy (Hewson) had some 'very nervous' first weeks, as the youngest in Soho fire station, 'but the Leading Firemen on my watch (blue) looked after me'. Kathleen Clayden's account reveals perhaps the truth of the situation: women were just not taken seriously.

From the day I joined up I enjoyed every minute of it. The only woman among sixty men, I was thoroughly spoiled . . . also the butt for the jokes and tricks the firemen played, like putting snooker balls or a plate of jelly in my bed.

The men were in charge; and this included jurisdiction over catering and kitchen staff. Mary Palmer had the job of making 'snacks' for firemen on duty.

Our first visit was undertaken with great trepidation, and our worst fears were soon realised because they had bought a pile of sprats for us to cook. We coped as best we could but were mortified afterwards when one of them said: 'We thought you would have gutted and filleted them first!'

Kathleen Clayden found the food she was asked to cook a real problem, particularly with the rationing, because

the sausages were awful – 'breadcrumbs in battledress' – but I enjoyed the dried eggs, 'yellow peril' . . . though once I made a sponge cake with it for the firemen, and they bowled it along the floor and it didn't even break into pieces. They didn't let me cook them anything ever again.

100   It was during the Blitz that the firewomen were properly tested. 'These

ARP warden comforting child, June 1944.

Kathleen Clayden (Cracknell) of
Wandsworth Fire Station; the youngest
to join in 1938.

Mary Hetherington (Marshall) joined
Chatham Police Station when she was
eighteen in November 1942.

Pat Musson of Woolwich Fire Station (*right*), and her pals, 1941.

Officers in training at the National Fire Service College, Brighton, February 1942.

Two porters haul heavily loaded barrows at a London station in March 1941.

Florence Field (Gooding) was a clippie in Exeter in 1941. She met her future husband, a GI, on the back platform of her double-decker bus in December 1943.

were the bad times,' said Kathleen Clayden. 'Five of my colleagues were burned to death.' Pat Newman, marking time in Woolwich, found herself suddenly right in the thick of it on day 1 of the Blitz.

During the 'phoney' war, we had to work with the men filling those dreadful sandbags in very hot weather, and there were always exercises and drill to keep us occupied until that fateful day of 7 September 1940, when the Blitz started. I took the call-out from the main station, and it was 'All units to the light gun factory, Woolwich Arsenal', which meant that all active personnel left immediately; myself and two colleagues were left in the school with the Watchmen. Being stationed in the centre of Woolwich Arsenal, Royal Artillery Barracks, River Thames and the railway, we got the full force of bombs coming down and shells going up, searchlights, etc. . . . the awful smell of the butter, sugar, oil, etc., warehouses all in flames, coupled with the dust of bombed houses. Meantime we had to take calls requesting help which we had to pass on to other stations, many of them in the same situation with no crews left on duty.

From November onwards, when Bristol was constantly blitzed, Mary Palmer found herself at the station sometimes several times a night, sometimes not at all.

When on 'alert', we mainly made cups of tea and chatted. It was a hazardous journey reporting for duty with ack-ack shrapnel falling all around. Many a time we have laid down on the street and on one occasion a large piece of shrapnel hit me on the tin hat! The Firemen loved to see us arrive; not that we did anything special, but I think they got a morale-booster because we used to laugh and chat and it eased the tension. We had the greatest admiration for them because they were obviously scared at times but wouldn't show it. Quite often they were sent night after night to various blitzes around – Cardiff, Bath, Plymouth, etc.

As the raids increased, Rosemary Joy, in the Soho fire station, found that she was 'always too busy plotting the fires to notice the air raids. My poor mother was always worried about me, though she herself was in the wvs looking after evacuees from raids.'

And there were other 'problems' that firewomen had to deal with. Pat Newman found the cockroaches at Shooters Hill fire station 'scared us at night more than the raids'. Kathleen Clayden, discovering one station over-run with rats, put bicycle-clips on her trousers 'in case one ran up my leg'. These full-timers soon got used to such minor inconveniences. Janet MacHardy, a voluntary part-time firewoman in Wisbech, Cambridgeshire, remembers how once when the siren went on her night on standby

I grabbed my tin hat and gas-mask and hurried to the station. I saw and heard the German plane in the searchlight and knew if it dropped anything it wouldn't touch me as it would 'filter' as it came down, passing over Wisbech. However, I ran like the wind and was out of breath by the time I arrived, and when the men on duty told me I needn't have hurried, explaining about the 'filtering', they nearly died laughing when I said I wasn't afraid of the planes but I was afraid of the dark.

As the war progressed, the firewomen's duties ranged from those of despatch rider, fire-engine driver, mechanic and hose-repairer to cooks, control-room staff or wireless operators. Pat Newman was eventually privileged to be chosen as one of six ladies to work in the London River Service HQ at Southwark, where 'we were the only ladies allowed and became secretaries to the various officers. We had to parade every morning when the flag was raised and had to stand to attention very smartly.'

But it wasn't all work. Kitty Harris-Rushton, who joined as a teenager in 1939, became a member of the Fire Station Entertainment Unit, a show-band consisting of professional musicians, comedians and singers – 'all telephonists or drivers, doing our share of work as well as entertaining – but it was all good fun'. Their first big show, *Blitz and Pieces*, was so successful that *Pathé Gazette* did a film of her friend Renée Champion and herself dancing with the band. They played not only for the fire service, but at American officers' clubs, Stoke Mandeville and Shenley hospitals, Woolwich Garrison, etc., and with such success that they followed it up with *On Parade*.

All the firewomen who wrote enjoyed their work, especially during the Blitz. 'After 1941', Mary Palmer said, 'it wasn't the same for us because by then the AFS had become the NFS, most of the Blitz was over and the "spirit" wasn't quite the same.' (Mary joined the WAAF in 1942, and we hear of her life there in other chapters.) Rosemary Joy was 'always so pleased to do my bit as Firewoman 829529. My life changed me very quickly from being a teenage girl to being a woman.' 'Life lacked excitement after the war,' added Kathleen Clayden, 'but, oh, what memories to look back on.' Pat Newman was rewarded at the war's end by being allowed to travel down to Tilbury from Blackfriars on the Massey Shaw fire-float which had taken part in the rescue of the troops at Dunkirk. 'It was an achievement for a woman to board a fire-float, but to sail down the river was making history.'

Altogether, the war had claimed the lives of twenty-five firewomen as well as 793 firemen.

Police

During the war 340 women volunteered to join the WAPC (Women's Auxiliary Police Corps). 'We were a very élite corps,' said Mary Rose

Hetherington (Marshall), who left her apprenticeship with the drapery trade to join:

> there were very few of us in July 1942 – only about fifteen to maybe hundreds of Wrens and Ats. We took over the office jobs so that the young police constables could join the armed forces. I was one of the youngest to join at eighteen; most were in their thirties. As a telephonist, stationed at Chatham in the Medway, my main duties were taking police messages and transmitting them to all stations in the country, then writing everything in long hand in huge volumes (no photocopying then).

The only difficulty she encountered being a female police auxiliary was

> when the Sailors were on leave from a food convoy that had a pretty bad time of it at sea bringing the food in. What do they find when they arrive at Chatham? Only that the bus drivers were on strike. Needless to say, fights ensued, and the Sailors were locked up for their own good. I went on early duty at 5 a.m. and had to pass the cells to get to my underground office. The cells were on one side of a long corridor. Every little flap in the doors opened – with a head on each one as if they were served up on trays – each head wolf-whistling at me. I had to walk the full length of that corridor. I did with head held high.

Mary Rose reckoned that being a WAPC was one of the happiest times in her life; but when Winifred Hipwell decided to wear the dark blue overalls of a 'special' constable at the police station in Market Weighton, near Hull, she found life

> very boring after working for the Women's Voluntary Service. I spent hours turning over the pictures of criminals and waiting for telephone messages. There was usually a regular Policeman on duty as well, but if I happened to be left alone I spent time working out the hours on the 24-hour clock in case a message came through, as they had to be recorded in 24 time.

Winifred Hipwell left the police to become a successful farm secretary; but when, in 1945, Mary Rose was asked to be a *real* policewoman, she declined. 'At that time, policewomen only dealt with wronged or "fallen" women and neglected children. This didn't appeal to me at all.' Instead, Mary Rose realised an earlier dream of running a department of her own, at Gorringes, Victoria, in 1959.

Porters

Kathy Gibbons and Jean Elizabeth Houghton (Webster) had both been machinists in London's East End before volunteering to go on the railways. They were detailed to become porters, loading and unloading 107 the goods-trains in two busy London stations. Kathy joined Broad Street Station in 1944, where her job was

> to wait till the trains come in, go up and unload them, fetch the goods down to the platform downstairs and put them on to the wagons – either lorries or cart and horses. I worked on the fish-wagons most of the time which went to Billingsgate market first thing in the morning. We done shift-work then: 6–10, 2–10, 10–6 next morning. We changed shifts every week. I enjoyed night work best because you had more free time. Then I went shopping with me mum or looked after me four younger sisters.

Jean Elizabeth had been posted to Liverpool Street Station earlier in 1942. She, too, preferred the various perks that working nights gave:

> Us girls used to like loading the paper-trains because we would start work at 12 p.m. and work till 4 a.m., but would get a full night's pay because we were paid by the newspapers. Other times, we had to unload crates of live chickens, so if we put our hands in the crates we would often find some fresh new-laid eggs for our breakfast.

Night work also included loading supplies for the forces. This meant for Jean Elizabeth trays of Telfers pies. 'Now whenever I see "Telfers pies" being brought into our local fish and chip shop these days, I always shout out: "Our troops won the war on Telfers pies." '

Jean Elizabeth developed a special 'understanding' with the troops who passed through her station. The railway would put a couple of extra carriages on the goods-train at night for servicemen going back off leave.

> Some of the men would ask us if there were any 'redcaps' about, and we would know immediately they hadn't got passes. When the 'redcaps' were in sight we would run along the carriages and shout through the windows 'red-caps about'! Then you should see them scarper; they would jump out the other doors on to the lines and hide under the train till they had gone.

Stations were an obvious target for enemy action. One night the station did get hit. Jean Elizabeth managed to avoid the danger, but

> several people got injured, including our male porter who had his leg blown off, but he lived to tell the tale. Apart from that danger, I don't regret the few years I had on Liverpool Street Station, I grew up very quick and learned a lot about life. We didn't have any problems of doing jobs normally done by men; in fact the foreman used to tell us we girls were more reliable than the men. The men that were left used to like to slope off to have their amber nectar and perhaps forget to put something important on a certain train. As soon as the war was over, though, they made it quite plain to the girls they must go, and give the jobs up to returning servicemen. That's when all our problems started, trying to fit our lives back to where they were before war broke out. But we couldn't; we were different people, we had all seen too much suffering and heartache. So we all had to make a fresh start in life.

Clippies

Some volunteered to go on the buses as 'clippies'. In 1942, Blanche Alice Davis (Grieves) joined London Transport, working on an electric overhead-cable trolleybus; while, from 1941, Florence Field (Gooding) worked on the corporation buses in Exeter, where 'it was hard work and long hours, but I loved it. We got good pay and good benefits, and it was exciting for me after being a maid in a private home since leaving school at fourteen.'

Both worked through the disruptions of the Blitz. Florence, for example, was in Exeter during the big raid of May 1942, and 'for a whole week following, the buses couldn't run at all because the streets were all blocked, so we were all put on canteen trucks and went around serving tea and sandwiches to the rescue workers'.

Wartime conditions only increased the normal problems involved in working the buses. Blanche had to tackle pea-soup fogs that descended on London during winter months, made worse by the blackout and inadequate lighting. 'I would slowly walk at the kerb-side with a flashlight, showing my driver the way back to the depot. Meanwhile passengers were jumping on and off the bus as we proceeded along.'

Margaret Turner, a 'clippie' in High Wycombe, was put straight on late shift night duty and says that it was weeks before she saw some of the routes in daylight. In Exeter, Florence had to contend with 'a lot of obnoxious people when the bus was full up and people could not get on, especially when the pubs turned out or when the dog-track let out'.

But there were also benefits; Florence was to meet her future husband, a GI, on the back platform of her double-decker bus in December 1943. 'At first I didn't like the American soldiers when they came to Exeter, but after a couple of hours talking to him while he was riding on the bus I agreed to meet him the next week.' (Now they live happily in St Louis, Missouri.)

When Blanche looks back – especially at the Blitz – she remembers the camaraderie of the people who were 'always willing to help those less fortunate than themselves. Also I remember being afraid, but being more afraid of showing it.'

SEVEN
The NAAFI

Many of us 'did our bit' but with no medals to show for it!

ETHEL HALL (GRIMES)

The NAAFI ladies, too, must not be forgotten. Wherever the armed forces needed them, the NAAFI was there to give tea and sustenance. 'Servitor servientum' – 'Servant of those who serve' – was its motto. Abroad, it was installed to follow the troops as soon as the situation became stable enough; while at home 1,400 canteens had been set up by April 1940. The NAAFI (Navy, Army and Air Force Institutes), formed in 1920, had stemmed from the old Expeditionary Forces Canteens, and because these institutes were run on the lines of a co-operative society controlled jointly by the three services, NAAFI women were not counted as war personnel but as civilians attached to the services. They did no square-bashing, nor did they have to salute; and they were able to resign at one week's notice.

Accommodation for the NAAFI was usually no more than adequate; probably in Nissen huts with a solid-fuel stove in the centre. Mrs Kathleen Allen recalls that they had 'good clean beds and nice food'. The redesigned blue cap and overall for counter work were now much smarter than the original dress with the mob-cap, and they wore khaki 'for walking out'. The khaki uniform was similar to that of the ATS but distinguished by a 'pork pie' hat with NAAFI badge.

Joan Bennet (Mrs Downes), once an under-nanny in Park Lane, joined the NAAFI early in 1938. By late 1945 she had worked her way up through the NAAFI hierarchy and through various sets of uniform.

At first my duties consisted of general cleaning and washing up (stacks of it), but I graduated in time to counter service. After serving at various locations in Essex, I was pleased to don a brown overall and take over at twenty-two as one of the youngest manageresses to date at Aylett's Army Camp, Rainham. Now I had a room of my own which had blue bedspreads with the NAAFI crest.

Equally important were the cooks. The number required naturally depended upon the size of canteen. Thelma Everden (Child) was employed as third cook on a large convalescent camp at Kingston upon

110

Thames, serving 1,500 men. She wore white overalls, apron and hat, and had to manage without the convenience that electricity or gas were to bring later. 'We cooked by coal, and the end product depended on the wind direction and state of the flues and what sort of coal we'd been issued with that week.'

Her most popular foods were 'rock cakes', 'Nelson' (a pastry slice filled with stale cakes and bread soaked in water and squeezed out, with sugar and spice added, cooked, and cut in squares), 'Tottenham' (a slightly richer rock-cake mix cooked in slabs), custard tarts and sticky buns; while Joan Bennet's Forces' Favourites were 'Raspberry buns, rock cakes, Australian flapjacks, maid-of-honour tarts, and doughnuts. Fried eggs and chips, pies and pasties were "tops" for evening snacks . . . and what can I say about NAAFI tea? Much maligned at times, I'm afraid. Served either straight from an urn or poured from twenty-cup metal tea-pots, depending on how busy we were.'

In addition to the main canteens, green mobile wagons were stationed on an aerodrome: for example, near the hangars. Joan often delayed pulling down the shutters if an aircrew pleaded for 'just a few more seconds' so that a pilot could land his aircraft and come over for a cuppa.

The men, Kathleen Allen says, were 'very young, some only eighteen years old, most of them full of fun, asking for "char and a wad"' (tea and cake). These were not served during main meals lest the temptation to fill up with snacks might replace having proper nourishing food. Problems arose, however, when the Americans came over in 1942 to Margery Leigh's canteen and

created havoc by asking for more. I was at my camp when the first 'truck' of GIs rolled in. The American gentlemen came into our canteen until such time as their own PX would be ready, and our cooks were hard put to it to keep up with their voracious appetites; whereas our lads and girls would have one, two or even three slices of plate apple pie, they would have the whole plate *per man*, and when we had Swiss rolls brought in they proceeded to turn down the Cellophane and eat the same like a banana.

Cigarettes, tobacco, chocolate, toiletries, polish and other essentials were as important as food, and vital to life on isolated stations. Ethel Hall, serving on a small aerodrome in the depths of Lincolnshire, remembers 'how excited the WAAF got whenever we had make-up or lipstick, shampoo, etc., to sell'.

Stock-taking was quite a chore and often meant working longer for no extra pay. Unforeseen events could also increase the workload. Ethel was in the Halifax barracks when the men of the 'Chindits' returned before rejoining their regiments. 'This meant we stayed open as long as we had food or razor blades.'

Duties usually stretched from 6 a.m. to 10 p.m. with two hours off in 111 the afternoon. Margery Leigh, canteen assistant on an RAF base in the Wirral, described a typical day when

> before anybody could have their first cuppa, the flues had to be cleaned, the fires got going; then staff breakfast cooked, and cooks getting on with cakes and what have you for the bar. Then the bar had to be cleaned, cups, saucers, plates, etc., laid out, cigarettes, chocolates, soap, etc., on display. The tea and coffee made in urns, for the customers' morning break – this was only about twenty minutes to half an hour. Then, that over, preparation of lunch. If the cook-house fare was not up to their liking ... well, it was NAAFI sandwiches. The evening sessions 6–10 were usually regaled with someone on the piano.

If there was a dance on, 'it was 12 p.m.', Ethel recalls – 'and then we had some beer'. Thelma remembers making lemonade from old-fashioned crystals.

NAAFI dances, the most important entertainment for the forces throughout the war, were 'something for the airmen to look forward to', Joan Bennet describes. 'We would set up the NAAFI bar for the evening. One or two of us would possibly manage a dance, perhaps, but usually we were kept too busy selling the beer.'

This was when Margery Leigh came into her own. 'I had had my voice trained, so sang when the occasion arose, sometimes at an official concert, sometimes with the NAAFI piano and sometimes on my knees scrubbing the bar floor afterwards.'

When the dance was over, the men often helped to clear up. Kathleen told us that on her army gun-site near Coventry 'the men would always give us NAAFI girls a hand to wash up when we were very busy'. Thelma, the cook, positively relied on the fact that there were 'nearly always a couple of men on fatigues who peeled potatoes for us or collected dirty cups and saucers, in a big bath, from the canteen'.

During much-earned off-duty hours between two and five, most girls rested in or on their beds to chat, read and write letters. Joan recalls 'lovely afternoons cycling along the country lanes during those wonderfully warm summers'. Ethel, however, devoted her free time to learning Polish 'so as to communicate with the Polish boys in the camp'.

Such golden hours were most precious, especially during the raids. NAAFI girls working on aerodromes or gun-sites were in constant danger and some, indeed, were killed or injured. Joan was charge-hand at NAAFI Chigwell Barrage Balloon Station during the Battle of Britain, and

> when the Alert sounded covers had to be put over the open fire, the chip-pan pulled off, the cash-tills locked in the safe and the shutters closed. We kept handy a small case containing such items as Quickies, hair-curlers and, possibly, a hot-water bottle, which was grabbed as we ran to the shelter, flashes from the gun-site opposite lighting our way; fires burning in the City and the searchlights picking out the planes. When the 'all-clear' sounded in

No place like home . . .

but, to the serving man, the next best thing is Naafi. He can always depend on it. In peace or in war, in the long, slow periods of waiting and between fast, fierce battles Naafi canteens provide him not only with good food and hot drinks but also with the hundred and one small extra comforts that take the edge off the hardships of Service life. Like home . . . Naafi is always there. To keep up this high standard of service to the Forces Naafi must have a steady flow of recruits. A break in the supply of recruits means that fighting men go short of little luxuries, warmth and comfort. Manageresses, cooks and counter assistants are urgently needed *now*. For full details about pay, uniform and conditions of service apply to Navy, Army & Air Force Institutes, Imperial Court, Kennington Lane, London, S.E.11.

Serve with **NAAFI**

Margery Leigh at her NAAFI canteen.

Jean Wood (Whiteley), Restaurant and Welfare Superintendent.

the morning, up we all trooped, bleary-eyed, and most wearing a knitted hood to cover the curlers.

The Blitz brought increased difficulties. Much was expected from the staff. Margery told us that, in September 1940, 'no sooner had you closed at ten than there was the wailing of the sirens which meant down to the shelters, and whatever time you emerged after the "all-clear" the dishes had to be tackled, be it 2 or 3 a.m. ready for next morning's break'.

And when, later, Margery was posted to a gun-site near Wallasey she remembers appalling conditions:

By this time the bombing was hotting up, and my colleagues and I spent a great deal of time, both night and day, in a sandbagged 'dugout' during what turned out to be the May 'seven-day blitz on Merseyside' with the gunners bringing *us* cups of tea instead of the other way round.

Increasingly the NAAFI girls were called upon for work that involved far more than their normal duties in the canteen. Jean Wood (Whiteley) remembers the hours they put in when RAF Kelston was being set up in 1944.

We unpacked bedding and cooking equipment in horrible winter weather. Boxes of blankets arrived, and as we hung them up near any warmth available they steamed. How we managed without severe cases of pneumonia or rheumatism, I marvel. The cook was a wonder. She worked miracles at the new 72-inch ranges – back to back. We had dried apple delivered in large chests, and she churned out pies twenty-four at a time *ad infinitum*. All the staff worked long hours. Soon the aerodrome was operational.

Later, during preparations for the highly secret Arnhem drop by the 7th division, Jean adds,

the NAAFI girls worked like slaves and had the experience of seeing the men go and then many come back to camp still with blackened faces, exhausted, many injured and carrying bad news of many of the boys who a few days before had been served over the NAAFI canteen. I well remember the sadness and the joy when the familiar 'Cherry Berries' returned. There would be a shout of greeting.

Jean herself was a Restaurant and Welfare Superintendent for the NAAFI. Aged twenty-two, she left her domestic science course to apply for and win the job of RWS – a post usually given to married women over thirty-five. She controlled an area together with two or three District Managers and one male Group Supervisor. They dealt with the business side; Jean attended to staff welfare, billets and uniform, while visiting every institute each week to see to the quality and profitability of the restaurant service.

My life in uniform was amazing! Officer uniform was provided by a posh tailor in London. It was a beautiful barathea uniform with gilt buttons with shoulder-flashes of light blue (Air Force), dark blue (Navy) and red (Army); a good-quality Sam Browne belt, cream shirt and khaki tie. The greatcoat was excellent quality (many the time I slept with it on my bed in unheated lodgings!).

Soon, however, she found it

very pressurised work. I felt that I was doing a job far beyond my capabilities with inadequate training of one fortnight – then, mostly to learn the use of the hundreds of numbered forms that were used – nothing to do with welfare matters and no cookery training. My very sheltered life in a girls' Methodist boarding school was about the greatest contrast one could muster up! We had no secretary, no driver or batwoman, and I often wrote records and letters – always in triplicate – until the early hours of the morning after long days touring canteens. Many times I was stretched almost to breaking-point. Older manageresses were in many cases resentful of my youth and inexperience.

Though I had learned to drive when I was seventeen, because of petrol rationing I hadn't driven many miles. For this job, I was immediately given an A40 car – briefly told to drive round Kelston on a market day and then told the car was mine – off you go! Travelling about at all hours of the day and night should have been frightening (there was very little traffic on the roads in those days, and I was often on the roads alone). Or when amongst a crowd of rowdy troops I learned to lock all doors; but usually there would be one or two who would say 'Leave her alone, lads – let her get on her way'. In other areas I got to know the villages well – shopkeepers, doctors, district nurse, clergy, garage owners, etc. – and when the York district supervisor came to check up on me I drove her around, waving to the right and waving to the left!! She said: 'My! My! It's like driving with the Queen!!'

This life continued for Jean until, in November 1945, she was posted abroad to be responsible for the catering side of the clubs and staff welfare at all receiving establishments in Belgium, and later promoted to the post of the one and only RWS for France. Margery Leigh also served in Belgium during 1944–5. After the war in Europe was over, many NAAFI girls accepted postings abroad to help cater for members of the forces going on leave or awaiting demobilisation. (See Chapter 11.)

They were the lucky ones. Most NAAFI workers feel that they had very little recognition for their work. 'It was a good life, which I enjoyed, but believe me, doing a very hard job, *and* very poorly paid for long hours and mostly living in very uncomfortable quarters,' says Mrs M. Darnan.

Kathleen Allen was an exception:

Lots of girls fell in love with the servicemen and married them. My husband was serving overseas with the 8th Army in Italy. I didn't see him for over four years. We worked very hard scrubbing the big kitchen floor on our hands and knees, blacking the big old-fashioned cooking range and endless washing up besides serving at the counter to the troops, but I loved every minute.

Ethel Hall, coming from a small mining village outside Barnsley, found on her demob in September 1946 that she 'didn't fit into village life any more', so trained to become a foster mother in a children's home. As for Thelma Everden, her canteen was completely destroyed by a doodlebug while the staff were safely in the shelter:

So ended my days in the NAAFI. But I shall always relive the day the Sunday joint caught fire and we put it out with sand; a military policeman who used to clean our shoes with a piece of bone and beer-dregs; Mabel who used to drink condensed milk straight from the tin; Maud who could make camiknickers out of one yard of material; and the girl who borrowed my honeymoon nightie because she hadn't enough clothing coupons to buy one for herself.

EIGHT
Nursing

Unlike those working in the services, the nurses had already won their battle for recognition. From the very start of the war they were 'safe', recognisable as 'nurse' wherever they went, whether through Blitz-torn London in the dead of night or working in a military hospital with sometimes thousands of men passing through. Lucilla Andrews, in her excellent book *No Time for Romance* (1977), wrote that her friends in the ATS and WAAF said: 'Takes a right bastard to accuse anyone wearing a red cross of being a tart, but we get it all the time.' Later she writes: 'I took this safety for granted and only much later realised how much of it we owed to the legacy of affection and respect we had inherited from VADs in the First World War . . . we were "their" nurses; they were "our" soldiers.'

The VADs (Voluntary Aid Detachments), formed in 1908, were young women who had undergone basic training in first aid through joining the voluntary organisations of the British Red Cross Society or St John Ambulance Brigade. Together with the trained and assistant nurses, they formed the Civil Nursing Reserve. So urgent was the need for VADs that after a few lectures and only ninety hours' basic training they went straight on to the wards before becoming 'mobile', which meant being able to work in any military hospital in the country, or 'non-mobile', which meant they could stay in their own area.

Before long, many volunteers were coming from other jobs which had been found unsatisfactory or unrewarding. Grace A. Walton (Mitchell), evacuated with thousands of other civil servants to Blackpool, found that she 'hated every minute of it from the mean landladies and freezing weather – so volunteered to go nursing back in London'. Peggy Scott (Telling) had already changed jobs twice. She writes that

> When war broke out, and I realised that this was 'it' and that hairdressing was certainly not going to be of prime importance for a long time, first I joined the WVS, helping several nights a week in the local services canteen and meeting more men than I had ever dreamed of. However, I knew there was more to life than sausage, egg and chips and decided on nursing. Soon I was informed that the Gloucester City General was to be my home and away I went as a Civil Nursing Reserve, complete with three suitcases.

118   A wartime hospital like the Gloucester City General would have its

wards run by one trained sister and staff nurse, and their complement of VADs. The trained nurses who had once staffed the wards had been spread around, many snapped up by the armed forces. The Army recruited QAIMNS (Queen Alexandra's Imperial Military Nursing Service), the Navy QARNNS (Queen Alexandra's Royal Naval Nursing Service), and the Air Force PMRAFNS (Princess Mary's Royal Air Force Nursing Service). There was usually a 'QA' attached to every sick-bay and training wing, while others were posted to camp reception units or to convalescent centres. Mary Staples (Howells) looked after 180 Wrens in a lovely sick-bay 'surrounded by daffodils with a "ward" of three beds and a surgery/sitting-room', at HMS *Foliat*, Plymouth. Joan Greatrex (Water-house) was not so lucky. She was posted to the ATS Training Centre at Guildford, where

we VADs together with a medical officer RAMC and a QA sister assisted with the weekly intake of new ATS recruits, approximately 200. All of whom were medically examined, vaccinations carried out, 'hair searches' for you know what. A small proportion of those heads inspected were found to be infected, and in a few cases alive! These cases were isolated for as long as it took for the unfortunate VAD seconded to the isolation hut to rid them of the aforementioned. After thorough treatment, each hair of the head had to be gone over. As can be imagined, this was very time-consuming, much to the annoyance of the poor recruit, who tended to blame us for their isolation and loss of leave until pronounced clear. Some threatened to tell their mums!! The treatment of scabies (unheard of by me at the time) was another hilarious duty. The smell of the disinfectant of clothes lingered long in my nostrils, as did the special treatment meted out to the unfortunate victim. This involved the brushing on of a special mixture all over a naked soapy body!

Meanwhile, all over the country, the younger girls were joining the British Red Cross or St John Ambulance Brigade. One eager sixteen-year-old, Sylvia Parker (Chaple) gave her age as seventeen to join the BRC.

I had just passed my first-aid exam and was wearing my smart outdoor uniform that my parents had bought for me. Indeed, I felt very proud. I got off the trolleybus at Ordnance Road when I saw a crowd of people who were saying there had been an accident. I pushed through the crowd saying, 'I can do first aid,' thinking to myself: This is really happening. I had bandages, etc., in my shoulder-bag along with my gas-mask . . . only to be confronted by this really rough-looking rag-and-bone man who said: 'It's me horse, duck. Can you do anything for him?' I turned away disappointed at not being able to put my first aid to use. But I had plenty of practice later.

With more fully trained staff likely to be needed, many young women were persuaded to take up nursing professionally despite the low pay. Phyllis Stevens had faced opposition from her father, who said of her   119 wish to nurse: 'Oh, rubbish! It's finishing school in France for you to be finished off.' But when she was accepted in 1937 at the Nightingale School, St Thomas's, London, he was very proud – qualified St Thomas's nurses were allowed to wear special prettily goffered hats.

In event of war, the Ministry of Defence had realised that large London hospitals such as St Thomas's would be at greater risk from air raids than those in other parts of the country. It was decided that their student nurses would be moved to the country for long periods of work and study. These 'safe' centres would be shared by students from various hospitals. In addition, many buildings throughout the country had already been requisitioned as emergency hospitals to make a total of 250,000 beds ready for air-raid victims. Hospitals remaining open in London had to improve safety conditions: blackout curtains were put up, lightbulbs painted blue, wards and surgeries moved into basements, while walls of sandbags arose outside ground-floor windows.

When war was declared, surgeons cancelled their operating-lists and evacuated their patients from city hospitals to the country. Rhoda Evans (Gunn) and her friend Alice, working as nursing auxiliaries on number 7 ambulance train, were to help with the evacuation. Rhoda had registered a few months earlier to do nursing and was prepared when a telegram arrived on 1 September asking her to report in uniform to Moor Street Station at noon the next day with sufficient food for twenty-four hours.

We all knew what it meant – England would soon be at war. When we arrived at the station we found a long train composed of cattle-trucks with a gutter down the centre of each truck. Standing around were a doctor, about six sisters (two had been sent to Siberia in the First World War and one had served on the Front in France). There was a dozen assorted females aged from seventeen and a half to fifty-six, each with a minimum of ninety hours' training. A little apart were a dozen or so orderlies (mostly St John Ambulance men) of all ages. And on another platform children waiting to be evacuated. They had a long label on their coats and white bags and gas-masks.

Suddenly everything seemed to happen at once. The long benches on the platform were commandeered and manhandled into the coaches. All the newsagent's papers likewise for use as toilet paper, etc. No sooner was this done than the patients arrived (the entire complement of Hallam Hospital, West Bromwich). There were stretcher cases, patients in chairs and some ambulant (able to walk) who sat on the benches. One small boy sat on a pile of newspapers for the whole journey looking through a hole at the passing scene. He had never been on a train before. We had to count and fold the blankets which the hospital had given us in exchange for those on the patients. This had to be done after every journey. So began our war work. We returned home with the milk – very tired indeed.

For Peggy Scott and her fellow-auxiliaries, in Gloucester City General 'day one' was panic.

There were ten of us, all shapes and sizes. This didn't matter to the linen room; we all got approximately the same uniform, long blue dresses with red NA on the front, white bibbed aprons, pieces of white material which we somehow had to turn into caps, grey-blue raincoats with red piping and blue felt hats with red bands – it did nothing for my looks and figure, I might say! All sent out haphazardly to digs, we spent the first evening feverishly trying to shorten or lengthen those dreadful dresses and trying to make sense of the caps, but it needed help next day from already-established CNRs to make anything of these.

First days on the ward were daunting. Joan Piper, a probationer nurse at Dulwich, had as her very first patient in her first ward 'an elderly lady who shook and trembled continuously. The ward sister gave me a plate of red jelly to feed her. I don't know who was shaking most!' Others, like the very young VAD Nurse 'Sunshine' Watson, felt discouraged:

After being called at half-past six with a handbell the next morning, I dressed carefully in my smart new Red Cross uniform and I could not manage to arrange my cap, a square of cotton with the Red Cross worn at the front. After reporting to Matron, I was sent to the women's orthopaedic ward where I was very disappointed to find that most or all of the women were in plaster – there would be no bandaging to do, which I had been taught in my first-aid classes.

But Eleanor Cook (Driscoll), a VAD at Lodge Hospital, Orsett, Essex, experienced no problems. 'After a week of intensive lectures, it was on to the wards then and Male Medical for me. I took to it like a duck to water, made some friends, and so began some of the happiest years of my life.'

The VADs began working from 7.30 a.m. to 8 p.m. with three hours off some time during the day, and a half-day off a week; but there were many part-timers working only Friday evenings and weekends who soon found that they were the 'dogsbodies' and given, as Joan Farmer (Old) recalls, 'the menial jobs to do. The junior nurse was more than grateful for my appearance so that she could delegate her regular unpleasant duties. Can you blame her for wanting a reprieve for a few hours? Even so, I mainly enjoyed the work.'

But probationer nurses, too, were given these jobs to start with. Joan Piper says: 'I was always getting told off about the oily stain down the front of my white coat from getting too near the old-fashioned bed-pan washer.' It was only when Joan passed her First-Year Preliminary State Exam that her 'ego was boosted', and she felt 'fairly useful'.

Nurse Watson, too, found that she was always in the sluice room or sweeping wards, and

because the hospital was filled almost entirely with civilian patients I was afraid that I was not doing real war work. Only one military ward was open for soldiers from the nearby camp, and I hoped very much that I would be sent to that. However, I remember one evening, soon after I had arrived, standing in the great hall in the tower, where everyone congregated in their off-duty periods. We were having a sing-song and, as I joined in with the songs, felt an uprush of emotion of being grown-up at last, of proudly wearing the uniform of a Red Cross nurse, of being a war worker, of doing my bit for the war effort.

Inevitably some VADs as well as young students gave up. The work was too hard, the conditions too grim, the discipline too irksome. But most carried on. Joan Farmer learned that 'it takes more than dedication or a sympathetic nature to make a competent nurse; it needs guts to tackle the many and unexpected happenings on a hospital ward'. And Red Cross Nurse Peggy Scott was soon to say: 'I saw my first death; in fact I saw so many in quick succession that I lost all fear of it.'

Those attached to the forces encountered forms of discipline on top of those normal in hospital life. Mary Staples, for example, while feeling that it was 'a very great privilege' to work on her naval sick-bay, found it 'a nerve-racking experience! Life was controlled by bells and watches and Liberty "boats". Orders were piped and relayed by the loud-hailer.' Army establishments were even worse. Joan Greatrex was now transferred to the Cambridge Military Hospital in Aldershot, where a very strict régime prevailed.

Try to imagine a long 24-bed ward, containing soldiers with various ailments, not all necessarily the result of the war, lying to attention for the Colonel's rounds – VADs at strategic points were also stood to attention in between beds holding aloft temperature-charts, and endeavouring to keep straight faces in spite of goading by the patients. The monocled Colonel plus his entourage would approach a bed, peer perfunctorily at a chart, whilst feeling for dust on a bed-rail!! Creased bedcovers or an untidy locker unheard of. Lots of elbow grease required using the correct polish for lockers, bed-tables, etc. Woe betide you if any smears appeared.

Living conditions, too, were tough. Olive Moffitt (Algar), clerking at a military hospital in Southampton, 'roughed it, barrack-room style, sleeping about eight people, toilets along a cold balcony with only cold water to wash. Hot baths were to be had but were downstairs across a square. One got a hot bath but a cold walk back to bed!'

A nurse's life *after* working hours was also kept under strict control. Rhoda Evans remembers the first talk Sister gave before they embarked on their life on the ambulance trains:

we were there to do a job and she didn't want any hanky-panky. She said when she was a young nurse in the First World War they were taken to France on a troopship and half the nurses got pregnant going over. We were very embarrassed at the time as the orderlies were there as well. We respected her wishes, but I understand that two nurses on number 3 train at Kings Norton did get pregnant.

Yet there were dances and socials and a little time for romance for VADs.

Rhoda remembers that it was 'easy to kiss and cuddle in the blackout'. Olive Moffitt, too, smiles when she looks back on dances in the YMCA hut in the military hospital grounds when

> dancing the last waltz was always to the tune of 'Who's Taking You Home Tonight'. And walking across the barrack square about fifty yards – no privacy – a hurried good-night kiss, then up stone steps to barrack room, perhaps bombs falling in the distance, guns firing and searchlights in accompaniment.

For student nurses, discipline was so strict that it was impossible even to meet the opposite sex. At St Thomas's, Probationer Nurse Phyllis Stevens soon found that they were to

> walk in crocodiles to the dining-room where we were waited upon. Hats were to be worn at all times. We only called one another by our surnames, lights out was at half-past ten . . . and if you were seen talking to a member of the opposite sex, even in mufti, you were 'out on your ear'. No one was allowed to marry before they finished their training or they had to leave.

Mary Morris (Mulrey), studying for her finals at Kent and West Sussex Hospital before returning to Guy's in London, found the internal hierarchy of hospital 'quite amazing':

> I wonder if matrons and sisters realise the terror they strike into the hearts of young probationers? I made an awful bloomer once on Men's Surgical. There was an urgent telephone call for the consultant during his ward round. He was accompanied on this regal round by his usual retinue of deferential students, his house surgeons and the ward sister. I excused myself to the great man, relayed the message and suddenly found myself in an awful row. Sister said icily: 'See me in my office later, Nurse.' I slunk off wondering what I had done wrong this time, but was soon to learn that junior nurses must never presume to talk to a consultant; messages must always be conveyed via Sister or a Staff.

But the months of discipline and hard training proved invaluable as the 'phoney war' came to an end. The rapid advance of German armour drove the British Expeditionary Force back to the Channel, with most being evacuated from Dunkirk between 26 May and 4 June. On 31 May – at the climax of the evacuation – Mary Morris was told by Matron that the ward was to be cleared at once with no questions asked.

> As I entered the casualty department, I was astounded to see so many wet, dirty and injured people there. Some were soldiers, others were civilians. They were all laid out on stretchers on the floor, and most of our surgeons and physicians were there, assisted by several senior sisters and staff nurses. I was given the job of removing dirty wet clothing, so that they could be examined by the doctors. Several of the men had their skin flayed by oil burns, a very painful condition, and others were injured by bomb splinters, and some were injured by machine-gun fire from the air as they came across the Channel.

Up to this point the hospitals had had to deal with nothing more alarming than bronchitis and pneumonia due to the severe weather conditions. Now they were faced with the full range of war wounds, and this without the benefit of penicillin, or any other form of antibiotics. Post-operative physiotherapy was a new development, though, and there were the recently developed sulpha drugs, all of which improved the lot of the wounded.

The way they were received was rather disorganised, however. Student Phyllis Stevens, doing theatre training at Brookfield Hospital, Surrey, was to expect eye casualties from Dunkirk. 'We waited, but didn't get them, and we sat outside in the sun with nothing to do but knit.' While in other places staff were suddenly overworked. Daphne Page (Davis), a VAD cook at her new barracks near Bovington, tells a queer tale.

> Many hundreds of men, the survivors who had reported sick, were sent here. They were given beds, tea and soup and aspirins, and the theory was that it was so uncomfortable that if after forty-eight hours they still reported sick, then they really must be! We were horrified and thought that they should be 'spoilt' after all they had gone through. However, the doctor was proved right and we wrong, for we never heard any complaints and only a very small proportion needed real hospital treatment.

The last wounded from the evacuation of Dunkirk were still in the wards when they began to be joined by the first casualties from the Battle of Britain. This raged from 10 July to 27 September, with its peak in mid-August, as these extracts from Mary Morris's diary show.

> *August 14th:* The Dunkirk men have gone home now or back to their units. In addition to the usual civilian surgical cases, we have several young RAF officers most of them with burns. They are Spitfire and Hurricane pilots. They usually remain with us for a few weeks' treatment prior to being transferred to Mr McIndoe's unit at East Grinstead Hospital. Have heard a great deal about his incredible powers in rebuilding faces for these young men who are so disfigured.

> *August 15th:* I went out on to the balcony at dawn just before washing the patients. The early mornings here are so beautiful. The air-raid warning usually goes off after our meal at 9.30 a.m., and soon afterwards we hear planes and the ack-ack guns. I watched another dog-fight this afternoon, the plane bursting into flame up there in the blue sky and the white parachute opening up like a flower and then dropping gracefully onto a field. Sometimes the parachute becomes entangled in a tree or even a church tower. All this has become a commonplace everyday event now. We had four German POW pilots admitted today, three were Messerschmidt pilots, the fourth a crew member of a Dornier, a 'flying pencil' bomber. Helmut's parachute landed on top of the church steeple, and there he sat refusing to come down. . . . He came down eventually when he was hungry.

124   Soon, however, as the Battle of Britain gave way to the Blitz, space had

A VAD nurse (Sheila Annesley) with a wounded RAF officer in a convalescent home, May 1941.

QA Mary Morris (Mulrey).

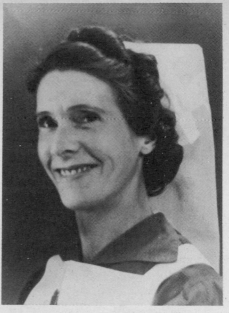

Portrait of Nurse Brading. Civil Nursing Reserve in Portsmouth 1939–46.

Rhoda Evans (*front, second from right*) with her No. 7 Ambulance crew.

to be made in the wards for the civilian victims of war. There was no more than a couple of weeks from the time of the first 'accidental' bombing of London on 24 August to the start of the mass raids. Phyllis Stevens witnessed her first bombing at four o'clock on the afternoon of 9 September. Phyllis, then twenty-two, had been training at St Thomas's for two and a half years, and doing her stint of night duty, when she saw 'masses of these huge black things dropping from the planes and heard the roaring and the thud of the bombs. There were no anti-aircraft guns that early on. So Matron moved us down to sleep in the basement.'

This was just as well, for the following night the hospital was hit. St Thomas's made a sitting target with the Houses of Parliament opposite, Westminster and Lambeth Bridges on either side, and Waterloo Station to the south. In Phyllis's ward,

all the men had woken up with fright, and I had to give them all phenobarbitone as most were cardiac patients, to try to settle them down. We walked along the main corridor to see what had happened and saw this enormous gap where the nurses' home had been hit. You could see County Hall through it. There was this thick cloud of smoke, brick-dust and this awful smell of cordite. So not one single patient was killed; but, although all the nurses were sleeping in the basement, four qualified physiotherapists not under Matron's jurisdiction had decided to stay and they got killed. Also one midwife home late after attending to a case and another girl who had been on leave seeing her parents and got back late delayed by the Blitz had both reported in, and so as not to disturb anyone would stay up in their rooms. They both got killed as the bomb fell at 1.30.

The following week, 15 September, we were just getting dressed to go on night duty when there was this almighty bang. A huge bomb had fallen on the dispensary, which was alight, then had fallen through the main corridor to the basement and hit the staff canteen. There were a lot of casualties. Matron came over for six volunteers to look after the patients who had been injured, and many burned. They had been laid head to tail in the basement wards. You had no idea who you would find in the beds. They were all staff who you might know. I remember a senior sister saying: 'You can't really nurse them. Just keep them comfortable. But whatever you do don't try to smooth the sheets under them because you'll cut your hands to bits.' Apparently, they had just literally picked the casualties up and put them into bed, glass splinters under them and their hair white with brick-dust. We had to cut their uniforms off, put them in clean nighties. All the lighting went. All the water went. Everything went that night in St Thomas's. After that, most of the remaining nurses were evacuated. The basement wards kept open, but there was very little going on up above.

And this was to be the pattern of things over the following years. Red Cross Nurses like Sylvia Parker manned the first-aid posts and rest centres for bombed-out victims from London and surrounding areas. During the day, Sylvia worked in a laundry, but three nights a week she helped to wash and bath the children and to attend to any injuries they had. 'During the night we would walk round to make sure everyone was all right.' The midwives, too, were having a hard time of it. It seems that, in 1940, 75 per cent of all babies in Britain were born at night. Lucilla Andrews wrote that 'every wartime midwife and obstetrician I met agreed that nothing so swiftly induced a baby as the sound of a falling bomb'.

Meanwhile in Dulwich, Joan Piper was coping in all sorts of ways. In her hospital, when air-raid victims were brought in,

> extra nurses were drafted from wards to help out in Casualty and Operating Theatre. Those off duty ran to help, and the hospital chaplain was excellent as a trolley-pusher or porter. A colleague of mine used to give her patients enamel wash-bowls to wear on their heads during air raids to protect them from any flying glass or debris! Our spare time was sparse. We were supposed to work forty-eight hours per week but were always working overtime, and there was no payment for it in those days. We also fitted in our fire-watching rotas, or volunteered for extra duties like helping with the evacuation. This meant getting up at 5 a.m., an early breakfast and then taking stretcher cases to the large ambulances which were converted Green Line coaches each taking at least six patients. We set off in convoy, about twelve coaches, one nurse to each, to Marylebone railway station. There, the patients were put on the hospital train to take them north away from bomb-strewn London. When we returned we made up the beds in the empty wards and soon received the next tide of patients.

Such patients were probably taken on board by Rhoda and Alice (who were now called the 'Milkmaids' because they had recently acquired uniforms of blue and white striped dresses, white pleated aprons and unusual caps made from flat pieces of material). They had scrubbed and cleaned out a banana-train at Monument Lane Station which had been refitted for evacuating people in London and the east coast to safer places. She remembers

> battling through the dangers of the Blitz. Once we had just left Aylesbury when a German plane began to pass and repass us. We looked like an ammunition-train except for red crosses painted on the roof, so we reduced speed to 4 miles an hour as they said we were a harder target to hit at that speed. Another time we had just crossed Vauxhall bridge when a bomb was dropped on it.

Now, all nurses were issued with special identity-cards which gave them priority transport to their hospitals when off duty during air raids. Also, with the danger of flying shrapnel, all VADs had to carry respirators and tin hats. Rhoda, however, hated her tin hat and

> used it as a shopping-basket. One day I got a good telling-off when Sister caught me with the rations and a bunch of flowers in it. I soon learned my lesson, for one night when walking home with my orderly who lived near me

he insisted I put it on. As we stood at the end of my road, Adolf treated us to a firework display and a red-hot piece of shrapnel about eight inches long hit my hat – it had a permanent dent ever after.

Olive Moffitt, in her Southampton military hospital, found 'working in, speaking, telephoning, etc., with respirators on, somewhat difficult'. On night duty with continual bombing, she received urgent orders from Command or sent reports from the CO

especially if naval craft were in the docks for repairs. Often the ships would put up a 'smokescreen', and everything was enveloped in a fog. Also, I was proud but sad to witness the first ATS woman to be killed in action on one such night. She was given a full military funeral in the chapel and buried at the hospital cemetery. A very moving occasion.

Nurses like VAD Grace Walton took the Blitz in their stride. 'I had to cope with all the air raids,' she writes. 'The casualties were massive. I never worked so hard in my life – but I wouldn't have missed it for all the world. The courage – dirt – blood and death – but the comradeship was something that had to be experienced.'

Many nurses, though, were irked by the seemingly unnecessary duties they were asked to perform in addition to normal work. Helen Gray (Joyce), day-probationer at the Nottingham Children's Hospital, suffered the nightmare of a diphtheria epidemic creating havoc amidst the Blitz. Having recovered from diphtheria herself, she was

working day or night as required 8 a.m.–8 p.m. and 8 p.m.–8 a.m., having to resort to living in because of transport difficulties during air raids. The night bombers were mostly *en route* for Sheffield, some gunfire overhead and odd bombs jettisoned on return usually before daybreak ... but washing and bed-making had to start at 5 a.m., bombs or no bombs. Although the top floor of the three-storey building was evacuated of its long-stay patients, the remaining four wards of approximately thirty beds each were served by one central light and staircase. When the warning siren went patients had to be taken downstairs into the cellar, bed patients one at a time by lift, the others carried by scurrying nurses, wrapped in red blankets with labelled gas-masks around their necks to be laid on a continuous line of mattresses. So often the red blankets and gas-masks were either not out ready or had been tidied away when needed. Often the 'all-clear' siren went before we had all the patients in the safety of the cellars. The futility of the operation seemed so obvious it left a lasting impression.

All nurses were expected to be in places of danger; night duty was no exception. Phyllis Stevens always had to go up to the first-floor ward and attend any emergency casualties admitted during the night. 'There was only me above ground. I waited, and listened to the bombs dropping. I had taken up my knitting as there was nothing to do. I never dropped so many stitches in my life.'

129

Long hours, extra duties, bad transport and, above all, tiredness took their toll as the war went on. No wonder, then, that nurses felt their efforts unappreciated. They resented in particular the injustice of punishments casually meted out for being late. Sylvia Parker, going to work one morning after being up most of a particularly bad night, was ten minutes late for work. 'I was stopped a whole hour's pay for this – a lot of money in those days. No excuses. What you did in your spare time was your own fault.' Mary Snow (Johnson), on leave to her home in Mallaig, recalled spending hours on a station platform before she discovered that there was no connection and eventually returning a day late. 'I received little sympathy; several of us were missing that night.'

Rhoda remembered one raid when she was unable to get into town to work.

The only way was to crawl round a bomb crater and walk. I arrived about half an hour late and got a telling-off from Doctor, who rightly said sick people wouldn't wait for a nurse who was late. Juniors arrived about half an hour later and got the same telling-off and we were told we would be sent to Western Road workhouse as a punishment. Two hours later Sister arrived from the same area as junior and nothing was said. I disliked the injustice, was fed up, but worked the month at the infirmary.

Sisters and matrons may have received superior treatment, but not all were daunting or unapproachable. Many inspired confidence and courage in their staff. Mary Pulham (Abbott), working at a convalescent home for British servicemen presented by the Earl of Clarendon, recalls that when

one of our St John Ambulance nurses received a letter from her husband – a flight lieutenant in the RAF and then a POW – he was completely well, but his letter made no sense at all. He was mentally a total wreck. I suggested she go to Matron and ask for leave for several days as she was so distressed. It was a great revelation to me when she came from Matron's room later, smiling and prepared to carry on as usual. Later this proved to be a great help to me when my fiancé was killed in Normandy and I thought if she could carry on so could I, and I served the patients' lunches before going off to visit his mother.

As the war progressed, duties changed. One of Sylvia Parker's new jobs at the Red Cross Centre, was to

pack prisoner-of-war parcels which were sent to the various camps in Germany, Italy and Japan, or we would hold parties for the next of kin of prisoners who would exchange little scraps of news they received from their loved ones. How sorry we felt for the relatives of POWs interned in Japan camps. News was very infrequent. The young ones amongst us would write little notes and put them amongst the socks, scarves, tins of boiled sweets and cigarettes. One note that we wrote went like this: 'If you're single drop me a line. If you're married never mind!' At the bottom of the note we would put our name and address. Needless to say, I never had a reply. Perhaps the Jerries found them and removed them before the lads got them.

And nursing conditions had deteriorated sadly. In London's East End, Mary Morris was now doing her 'fever training' at Brookfield Hospital, as well as studying for her exams. She found conditions there deplorable, nursing TB, meningitis, diphtheria, whooping cough. An entry in her diary states:

Oct 1942: I am feeling tired. My State Exams are coming up soon and there is too little time for study. All lectures are in our 'off-duty' periods. I set my alarm clock for 4.30 and work on my notes and text books until it is time for breakfast at 6.30. . . . Fever Nursing is very demanding, time-consuming and more than a little frightening. We are short of nurses, probably because so many of us seem to pick up infections from the patients.

Aug 2nd: Their high-pitched screams are horrific. They are like terrified young animals. We give them sedatives for pain, but it never seems to help. I remember the ONE LINE in my text book relating to this awful disease which simply states 'there is no treatment beyond meeting symptoms as they arise'.

Feb 1943: On night duty in Children's Whooping Cough Ward. It is quite impossible to sleep with the noise of guns all day and the coughing and vomiting and screaming of children all night is quite intolerable. My heart sinks as I climb the iron stairs and start another 12 hours' stint of coping alone with 32 sick children, cleaning up the continual vomit and wet and dirty beds. Most of them come from the East End of London and are very undernourished.

Mar 28th: Once as I climbed the iron stairs as I was nearing the top I saw them – big black furry rats – I was hypnotised with terror for a few dreadful seconds while they stood their ground and looked at me. My knees were beginning to buckle when suddenly they scurried away. I reported the rats to the day Staff Nurse, but she said that there was nothing that could be done. The food bins were not emptied very often because of shortage of porters. She said: 'After all, there is a war on.' This is a common excuse for every type of incompetence and inefficiency these days. There is no answer to it.

Bad food was a problem for both nurses and patients alike. Nurses were given no extra rations. Mary Morris writes:

I am always hungry. There are times particularly in the fore-noon when I feel so faint from hunger that it is almost impossible to carry out my innumerable duties. Our food ration is totally inadequate: 1 oz cheese, 2 ozs butter per week and one egg each fortnight . . . and of course an orange each month (which seems almost too valuable to eat!). We tend to make up with bread – the 'National loaf' is not bad, but once the butter ration is finished there is only dripping to put on the bread. It is hateful stuff but better than starving. Serving the patients' dinner is a painful experience. It is quite exquisite agony to have to serve their food when one is so hungry.

Peggy Scott found on numerous occasions that her cheese contained maggots: 'No amount of complaining did any good, so my mother used to save me some.' Occasionally nurses were lucky enough to have their rations augmented by visiting teams of doctors and nurses from abroad. VAD Mary Mills (Macdonald) had one arrive from Canada at her military hospital at Hairmyris, East Kilbride, Scotland, who 'shared their food parcels with us and as our meals were of the poorest wartime standard it did help to keep us going'.

Joan Piper, however, put on a stone in weight after her first year as probationer nurse. It was 'probably due to the stodgy hospital diet. A senior sister said my uniform was much too tight, or words to that effect! She sent me to the needle-room and three-inch strips of material were inserted in both sides of every one of my uniform dresses.'

Perhaps the luckiest nurse was Mary Pulham at her convalescent hospital.

> As this was only nine miles from my home, it was thought that I would know the local tradesmen well, so instead of actually nursing I was to assist the Quartermaster. Every effort was made to obtain what was needed. I remember a supplies officer saying: 'I have your list, but now tell me what you *really* need.' All in all, with gifts of fruit and vegetables from the local people, our rations went round well. We had one or two lunches of bread and dripping, when the meat ration would not spread to us as well as the patients, but we did not come to any harm as a result. We were so spoilt that, when one day, a young soldier complained of finding a grub in his cabbage, 'Bring it to me,' said the Nursing Sister, and promptly ate it, saying that it was an extra meat ration for her!

It was no wonder that most of the nurses' treasured spare time was taken up with eating and sleeping. Mary Morris recounts how once when travelling on leave to her home in Caltara, Ireland, she was treated to a memorable breakfast at the Sherbourne Hotel, Dublin. 'We tucked into the kind of breakfast I dreamed about at the Kent and Sussex. Lovely rashers of Irish bacon, two eggs, sausage, mushrooms and tomatoes. Delicious home-made wheat bread and lashings of butter.'

And there were Christmases and birthdays to look forward to. Nurse Watson remembered that

> The sisters and nurses always worked very hard indeed to give the patients a good Christmas, and each in her own way used imagination to decorate her ward . . . the patients had a traditional Christmas lunch and, as in every hospital at Christmas-time, a surgeon carved the turkey.

Mary Pulham celebrated her twenty-first birthday during the years at Kyre Convalescent Hospital, and 'the patients presented me with a huge and very heavy key – wrapped in a beautiful mauve ribbon. I thought it was wonderful. However, some days later they rather hesitatingly asked me to return it: the Vicar wanted to get into the church!'

She remembers, too, monthly ENSA concerts, tickets pinned up in Matron's office for free theatre seats, and the film shows 'which gave us the opportunity to get on with our knitting for the merchant navy'.

When the war finally ended in the small hours of 15 August Mary Staples, at HMS *Foliat*, listened to the sirens of the ships far away in Plymouth Sound. 'A wonderful day followed laced with tears with remembered friends and lovers lost for ever, and then the marvellous anticipation *home* at last!' Going home was precious for these volunteers, many of whom had worked in quite atrocious conditions. This was especially true of those who had signed up for overseas service (and whose stories will be looked at in the next chapter). Initially for these recruits, however, there had been the excitement of becoming transformed almost overnight, as Mary Snow says,

from a young nurse to a nursing sister and army officer. Having been for so many years at the bottom of the nursing hierarchy and deferring to staff nurses, sisters, matrons and doctors, it came as somewhat of a surprise to find that my two pips produced salutes from all parts of the compass.

NINE
Going Abroad

The first women to go abroad were the handful of nurses and FANY/ATS ambulance drivers who accompanied the British Expeditionary Force in early 1940. Following the fall of France, a few were posted to places such as Singapore and Washington; but it was not until 1943, once Suez had been reopened, that women started going abroad in any significant numbers. They were needed to replace men returning in preparation for the Second Front, or later for demobilisation. Some, finally, went out to replace other women in uncongenial places such as the Persian Gulf where the maximum tour of duty was a year.

All those serving abroad were volunteers, and they did so for much the same reasons as had prompted the volunteers of 1938 and 1939: for a change, to add excitement to their lives, or maybe because a boyfriend, brother or husband was serving abroad or had become a POW. Wren Tremain Troop (Milner-Gibson) was serving at HMS *Duke*, Malvern, when she heard that her husband was missing and later that his ship had been lost with all hands. 'It was after that that the 1/0 suggested I might like to apply for overseas service, and this I did.'

New recruits were given additional medical examinations, which included vaccinations and inoculations. As well as the usual TAB typhus and anti-tetanus, Waaf Barbara Charters, sailing to Egypt, reckoned that the worst inoculation was for 'Yellow Jack' – 'My arm felt as if it had been crushed with a hammer'. And there were lectures and training for the new life overseas – as well as warnings. 'The hotter the climate, the hotter a man's passion. Beware!' Wren Patricia Pern was told.

They knew that the journey out could be dangerous, especially during 1943 when some 4,000 U-boats were at large, but this did not deter the stream of volunteers. QA Mary Snow, who went out to India that year, remembers being 'so excited at the prospect of going overseas in spite of the knowledge that a troopship had been sunk in the Indian Ocean and some of the girls I had known were lost'.

Some of the Fanys were to be involved with clandestine operations, which added the spice of excitement to any feelings of danger. Kay Kerrvish, who was to end up coding messages for agents behind enemy lines, came away from a 'terrifying day' at SOE HQ in Baker Street, 'convinced that I was to be dropped into Italy as an agent'. Pam Batt (Daniels), whose job would be to transmit such messages, spent some time before posting at the training school in Henley learning 'Morse code up to twenty-two words a minute! i.e., blocks of five letters – no plain English'. Following training, all Fanys going abroad were then, as Ruth Middleton has told us, promoted to the rank of cadet ensign (2nd lieutenant). 'Although we got no more pay as officers, the reason, we found out later, was that it enabled us to travel in easier circumstances, e.g., first class on trains.'

Various matters had to be attended to before departure, as Mary Snow writes:

> Now things were really beginning to happen – bank accounts had to be opened, a will made. (The will seems odd to a young girl in her early twenties.) Letters had to be written to next of kin – our letters were held back for several weeks by the Matron as our destination could not be revealed.

A week or so of embarkation leave was normally given. Kay Kerrvish nearly didn't make it back from hers because the train was machine-gunned near Wimbledon – 'luckily only one person was killed. We hid under the seats.' Parents were naturally filled with anxiety: some girls chosen for overseas were terribly young. Indeed, it was for this reason that parents, who had to give permission for under-age Wrens like Prim Taylor (Shepard), signed 'with mixed feelings': she had never been far from home and was under twenty-one. Priscilla Inverarity's father, though, had a more down-to-earth reason for signing 'only grudgingly': 'You should wait until you are an officer as, if taken prisoner, you'll have better treatment.'

Packing the strange 'tropical kit' which had arrived filled the girls with amusement. Wrens Priscilla Inverarity and Joan Dinwoodie (Sprinks), sailing early on in 1941 and 1942, received 'awful uniforms made from heavy white drill, white cotton stockings, white canvas shoes and topi'. Priscilla's kit included 'two pairs of white *woollen* knickers! And a regulation white skull-cap to put over our navy "pudding basin" hat once we reached the tropics.'

Joan Crane (Carson) and her fellow QAs bound for Egypt in 1942

> were given a list of necessities dating from the Boer War by the odd things like flannel petticoats and lantern with candle. Instead, we bought all aertex underwear – the only place we could acquire white stockings was a shop which sold them to undertakers! But we did have grey flannel trousers, non-uniform, for wearing on board ship – we might be torpedoed and we could not climb down rope ladders in skirts with men looking up!

By 1943–4, when the bulk of women went out, things had improved. Wren officer Tremain Troop had

> white felt hat with band and badge as for tricorne; white dress mostly worn in the evenings and 'on occasions', otherwise white cotton blouse and skirt, white canvas shoes, no stockings but ankle-socks optional. (Wren rating to wear the same except for headgear. Wren CPOs and POs white felt hats like the officers.)

But, even as late as 1944, Waaf Eileen Shaw, a teleprinter and wireless operator *en route* for the Middle East, was finding trouble with her kit, which included 'thirteen pairs of knickers, some thin blue and some khaki!'

In contrast, QA Mary Morris found her uniform 'very attractive – a simple grey dress, scarlet cape and white organdie head-dress, two lovely shiny pips on the shoulder and our own QA badge'. It was the other pieces of tropical equipment that had arrived she found 'fascinating' – things like a canvas bowl on tripod, canvas bucket, a tilly lamp and even a collapsible bath.

> We had great fun trying out the latter. Put it on the bathroom floor, filled with water. It was useless, so dreadfully 'wobbly' and 'swishy'. The others held on to the sides whilst I tried to get in; the result was disastrous and water everywhere. We were convulsed with laughter.

Women in France

Long before the bulk of servicewomen ventured farther afield, Fany Moyra MacLeod (Charlton) had joined the No. 2 Ambulance/Car Company, Royal Army Service Corps, on active service with the BEF, having boarded SS *Archangel* in April 1940 for France. Mary Nairne (Evans) was called at the same time to be a QAIMNS in the hospital-ship *Somersetshire*, after training at Guy's Hospital, London.

Moyra had been working since the outbreak of war in the Colchester Military Hospital driving an ambulance on a 78-hour week for 1s 4d (7p) a day. Now, in Dieppe, her unit was detailed to meet hospital-trains and ferry stretcher cases to the hospital-ships. But when, on 10 May, Germany invaded Belgium and Holland the hospital-town of Dieppe was soon crowded with refugees 'stretching down the road and out in one continuous procession'. On the 19th, Dieppe itself was being bombed, and on 23 May they were all given barely an hour to pack everything, load up the ambulances and move out. So began the painful retreat.

They left in convoy for Le Mans. There they ferried patients off trains arriving straight from the Front (mainly the Somme), moving them from

Number 9 Hospital to trains which took them to the British General Hospital at La Baule. And Moyra writes in her diary:

June 8th: There is a horrid fascination about an ambulance-train coming in; it snorts and steams in the noon-day sun and there is a few minutes' pause; then the walking wounded begin to appear, hobbling and helping each other along – bandaged heads, arms in slings, dirty and hot in their tin hats and battledress in the sweltering heat. That is the worst time for us, while waiting in line to load up with nothing to do but watch and think. One feels sick and cold with apprehension. The rest of it – negotiating the rails and the platforms, seeing to the loading up and to the doors and steps, and trying to avoid bumps all the way to the Casino (no. 4 BGH) – is a full-time job. One is so scared of recognising, in one of the dirty, haggard, unshaven faces, somebody who is a friend . . . It is rather cheering to see how different the men are when they leave the hospital washed and shaved and changed, with wounds properly dressed.

June 10th: Italy has come into the war. The Germans have reached Dieppe. We are to leave for England, and men are coming over here to relieve us of our beloved ambulances.

June 13th: St-Nazaire harbour has been bombed. All hospitals had to be evacuated and taken to the hospital-ships, fast. We drove in full convoy. I had four stretchers and one sitter, an RAF man. We put them off in a big Customs shed by the hospital-troopship *Dorsetshire*. There is a big convoy of some ten or twelve ships lying out to sea.

It was in this convoy that Mary Nairne's ship, HMS *Somersetshire*, was evacuating the wounded as fast as it was able.

On our third trip from St-Nazaire, we had nearly 1,000 wounded on board – our normal complement is 600. We are heartbroken to have to leave behind hundreds of healthy troops on the quays (Red Cross rules and regulations forbid the carrying of active troops), knowing they will expect to spend the next few years in German hands. *Somersetshire* is the last ship to leave St-Nazaire and set sail with all lights burning to identify itself. . . . An attack by aerial torpedo soon decides us to switch off all lights and high-tail it for home.

Meanwhile Moyra's unit had handed over to their new drivers and, after a wild rush of packing, squashed into nine ambulances which drove them to Rennes; then train to St-Malo to board *Princess Astrid* for home.

June 14th: We moved slowly, and with some manoeuvring, out of the narrow harbour mouth and an accordion playing and the troops singing 'Somewhere in France with You'. Our throats felt lumpy, and we were thoroughly fed up that we were leaving when there was still work to be done.

June 19th: (Home.) Paris has fallen and France has asked Hitler for peace terms, so we are left alone to champion the cause of truth and beauty, and all that makes life worth living. I have never loved England so much. Once or twice I have rather wished I could die now – but one must face the odds and go through with it. One thing I know: I couldn't live in a conquered England. We will win all right in the end; it's worth it.

The Voyage Out

After Dunkirk, women were sent farther afield, travelling out in the relative safety of a convoy. QA Joy Hobley (Wilson), sailing in SS *Strananava* to India in 1944, where both her brother and her fiancé were serving in the 14th Army, remembers 'grey destroyers always protecting us as we sailed through the Med'.

Once aboard, it was not uncommon for women to share accommodation for the first time in their lives. QA Mary Snow explained that 'in hospital I always had a room of my own and, still a somewhat sheltered Highland lass, it took some time to get used to taking clothes off and washing in the presence of others who made no allowance for shyness at all'.

Nevertheless she enjoyed the luxury of HMT *Monarch of Bermuda* in 1944. 'Carpets inches thick to sink into on the way to our cabins . . . and oh! the butter, marmalade, eggs and bacon . . . quite unbelievable and we all made the most of it.'

And Fany Kay Kermish, sailing in the *Athlone Castle*, remembers the joy of eating 'white bread and red American apples'.

No more than 250 women were to embark in any one ship. There were normally far fewer, often being allocated first-class cabins. Eileen Shaw was one of ten Waaf on board the *Reino del Pacifico* bound for the Middle East in 1944 who found themselves 'accommodated in bunks in the bridal suite! There were cupids dancing round walls and ceilings, and we had our own private bathroom although it was only sea-water.' Others were not so fortunate. New Zealander Honor Shelton (Flanagan), one of forty Waaf sailing from New Zealand to Fiji in 1942 to be a telephone operator, wondered what 'MOF' on her ticket signified. 'I soon found out – "mattress on floor"! And the ship zig-zagged for four days before we reached Suva. We were told that it was the roughest trip in twenty years, but thankfully I was a good sailor.'

Usually the ladies were spoilt – at least, for company. In the troopship SS *Moreton Bay* in July 1943 there were, for example, ninety Wrens and about 2,000 soldiers and airmen; while Waaf Ronnie Aamundsen (Walker) was faced with 500 Australian troops aboard her ship *en route* for the Middle East: 'the journey was not entirely boring. Excellent chaps. Not the least bit rough and ready!!'

Mary Snow describes how, as they passed Gibraltar in July 1943,

the colour of the sea and sky changed to a warm blue and the ship's crew appeared in spotless white. This was the signal for tropical kit. We ladies turned out feeling smart indeed but oh! the men when they appeared with their shorts – we had many a laugh. I don't think they had tried them on before leaving UK. Most were far too large and seemed to be near calf-length.

At this point in the journey her convoy joined another, in which Wren Tremain Troop was sailing, *en route* for Mombasa. 'We made a bit of history,' she writes. 'We were the first ship through the Med when it was opened up in 1943. Shortly after, we saw a ship totally enveloped in flames – a horrifying sight.' From farther away, Mary Snow had noted in the distance wrecks or fires; and Wren Prim Taylor, on board the *Reina del Pacifico* in the second convoy through, wrote that 'The first convoy had lost one of its vessels'.

Precautions for such dangers were to be taken at all times. In the *Monarch of Bermuda*, March 1943, Wren Daisy Baldwin (Henderson) was instructed to sleep in bell-bottoms, and QA Joan Crane, sailing to Suez in 1942, had her cabin doors 'fixed open because of people being trapped after a ship was torpedoed or shelled'. Priscilla Inverarity, in the third lot of Wrens to be sent to Bombay via South Africa in 1942, 'reached Durban on the SS *Tamaroa*, after dodging U-boats and having to wear life-jackets day and night. Sometimes we slept fully-clothed clutching a small waterproof bag containing our paybooks and a few personal belongings.' (The second boatload had all been sunk with no survivors.)

Discipline was strictly observed on board. For Waaf Mary Ker, daily boat-drill was compulsory when travelling to India in the SS *Cameronia* in 1944 – 'even in oppressive heat, and this was not pleasant especially in rough seas'. Joan Crane and her companions had to sit in a corner 'while the men were made to drill, and we used to wonder if we were torpedoed would they put one of us in each boat or just forget us'.

Working Abroad

Far and Middle East

Joan Dinwoodie was one of the very first draft of twenty-four Wren wireless telegraphists sent to Singapore in April 1941. After signing the Official Secrets Act, they sailed in the *Nestor*, with fifty other ships, having been given brass buttons and upgraded to Chief Wrens. The working conditions inside their watchroom in Singapore 'had to be experienced to be imagined. A windowless concrete block with no air-conditioning, and manned twenty-four hours a day so it was never aired. No wonder we went on watch armed with giant flasks of iced *ayer Lima* (lime water) and small towels to wear round our necks.'

Her quarters, too, left much to be desired. Although a Chinese *Amah* was provided for each block for cleaning and dhobying, the space beneath them was 'a happy hunting-ground for frogs and presumably to discourage snakes, etc., as well as to cope with sudden tropical downpours'.

On the night Pearl Harbor was bombed (7 December 1941), Singapore, too, was raided. All service personnel were ordered to report immediately to their units. Joan didn't set foot outside again until she was evacuated a month later, leaving Kranji for Colombo in the troopship *Devonshire*. But in Colombo a large force of Japanese attacked the city on Easter Sunday, and her house servants 'promptly stole our bikes and headed up-country. After that we were part of Admiral Somerville's Force A *en route* to Mombasa, arriving in May 1942.'

In Kilindini, Mombasa, her trials were still not over. 'We cursed the Arab dhows that came in from the sea beating drums so loud that we couldn't read the signals at times. And our watchroom was constantly plagued by a mass of flying insects, including praying mantises and bats.'

Mary Nairne also found herself in Eastern waters in 1941, in the hospital-ship *Somersetshire*, ferrying hundreds of Australian and New Zealander wounded back to their homelands – 'a long tiring journey, zig-zagging across the Atlantic, refuelling in Freetown and Cape Town prior to the final run across the Indian Ocean'. This accomplished, they were assigned to sail to Alexandria to provide the evacuation force from besieged Tobruk before its fall on 21 June. After twelve successive journeys, ferrying a total of nearly 6,000 injured to safety under constant shelling, *Somersetshire* (luckily empty) received a torpedo hit on its thirteenth run. 'Abandon ship!' was called, and they all spent seven hours in the boats with a Greek destroyer circling round them all night, until dawn saw them rescued by tug-boats from Alexandria. Casualties were few: six nursing orderlies and an Indian seaman.

By October 1941 it was safe to return to Cairo. Here, Mary helped set up a hospital to tend the wounded from the front lines, and this was where she stayed until 1945. (Mary Nairne died in May 1988. She was awarded the Atlantic Star – unusual for a woman.)

Later on, in 1942, QA Joan Crane was posted from the 63rd BGH in Cairo to Suez. Rommel was expected to invade any day. But they found they weren't needed and were sent to the Sudan 'with nothing to do but keep cool'; then back to Kantara to nurse the wounded from Alamein. It had been a great victory, but it meant that 'every day the trains landed more wounded. My first job was in reception, taking name, number and next of kin. It was very moving to see the effect we had on most of them, after

With the BEF (British Expeditionary Force). A ward inside the 'Casino', Dieppe, converted into a Base Hospital, April 1940.

Fany Moyra Charlton (Macleod) off to join the BEF, March 1940.

The medical staff on the Hospital Ship *Karapara*, India, 1944/5. Sister Johnson is third from right.

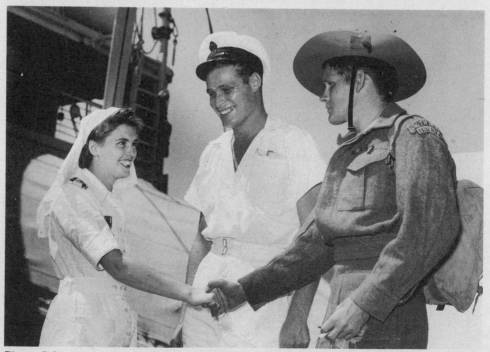

Sister Johnson saying goodbye to a Chindit she had nursed on the *Karapara*, 1945.

months of misery fighting in the desert – to be suddenly met by us was like a breath of home to them.'

Following in the wake of Monty's attack, Joan sailed to Benghazi in a hospital-ship, arriving on Christmas Eve 1942. They disembarked with extreme difficulty since the harbour was full of wrecks, then set up camp at Barce. But trouble started when,

> in a sudden storm, the lighters bringing our equipment ashore capsized. The retreating Germans had poured sump oil in the water-wells, our rations had difficulty getting through and our first convoy of wounded arrived. They had to stay on stretchers until we got help. Tankers brought us desalinated water for drinking only. The men had been short of water for some time and were in a filthy state, with desert sores and clothes fit only for burning. The operating theatre was working by tilly lamps, the rest of us had hurricane lamps. Gradually things improved.

Joan nursed the 8th Army for fourteen months, before being sent to Sicily and then back to Egypt to tend the African and Indian troops who were clearing up – and also to tend the POW camps.

It was now, following Rommel's final defeat in North Africa, that more women were sent out to relieve the men. Ronnie Aasmundsen remembers that

> the poor boys who had been fighting at the Front for a couple of years hadn't seen an English girl or heard one speaking for goodness knows how long; their ties were beautifully pressed, their trousers had seams you could have cut your fingers on, and they used to come up and say: 'Hope you don't mind if we just give you a clap on the shoulder; it's just so good to see you.' They were very nice to us, and very respectful – mind you, if they weren't nice, we just didn't speak to them!

Fellow-Waaf Barbara Charters arrived at the El Khanka Camp as corporal in charge of Central Registry in Station Headquarters. 'What a reception we had,' she says. 'We were the first Waaf to be stationed there. There was a dance organised for the night; us poor souls were danced off our feet.'

These dances continued, according to Prim Taylor, since

> word somehow got around at Ismailia, and the various Army and RAF camps were so delighted to see us as we were the first 'girls from home'. Parties of all kinds were the order of the day for miles around, and it was rumoured that there had never been so many practice flights over our camp from the not-too-distant RAF camp as there were whilst we were 'in residence'.

They weren't sent abroad to provide feminine company for servicemen, however; they had important work to do. And, just occasionally, they were given credit for what they did. Ronnie Aasmundsen told us that she and her fellow-Waaf

had to take over and run the entire telecommunications system in the   143

Levant, then we went on to run the whole of the Middle East section, and only after a couple of months a wing commander came out from Churchill to say that the Telecommunications Centre of the Middle East had never been better run!

Discipline was strict, too. There were still kit inspections, domestic nights and FFIs, while barracks life included new worries about bed-bugs, mosquitoes, scorpions and other assorted beasties.

Despite all this, most women look back nostalgically on their time in the Middle East. As Barbara Charters writes dreamily: 'We can say we have sat beneath the palm trees in the moonlight gazing at the pyramids with our boyfriends and drinking champagne.'

North Africa

A few women, particularly those working for secret organisations, were posted further west. One of these was Yvonne George, who was the only woman among 2,365 RAF who sailed in a 'nameless' P & O liner for Algiers in November 1943. (Apart from the captain, she was the only one on board who knew their destination.)

Yvonne, a Waaf intelligence officer, had already worked for two years as Controller in the A.I.2(c) Section of Air Ministry Intelligence, acting as liaison between RAF Tempsford in Bedfordshire and SOE. It was from this field that agents – 'joes' as they were called – left for France or other occupied countries in Europe.

In 1943, with too many aircraft being lost over France, it was decided to fly a squadron to Algiers, and Yvonne was posted to continue her work at the HQ of the Mediterranean Allied Air Forces. This was housed in the famous St George's Hotel – Air Vice-Marshal Tedder being the RAF chief with General Eisenhower as Supreme Commander. It seemed to Yvonne that she had 'suddenly fallen on to a different planet', coming direct from four years' continuous bombing, little heat, food and clothing rationing. Yvonne often visited the 'Club des Pins', situated on a lovely sandy beach just outside Algiers. Built for the French as a holiday place, this was now taken over by the SOE for their HQ. Here also was the ISSU 6 (International Service Signals Unit) where Fany Pan Batt had been posted a month or so earlier to work as a wireless operator.

The whole outfit was known in England as 'The Firm'. For cover we were all officers and civilians working as secretaries and typists – we had journeyed out on civilian passports. In England I got the name of 'Mopsy', having a mop of curly hair. Before I arrived the camp had received a coded message from India, 'Has Mopsy arrived yet?' Needless to say the CO was not amused, but everyone else was! We worked as wireless operators and others as coders, etc., to the Maquis in S. France. Some of them were on camp to be trained in operating a wireless set; blowing things up; trailing us and not be

144

seen in Algiers – that was fun – our main object to lose them, which we did quite easily. They were also trained to parachute jump by the Americans on camp.

In 1944, Pan and Yvonne followed the Allied armies into Italy. At first they were stationed in Bari, where intelligence units were helping to supply both the Italian Resistance and the partisans in Yugoslavia. Yvonne was once again

a controller in a team of three – another WAAF officer and an RAF flight lieutenant. We worked in shifts – twenty-four hours on, forty-eight hours off – monitoring the activities of the planes. Our control work was now dealing with hundreds and hundreds of planes consisting of not only the RAF but squadrons from S. Africa, America, and we even had two Russian aircraft. The latter hardly ever informed us (which they were supposed to do) as to their movements, and it was a daily task to chase them to find out if they were operating or not each day.

Early in 1945 the Allies began their final assault northwards, chasing the Germans from north Italy. With all their Italian partisans and British agents now fully equipped, Pan and Yvonne's units prepared to fold up. Pan went on to work at HQ in Baker Street, while Yvonne was offered a job in the Army Mobile Broadcasting Unit attached to the 8th Army and Desert Air Force. Based in the battle-worn town of Cesena, with equipment housed in three 3-ton lorries parked in the moat of an old castle, for six days a week she sent 'words of comfort and love from home to the boys who were doing such a magnificent job fighting in the front line'. Her signature tune, 'All the Things You Are', and her opening words, 'Hello, this is Yvonne with another edition of "Home Mail" ', became familiar throughout the battle-fields of northern Italy, and the programme – a forerunner of 'Forces Favourites' – soon had thousands of letters pouring in from men who hadn't seen their families for two or even three years.

Following the Italian surrender on 9 September 1943, Sister Mary McCulloch (Turner) had meanwhile been dealing with the less pleasant side of things in the hospital-ship *St Andrew*. Amongst all the havoc, she found time to write vividly in her diary of these events.

October 6th: Took on 386 casualties at Salerno. How difficult it was. A heavy sea running and we were under shell-fire while doing so. The patients are glad to get into a comfortable bed and have some decent food. I gave lots of morphia to the badly injured ones.

October 30th: My patient dies. Only a young lad. He was alone. Somebody will now be alone, too. I wish they could know how he died, but we have no record of his address or next of kin. [He didn't even have his AB64.] We buried him at sea at about 10 p.m.

November 6th: Set sail for Bari and we were sitting down to tea when we were dive-bombed. Not hit fortunately. We increased our speed to 15 knots, having sent out a message to say we are being attacked. What a night! The first thing I found myself doing was to put a life-belt on a Gerry patient.

November 7th: The *St Andrew* is the first hospital-ship to enter Brindisi about 10 a.m. Ghastly off-loading to hospital at Bone. About fifteen miles away and only four ambulances to take about 240 patients.

January 1944: Arrived at Anzio 9 a.m. Continuous raiding. We are told to steam away from the battle area for the night. So we, together with the *St David* and *Leinster*, steam away fully lit. But we are persistently and deliberately pursued and attacked. The *Leinster* is hit and set afire. Very little damage, and no casualties. The dive-bombing continues, and the lights of the *St David* are missed. We discover the *St David* received two direct hits and went down in one minute. There were seventy patients on board. Several are saved just by jumping in the water and clinging on to rafts. There was no time to lower any boats. We returned to Naples with survivors. *We* were fortunate.

The Germans appeared to grant no immunity to hospital-ships, going so far as to attack fully lit hospital-ships with German patients aboard. But there are incidents, too, of needless risks taken on journeys involving British servicewomen. Priscilla Inverarity had been working for a year in the cypher office in Basra, and when she left to attend her OTC in Colombo in 1943 she 'travelled on a fully laden tanker called the *Sinclair HC*. I asked the captain about his rules for wearing life-jackets, and his reply was: "If we're hit, you won't know a thing." (Later it was declared too dangerous to transport Wrens on loaded tankers.)'

India and Ceylon

Those sent to work in India or Ceylon found them countries of extremes. The experience of another Wren, Prim Taylor, was not untypical. She started off in autumn 1943 as a first-class passenger aboard the luxurious Polish ship *Sobieski*, then travelled overland in India in 'utter discomfort'. Although 'security' had given her a special section on the train, she found herself at one point 'waking from a not very relaxing sleep ... to see a huge Indian, wearing a brightly coloured turban, standing over me and smoothing my cheek with his hand. I let out a shriek, whereupon our escorts came running.'

Her destination was the Fleet Air Arm base in Colombo where she worked in the captain's office.

I was often at my desk at 7 a.m., siesta break from two to four. Work until dinner back at the Wrennery, then a further two hours. The work load was really intense, but of course we had our time off. Best were invitations from kindly tea-planters, to share their homes – invariably in the most beautiful surroundings with lovely gardens and choice pieces of furniture.

QAs Mary Snow and Joy Hobley also found themselves switched from one extreme to another. Both stayed for a while at the modern hospital in Poona in India. 'There were dances every night for which we had long dresses made from fine sari material. The Indian tailors could study a picture of a dress in a magazine and make copies from a glorious array of cottons and silks. Later, there were happy days on a houseboat in Kashmir, and catching a glimpse of the Taj Mahal from the train.'

Then Mary was posted to an Indian hospital where everything was

oh, so very different. The patients were very sick men repatriated from Italy. Relatives virtually camped round the patients' beds. I was Theatre Sister, working under very hot conditions. We were given great consideration by the Muslim and Hindu doctors and surgeons while they carried on with the work. We had special food, because everyone else, including Matron, ate curry!

Joy Hobley was sent down to Comilla to nurse in a large bamboo hospital close to the jungle where the beds (charpoys) had their legs in tins of water to prevent the termites crawling up.

My favourite patients were the Gurkhas. Many had very bad wounds inflicted by the Japanese in hand-to-hand fighting. Night duty was somewhat unnerving, going round my three wards with hurricane lamp and my Indian orderly, lifting up mosquito-nets to give injections. We were given much more responsibility than in the UK.

QAs were accepted everywhere without any difficulty, but for the servicewomen it could be less easy. Mary Ker – the 'first and only Waaf in Bombay, Christmas 1944' – had to make all the quartering and messing arrangements for incoming Waaf, whether airwomen or officers.

In one unit the CO, a fierce group captain, said he'd 'not have any women eating with his RAF officers', and he and I had a strained lunch behind a beaded curtain in an anteroom. After lunch he said all the RAF would have left, so he would show me the rest of the mess. We got to the top of the stairs looking into the RAF dining-room and a flight lieutenant leaped to his feet, rushed up to me, kissed me on both cheeks and said: 'Hello, Mum.' He had been my son in *George and Margaret* at the Carnegie Theatre, Dunfermline. This shook the CO so much that he accepted the girls *in toto*.

The FANY, too, was represented in the subcontinent, and we have accounts from Ruth Middleton and Kay Kerrvish, both sent out in 1944. Ruth's journey to Colombo, Ceylon (Sri Lanka), was relatively quick.

I was taken to Lynham airfield with three others and we travelled on a large transport plane – no seats, just four of us squashed between the cargo. Once we stopped on a desert strip of Sharja where the plane was encircled by fierce-looking Arab tribesmen and the heat was terrific. Then by train from Karachi down to Colombo and by lorry to a camp at Gangadawhela in the jungle to join the Indian Group FANYs attached to Force 136, a branch of SOE.

147

From the Signals Station there, I worked on a shift basis, encoded and decoded messages to or from agents behind Japanese lines who provided vital information and requested supplies of all sorts, and we sent them details of arrangements for air-drops, etc. Occasionally we would meet some of these men, and in any case we came to know them by their code-names, and there would be concern if an agent was failing to report in at his scheduled contact-times, with general relief if he later came through or we learned that he was safe. There were sometimes messages where a mistake had been made by an agent during coding or transmission, and it was essential that these be unravelled – so we were always busy.

Kay Kerrvish was also part of Force 136, the first FANY Indian section stationed at Meerut, India, doing similar work. Her coding sessions were long, but in the daytime only. She, too, worried over messages.

It was difficult to sleep when one knew that an agent behind enemy lines had sent a vital request for equipment – but we could not decode it. Transmissions by agents were often interrupted or jammed, and the Morse code was received in a distorted way.

Kay enjoyed luxurious living conditions in India.

We each had our own hut or *basha* with a bath-hut and our own bearers who brought us tea in bed. One morning I nearly died of shock when Mohammet, my bearer, brought my tea. He had dyed his beard bright green (a sign of the Muslim new year).

However, conditions changed when she was posted to Ceylon. Travelling down, her six-day train journey was

interrupted by the monsoon, which broke early, and it was impossible for the Indians to carry the meals down the long length of the train. After we had finished our tinned food the rasher types amongst us forgot the warnings and bought up everything they could find to eat at the stations, with the result that when we reached Madras the ambulances were waiting and fifty to sixty service men and women were transported to hospital – mostly with dysentery. At Gangadawhela life was pretty grim. For the first time I realised that mosquito-nets also helped to protect us from the rats that ran all over our rooms at night, knocking down the photos of our friends and families and eating anything from soap upwards or downwards. The toilets were great pits dug down through the hills – the sides of the pits being hung with cow hides which were supposed to encourage the production of the right bacteria. The stench was incredible – they were named 'cow houses'. Snakes, lizards and all sorts of wild-life abounded, and young Sinhalese boys were always on patrol with choppers ready to keep the pests at bay.

Ruth, too, remembers the undersides of the toilet seats swarming with huge cockroaches

which didn't matter during the daylight, but putting a light on at night disturbed them. They also invaded the quarters, eating large holes in one's clothes, so every few days these needed to be taken out and inspected. During the monsoon period the open drains running through the camp would sometimes overflow.

The 'creepy crawlies' were often the worst things that those stationed abroad had to contend with. The mosquitoes, long ants, scorpions, lizards and bed-bugs experienced by those in the Middle East were as nothing compared with what was encountered farther east.

Although occasionally Ruth and Kay had Liberty trucks to take them swimming at Mount Lavinia beach, neither the conditions nor strict security were very enjoyable. 'Most of my friends finished up in hospital,' writes Kay. 'I soldiered on apart from a short bout of dysentery. We worked hard – often night shifts, and were escorted to the signal station by armed guards. The only people we saw outside the camp were the saffron-robed Buddhist monks who were rumoured to be fifth columnists.'

After the war was over in Europe, Kay found that she was decoding not so much messages from agents in Burma as teleprinted messages from London regarding troops from Europe being redeployed in India and Burma. There seemed to be movement everywhere. QA Mary Snow was soon to come face to face with women internees released from Japanese camps. She had been transferred to another hospital-ship, *Karapara*.

sailing down the murky Hoogly River carrying a hospital staff to Burma with the monsoon in full swing. And thus began trips sailing from places like Chittagong and Rangoon with sick patients to be treated before going back to the UK. Once we tied up alongside the cruiser *Sussex*, and it was on this ship that the Japanese came to sign part of the peace treaty in September. Afterwards, we were not allowed to go to Changi Jail because of the conditions there but we did get to Sima road-camp. All were under-nourished and in tattered clothes but had managed to save a little lipstick for THE DAY. We were invited to stay for lunch. I'm ashamed to say we could not drink the soup which they had been used to. It looked like dirty water. It took some time to get these ladies used to a better diet. (It was interesting to find that the Sisters who had carried out their usual job of nursing and caring were in much better shape than the others.) It was for us now to repatriate the prisoners. Our first trip to Madras carried soldiers who had lost a limb. The improvisations they achieved were marvellous. Eating utensils made and fixed with wire, cups from old jars and crutches from all sorts of things. We had to restrain ourselves; they were and wanted to be very independent and were a great help to one another. Four young men were in padded cells, and it was pathetic to hear the noises they made and their blank expressions. Many of the troubles were due to beriberi.

It was time now to repatriate the servicewomen themselves. Regulating Officer Tremain Troop, who in 1943 had been busily getting 'any-   149 thing up to a hundred or more Wrens – as well as their papers – ready for embarkation' in the regulating office at the naval dockyards in Kilindini, Mombasa, had been posted to India soon after VJ-Day to arrange everyone's passage back to Britain for demob. She stayed in what must have been the most fabulous Wrennery in the world: 'a palace belonging to the Maharajah of Jaipur; marble-floored and designed by Lutyens, complete with rose gardens'. Kay Kerrvish, too, was back in India, working in Calcutta. But in autumn 1945, with riots breaking out and most of the work done, it was time to go home; and Kay recalls that, while stopping off in Karachi for a few weeks, awaiting a flight to the UK, they were given 'courses in beauty treatment, etc., and talks on the problems of the Britain we were returning to'.

TEN
Love and Laughter

I used to do a bit of tap-dancing and was trying out a few steps one day when I was asked if I'd like to join a concert party. Most of us were in the Army, but there was a girl civilian singer who used to wow the lads with such songs as 'Somewhere in France', 'I'll Pray for You', 'Wish Me Luck' and so on. The concert party eventually broke up as the men were posted abroad. I remember having a very soft spot for the sax player and was very sorry to see them go. This, however, was life as it was lived then. We had many light-hearted relationships with the opposite sex, some perhaps a little more serious than others. Eventually we knew they would be posted abroad.

EILEEN HAZELL

Life was not all work for servicewomen in Britain during the war. Maybe it was less exotic, less exciting than for those serving abroad; but they made the most of what leisure-time they had. Not that everybody was out on the razzle every spare moment; many were posted too far from any form of entertainment, and in any case few could afford to go out very often. Winifred Parish (Jones) had 10s 4d [52p] a week, 'so you can guess it was a case of spending it wisely. You had to buy your own soap, toothpaste, make-up, shoe polish and everything out of your own pay, but my mum and dad used to put many a ten-bob [50p] note in a letter; what a help that was.'

Eileen Hazell, also in the ATS, recalls that her pay

was about 9s [45p] a week, pay parade being one of the highlights of the week. Needless to say, this didn't go very far. One had to be an expert to juggle all the little bits and pieces one needed. Parcels from home were always welcome, cakes, sweets (often home-made) being shared among friends, sometimes a nice bit of soap or a knitted cardigan (khaki, of course).

Most evenings – for those not on night duty – would have been spent doing quite simple things; reading, writing letters, knitting, just chatting to friends. For friends were very important; so important – as one Waaf told us – that people were prepared to forgo promotion to stay with them.

You had to go on special courses if you wanted to be an NCO. We could have put in for it, I suppose. There was nothing to stop anyone putting in, but then again, who wanted to? We had that atmosphere amongst us all that

151

you didn't want to. You wouldn't want to be separated from your mates, you wouldn't have such fun. I mean, who'd make your bed for you when you was on leave and you was coming back late so you wouldn't have to worry about making it in the dark?

Your best friends – your 'oppos' they were called in the Navy – tended to be from your own hut or cabin. And you usually stuck together off-duty when you went out. But in many places, particularly the most isolated camps, there was no need to go into the civilian world to find things to do. Janet Sykes (Jupp) was with the 2nd Battery, 1st Searchlight Regiment, stuck miles from anywhere in the middle of Romney Marsh.

We had to make our own entertainment out there. Our SL troops were scattered in the surrounding villages, and they sometimes ran dances where we Ats were in much demand to augment the local girls. We were sometimes fed up that we always had to go in our uniforms while civvies could wear pretty frocks, but we were allowed to unbind our hair, if it was long, so that was some compensation.

Our battery was fortunate in having a very good dance-band – piano supplied by Army Benevolent Fund and other instruments, drums, sax, double bass, owned by their players. On Sunday nights we had dances in the canteen, to which off-duty gunners from our outlying troops were allowed to come. I remember loving them, as I was a good dancer, specially quickstep and jitterbug, and then how we sang the romantic songs when the lights were out – 'Deep Purple', 'In the Still of the Night', 'We'll Meet Again', a release from the anxieties and tensions of droning bombers and burning towns.

Burrow Head HAA Firing Practice Camp, where Molly Gale was RSM, was 'so isolated that the RA and ATS worked and played together. Pigs were kept and when sold the profits went to buy instruments.' What Molly describes as their 'average week's entertainments' would be pretty impressive in a medium-sized town.

Monday	Staff dance (camp dance-band)
Tuesday	Films
Wednesday	Orchestra concert (thirty-three members)
Thursday	Play (drama group)
Friday	Concert
Saturday	Dance
Sunday	Sports

The Friday concert was given by the camp concert party, the Shooting Stars. Their name obviously came from the camp's main function, that of providing target practice for ack-ack gunners; but so, according to Molly, did their costumes. For the towing sleeve was made of red poplin, with yards and yards of red net or white nylon, and, if retrieved, was made into 'costumes, pyjamas or blouses; not a scrap was wasted'.

In other places, as Claire Lowry writes, relatives had to be badgered for spare coupons with which to provide material for costumes. She was an immobile Wren in Portsmouth and describes a flourishing scene where, for one concert, they were coached by a professional dance tutor in a high-kicking Tiller Girls routine, much appreciated by the matelots.

Not all the performers in such shows were amateurs, though. Many professionals were serving in the forces, and others visited troops at home and abroad, usually under the auspices of ENSA. Even up on Scapa Flow, according to Nancy Hammond, they were visited by a whole range of performers, including Tommy Handley, Evelyn Laye, Joan Hammond, John Mills, Bernard Lee and the pianists Moisewitch and Ponisoff.

The quality could not be guaranteed, however. With so many camps eager for entertainment, the organisers tended to accept on trust anyone willing to travel. Mary Palmer writes that

> some of the ENSA shows were made hilarious not by the performers but by the remarks fired at them by the audience. One show included an act called Peaches on Parade. This consisted of half a dozen oversize women singing and dancing in satin dresses. The audience encored them so many times in a send-up, but to their credit they still kept going amidst hoots of laughter. Another act was a conjuror who couldn't and never did do any of his tricks. We had the tables turned, though, because a ripple went round that a French ENSA party were coming and of course all the men had visions of the can-can etc. It was almost impossible to get any tickets, and bribes were being passed. On the night it turned out to be a cultural show, and we all sat through classical music.

But the men in the audience were quite prepared to shout out comments even when no live performers were involved. Lilian Bader (Bailey) remembers that at the weekly film show at RAF Shawbury 'whenever the hero embraced his loved one there would be loud Donald Duck sounds from the men and indignant shushes from us girls. Sometimes, a raucous voice would shout at such moments, "Roll on my seven days' leave," and there would be more laughter.'

Such leave was very precious. People usually spent their longer, seven- or nine-day leaves with their families. But in the case of 24- or 48-hour passes this depended on how much travelling was involved. For Ida Garland at RAF Linton-on-Ouse it meant a gentle stroll, since she was stationed on land built on her father's farm. For others it was not so easy.

Kathleen Burton, working on searchlights near Hitchen, had a 48-hour pass once a month.

> We worked a guard the night before and went off at 7 a.m., having missed our sleep. I came home to Torquay a couple of times like that, travelling thirteen hours to get home and twelve back. We had to risk not being picked up in London by red caps as our passes went from 2 p.m. Most trains were

full and standing-room only in the corridors as well. When I got the train back from Torquay my mother had to push me in and I stood between the people on the seats in the compartment all the way to London, with their feet in the way and no hand-holds anywhere.

Pat Sparks had an even more tiresome journey from RAF Sopley Park with two fellow-Waaf.

Three of us from the North of England could not get home on a Sunday; we were given permission to have our passes at midnight on the Saturday. We travelled to Waterloo on the milk-train, arriving there at about 3 a.m. We tried to find a hostel, but they were all full. We were advised to stay in the services canteen on the station instead. Well, Peggy and I could have got by unnoticed, but Janice was so beautiful everyone took notice. There were representatives of all our allies in that canteen, all eyeing three girls in blue. Three British sailors came and sat with us for a while, giving us protection, but they had to leave. We asked a policeman where we could have breakfast and were told the only place on a Sunday morning would be Lyon's Corner House at Piccadilly. Being very provincial girls, we set off blithely expecting, if not tea and sympathy, at least coffee and toast. Well, we were greeted with cold stares from the local ladies, leers from the lecherous males and even in the 'Ladies' got odd looks. So a quick retreat to King's Cross was indicated, even though it meant a long wait for a train. I don't recall that we ever did get to eat breakfast, either.

Some COs were sympathetic to those with great distances to travel. The cook at the WAAF convalescent home in western Scotland was from Dover, so Dora Sibley always gave her an extra day to make up for it. But such arrangements could not be guaranteed, and it is not surprising that many women headed for the nearest big town for their shorter leaves.

Quite often they would hitch-hike – a considerably safer way of travelling then than now – since travel warrants were usually issued only for longer leaves. This is how Hazel Williams used to get from Chichester to Brighton, spending 2s 6d [12½p] on a night's bed and breakfast at the YWCA. She would hire an iron to press her uniform 'and any money left was spent on dances in one of the many dance-halls Brighton had'. According to Elsie Brimson (Private Poulton), when not staying with family they were expected to put up at an approved hostel overnight 'and our sergeant-major (a woman) would check up on us'.

The biggest lure of all was London where many attractions were free for service personnel. For Bettine Rose, 'Saturday afternoon in London meant a free ticket for a matinée, the ballet at the Opera House, tea at a glittering Lyon's Corner House'. Pat Sparks 'visited the lunchtime concerts at the National Gallery and heard Myra Hess play'. Claire Lowry headed straight for the theatre, remembering in particular *The Lady's Not for Burning* with John Gielgud and Pamela Brown as well as two promising newcomers, Richard Burton and Claire Bloom. Then there was Ivor Novello in *The Dancing Years*, or *Strike a New Note* with Sid Field and Zoë Gail, whose hit song 'When the Lights Go on in London' would stop the show night after night.

Some preferred dancing at one of the big palais: the Astoria, Cricklewood or Hammersmith (Eileen and Ida, the ATS redcaps, spent many an evening on duty at Hammersmith, up on the balcony listening to Lou Preager). Others went to see Ivy Benson's All-Girls Band at Covent Garden where, as Elizabeth Houghton remembers,

> the Opera House was converted into a huge ballroom with a revolving stage in the middle of the floor. All around us there would be servicemen from all the countries in the world, in uniform, dancing the night away, never knowing whether they would be alive the next day, but still enjoying the evening. At the end when 'God Save the King' was played it was followed by these allies all singing their own national anthem, which brought tears into our eyes.

Most exciting of all was the Stage Door Canteen in Piccadilly. The place was always packed out, and you had to sit on the floor. But there was a show, and dancing – to Glenn Miller on a good night. It was here that AA gunner Margaret Hunt was once asked 'Can I borrow your frame for the next shuffle?' by a tall ginger-haired American soldier.

Not even the Blitz seems to have stopped them coming to London. Pat Sparks once found herself in a tunnel at Waterloo

> next to an American naval officer who was disgusted because it was his first visit to London and he had not much time. I offered to show him nearby, if he could brave the raid, and we crossed Westminster Bridge, dodging sprays of water from the Thames as it was being shot up. He enjoyed my guided tour past Boadicea, Central Hall, to Westminster, up the Embankment to Waterloo Bridge, then back to the station where we parted. I don't think we even exchanged names. It was that kind of war.

Many units, particularly in country areas, established friendly relations with the local community. Evelyn Hambley spent two years at a remote AA post in Wales

> waiting for a Luftwaffe attack on Pembroke docks which never came. We had a good site commander who liaised with the local farmers, and both men and girls were found work picking flax, potatoes and suchlike. This earned them a little extra pocket-money. Half was put towards a camp PA system and musical instruments, and when in due course the unit was disbanded all the equipment was sold and every member of the unit (some 170–80) was given a savings certificate.

Local people would often invite individuals or small groups on a regular basis to their homes. Joan Stewart, a Methodist, was stationed at an army camp near Wrexham, Denbigh, 'and to be a Methodist in Wales was almost as good as being Welsh. There were people absolutely   155 queuing up to take me home for supper after the Sunday-evening service.'

Freda Spowart remembers with affection an old couple who were happy to receive any member of her searchlight crew at any time. When the camp was finally disbanded the searchlight was attached to one of their lorries and off they drove 'with all the villagers waving and the poor old couple with tears streaming down their faces'.

Others have memories of moments out of war, cycling into a countryside criss-crossed by hedgerows, with wild flowers as yet unthreatened by chemicals. Marjorie Nott and her friends from a remote RAF camp in Pembrokeshire used to gather luscious blackberries in the autumn, while on winter afternoons the women of the 'Famous 93rd', always short of fuel, went wooding down by a stream nearby, using a hand-cart to bring it back.

Those out in the country were occasionally given a chance of getting away for an evening. Janet Sykes writes that

> sometimes a 'Liberty wagon' was laid on to take us to the nearest town. This was a large lorry, and we had to scramble into the back and stand there clinging to whatever came to hand, usually a strong arm proffered by a gunner. We spent our evenings at the cinema or in a dance-hall if we could afford them or in the Sally Army canteen, where we were made welcome and could buy a cheap cup of stewed tea, a Spam sandwich or a grotty wartime cake made out of what tasted like sawdust.

But for some it was just impossible to get to any towns. Nancy Hammond describes the island of Hoy as having

> no shops except for a post office and a cobbler. No transport, only bikes to hire. Transport by drifter between the different islands was free, if one had the leisure-time to go anywhere. A ship was selected each Saturday and Sunday from May to September for the Wrens to visit to cheer up the men, from 2.30 to 4.30. A drifter took us there and back. Also in summer a dance was held by one ship on Flotta Island from 6 to 8 p.m. in the Naafi. A roll-call had to be held before we sailed back! Two late passes to 10 p.m. were allowed each week. All dances held on the island by RAF, Army or Navy had to be signed for, and Wrens escorted by petty officers, either by walking there or in a lorry sent by the unit.

Olive Thompson (Croxton), who was also stationed on Scapa Flow, calculates that in the whole area there were no more than sixty Wrens to over 50,000 men. In such circumstances it was difficult for women – however well they did their work – to be regarded by men as anything other than a precious commodity, bringing a touch of femininity to an otherwise all-male world.

In places where women were not so rare it was easier for them to be accepted as workmates and to be treated as friends. Joan Stewart was 156 one of five women (two drivers, one orderly, one welder and one clerk) attached to a REME platoon. 'The men were lovely,' she says. 'They treated us like sisters. It was like belonging to a big family! We all went to dances and generally went about together.' And boats crew Wrens, says Pamela Burningham, eventually became such a common sight that they were always treated in a friendly way.

> When we were alongside *Campanula* or some other ship we were invariably offered a mug of cocoa by the crew down on their mess deck, or sometimes a hand would just appear through a porthole, holding a steaming mug. And perhaps a bar of 'nutty', as all chocolate was called in the Navy. Of course, if we had no officers aboard we were more than welcome, despite being lower-deck, to be invited into the wardroom for a gin! Quite illegal for us, of course. The Navy is very democratic and the crews never resented this and we were on a friendly basis with them as well as their officers.

Romance

> While there is no objection to members ATS going out with members of HM Forces, it is not considered desirable that members should make a habit of going out alone in these circumstances, or any other circumstances with the exception of relatives. Members will clearly realise that failure to behave themselves on any such occasions will result in this privilege being withdrawn altogether.
> *Part 1 Order, dated 25 May 1939*

The fact that women could become accepted as efficient fellow-workers did not, of course, preclude more intimate relationships with men. Indeed, the closer men and women worked together the more likely this was to occur. The mixed AA batteries, in particular, were places where, as Edna Smith puts it, 'there were lots of romances. All the soldiers and girls were young and working side by side. I expect it was natural.'

Some officers thought that such goings-on should be actively discouraged, and Hilda Mason reports that on her mixed gun-site things were very strict.

> Our first junior commander was more suited to the rôle of prison governor. Girls in the forces quite undeservedly had a doubtful reputation, and Madam was not having any hanky-panky in *her* unit. A girl observed sitting beside the same fellow twice in the canteen was promptly posted to another unit.

But on most camps, and in all three services, the atmosphere was more tolerant. The rather prim prewar order describing such activities as 'not desirable' for Ats must have been quietly forgotten after a while. The only type of relationship that was actively discouraged was between officers and other ranks. Janet Sykes had to be very discreet when, as an ATS private, she started seeing her future husband, a troop commander in her own regiment.

It was a strange courtship, meeting in the nearest town, snatching a   157 minute's chat when he had to come in the battery office on duty, seeing him at Troop HQ in the depths of the country, or managing to meet him at my home for a 24-hour leave. Eventually he was transferred to the infantry and we were married in April 1944, but this was OK as we were not in the same branch of the Army.

Things became rather more tolerant as the war progressed, and it is only during the early days that, according to Frances Annett

a Wren rating was not allowed to go out with or be seen with anyone of officer rank. As many of the earlier Wrens were from officers' families (thus keeping up the tradition), it was extremely difficult for us in our social life, and many a time three of us were smuggled on the floor of a taxi with our officer boyfriends' feet lightly resting on our dark coats and we trying not to sneeze or giggle as the guards at the dockyard gates looked in the taxi to check. I had many a dinner and evening on board a destroyer this way. It added spice to the evening.

None of our informants refers to instances of women involved with men of lower rank. Such relationships would have been difficult for most men to handle, creating as they would an irreconcilable tension between inferiority of rank and presumed superiority of status. Molly Gale, as that very rare creature, a female regimental sergeant-major, has some amusing stories to tell about such conflicts between rank and gender.

At Burrow Head, oilskins, sou'westers and rubber boots were issued for protection against the severe storms. One day when wearing them I met a soldier who said, 'Going fishing, my love?' and I replied it was the weather for it. The following day I met him on the same spot; his face was a study when he saw my rank. Bet he was the only private in the Army who had said that to the RSM.

At the Saturday-night dances I was often asked to dance by one of the ORs from the all-male RA battery which was in camp for practice. I knew when it had been a bet by the whistles from his mates as we circled the floor. I usually asked if I shared the bet.

In most cases, it seems, women went out with men of the same rank or slightly above. Some met at social events, others got to know each other through work. But, however they met, there was the constant risk of either party being posted away. Eve Sugden used to drive the male wireless mechanics out to work on the planes and tells how during moments of boredom she taught one of them to drive.

The other one never forgave me for not teaching him as well but, then, I was not in love with him. . . . Just before D-Day I was posted away to a bomber group. If hearts could break, mine did then as I left behind the Spitfires and my true love.

Couples were automatically separated if they married, which is what happened to Edna Smith after her wedding to a fellow-gunner. They used

With Best Wishes
"Yvonne"
"Home Mail"

WAAF officer Yvonne George in a makeshift Army Broadcasting Service studio in Northern Italy. 'Home Mail', her request programme, was immensely popular with the troops, and hundreds of copies of this photograph were sent to men of the 8th Army and Desert Air Force.

'Gunner' Edna Smith wearing her Hollywood wedding dress.

WAAF corporal Lilian Bader (née Bailey) and her husband Ramsay.

*" I forgot; did she say I was going to be married and have two
children or have two children and then get married?"*

Images of women (*above and overleaf*). 'Serious' cartoonists, such as Osbert Lancaster
and Vicky, often depicted women in uniform as parodies of men. Others saw them as
empty-headed or as playthings for the men. Women in adverts were told at first that it
was their 'duty to be beautiful', but in later years the advertisers vied with each other
to give tribute to the contributions made by women.

" *What do you mean—you don't see anything you fancy?* "

" *If the ensemble fails to meet with Moddom's satisfaction, Moddom has but to raise Moddom's little finger.* "

"*I don't care whose window you were dressing before the war—that is not the way to lay out your kit!*"

" *Absent without leave, resisting arrest—rather a poor show, isn't it, mater?* "

to go to cheap bed-and-breakfast places for their 24- or 48-hour leaves. 'Some were awful,' she recalls. 'One place we went to we sat up all night because the bed was so dirty and full of bugs.' But the Smiths were comparatively lucky; many couples were posted so far apart that they could not meet for short leaves at all; and men, increasingly, were posted abroad as women were trained to replace them.

The solid relationships, like that of the Smiths, managed to survive; and many of our informants are still happily married to their wartime loves or can look back, in widowhood, on many years of happiness. But enforced separation inevitably put many relationships under severe strain, a strain compounded by the presence of other men looking for female companionship. And from early 1942 onwards an increasing number of these men wore smart well-cut uniforms, had plenty of spending money and spoke with accents familiar from Hollywood films.

The Yanks Are Coming

It was always a fight to get your name down on the lists to go to the American dances. They used to send trucks for us; I can see them now coming along like glow-worms in convoy. When we arrived they had got used to us and stood aside while we dived for the food-laden tables, food we hadn't seen since the war began, and it was all *free*! Then we had a good evening dancing, which meant of course that we got back to camp late, got up late, no breakfast, no time for tea, lost weight. It was all well behaved, believe me, always someone in charge. Then they vanished and we heard that their boat had sunk, so who could blame anyone for having a good time?
Ivy Roberts (Sergeant Johnston, WAAF)

American troops stationed anywhere near a group of Ats, Waaf or Wrens would regularly send out invitations to parties and dances, and it was an opportunity few refused. Not only was there good music and plentiful food but, as Betty Stanbury says, they all came away with a gift, 'nylons, cigarettes or sweets!' Such gifts didn't always come without strings attached, however. Bettine Rose will never forget the one time she went to a big USAAF base.

A lorry with about forty Ats and two or three officers took us there late one afternoon. Large bonfires were burning on the runways, and huge lumps of meat were being roasted. Suddenly a large fleet of B52 bombers arrived back from a daylight raid over Germany. Those crazy pilots flew low over our heads and performed all kinds of low-level flying you could only imagine a fighter plane could do. Later in the evening there was dancing in a giant hangar; beer-barrels ranged round the hangar and lots of old East Anglian farmers who had been invited along were supping and slowly sinking to the floor. Most of the time was spent dodging the more undesirable types of Yanks who were offering cartons of Camels or stockings in exchange for a visit to their quarters. There seemed to be no discipline from their officers at

163

all. At about 2 a.m. after they had rounded up missing Ats the lorry took us back.

Elizabeth Houghton used to meet a lot of American servicemen while working at Liverpool Street Station and reports that

our own servicemen took a dim view of our fraternising with them and would give us the cold shoulder. Some of the girls used to go down to their camp at Diss, Norfolk. I remember one girl in particular who thought she was clever at this lark and didn't expect they wouldn't take no for an answer; when they got her in a hangar they really duffed her up. When we eventually saw her, her pretty face was black and blue; she had really taken a beating.

But, according to other women, it was possible to talk your way out of any unwanted advances. Joan Stewart says that

Lurid tales are told of the Yanks' amorous adventures, but to tell the truth I found them both polite and helpful. The trick I found was to produce a family snap. Immediately out would come the wallets and you would see pictures of wife, Mom, Dad, Junior, Aunt this and Uncle that. They were home-sick.

Another woman who developed strategies for dealing with importunate servicemen was Win Dowd, who often found herself alone, driving round East Anglia with her truckload of films.

Cambridge was full of American soldiers in the evenings who were brought in by Recreational Transport (Passion Wagons) from the US airbases, and there were always a few who didn't make it to the truck in time. The vehicles were parked off the town centre. The stragglers were invariably the worse for drink, and not really to be looked upon as the average GI. If when I was travelling between shows I had to pass one of the bases and would be going through the town *en route*, I would sometimes pull up outside the gate and give lifts to odd bods on early passes who didn't want to wait for the Passion Wagons. I found them to be polite and generous. They would give me bars of chocolate and gum, the first a treat and the second handy to pass on. However, the Yanks I encountered walking home after parking my vehicle were very different. They had either knowingly overstayed or been too drunk to find the carpark. As I couldn't see myself doing battle with what always seemed to be a six-foot hulk, I had to resort to more subtle ways of defending myself until I was within spitting distance of the billet. My first plot was the schoolmarm approach. They usually opened with 'Carry your bag, mam?' 'Why, thank you, young man,' I would reply, and hand over the case. That was one hand accounted for. 'And how are you liking England? We do so appreciate your help over here.' This often got rid of them at the first turning. 'Have to turn off here, mam. Nice to meet you, mam.' When one fellow came on a bit strong I tearfully told him that I had promised my sailor boyfriend that I would wait for him. The GI tried persuasion, telling me that with a war on we all had to take our fun where and when it came. I still kept on about the boy away at sea and our plans for when he came home. Eventually he went very quiet, and when we reached the door of my billet I found that he was in tears. He shook my hand in both of his, lifted it to his lips and kissed it, spluttering: 'I have a girl at home and I would like to believe that she is acting just like you.' He didn't know just how much I *was* acting.

But not all the advances were unwanted. As Elizabeth Houghton says,

The permissive society really took off when war broke out. People of my age were never told the facts of life by parents; that subject was taboo. We had to find out for ourselves. The subject of sex was only spoken in whispers by our elders but, having big ears, we learned a lot. So many young people of that era never knew whether they would see their loved ones again and threw all caution and reason to the wind.

Problems of Love

We had an enormous amount of very young girls who were taken in at seventeen and a half, and lots of them came to grief. I took an elementary midwifery course because there used to be a lot of abortions and things like that. I was twenty-four when I went in, older, married, and almost like a mother to them. Sometimes we'd have three or four in the ward at a time. But I'm not blaming the girls; they were young, and a seventeen-year-old then was not like a seventeen-year-old now. They were innocent, they were naïve, they came in, there were men there, married men, ready to go abroad, there was immense pressure on them. And we had to cope with these girls. . . . You see, these things are not known. I'm saying it to you because it's forty-odd years on. This did happen.

Florrie 'Blossom' Buck, corporal nursing orderly, WAAF

Fifty years ago the average young woman knew little or nothing about contraception; the Pill had not been invented, and the only reasonably effective device controlled by the woman – the 'Dutch cap' – was difficult to obtain and complicated to insert. Women, therefore, relied on the man using a condom or trusted to luck. And luck, far too often, ran out. The consequence for many of them was pregnancy, and this at a time when abortion was illegal and single parenthood almost literally unthinkable.

'Occasionally we would notice,' one Waaf told us, 'that we had not seen a particular girl for some time, and the explanation was that she had been "posted". The simple truth was that she was expecting and had been shuffled off to the place where the RAF sent such people; all very discreet.' The services were not unsympathetic towards unmarried women discovered to be pregnant – they would, for example, help to arrange for a home to be found for the child, or try to chase up the father for maintenance payments – but it was an offence against King's Regulations 165 and merited automatic discharge. 'Of course, if the father was an airman,' another Waaf added, '*he* wouldn't be dismissed. Nothing would happen to *him*. If they were on the same station, then the woman would be discharged on the spot and the man would be posted away.'

For a few women – those unhappy with service life and intending to marry the father of their child – this ruling was convenient. But for most it meant that they would lose the company and support of their friends at a time when they could look for little sympathy in the world outside. Another of the ex-Waaf with whom we talked about such matters told us that in her hut there was one pregnant girl who went back to her family only to be thrown out by her father.

> She had nowhere to go, so she came back to camp. She saw the officer, and the officer put her into the medical quarters where she stayed for a little while. She felt so unhappy there that the officer put her back into her hut, into her own bed. And she stayed with us until they found a home for her where she had her baby. Well, we all felt sorry for her; for that girl to walk around the camp in her civilian clothes was really a disgrace because everybody knew, men and women, what she was there for.

We must stress again that the wartime increase in sexual activity outside marriage affected British society as a whole and that incidences of unwanted pregnancy among servicewomen were in fact less than in the civilian population. Certainly, in view of the popular beliefs of the time, this would have come as a surprise to many people. For, as Hazel Williams reminds us, 'the average civilian didn't think much of service-women; "comforts for the troops" was their idea of us. It could have hurt, but on the whole didn't. We were young, beautiful (so we thought) and could look after ourselves.'

They needed to be able to do so, not just to get through the demands of work, often in the tough conditions we have already looked at, but also to cope with the pains of love; those which have always been a possibility – the disillusionment, the betrayals – as well as those which war carries with it as part of the baggage-train: separation and loss.

There were women throughout Britain whose menfolk were exposed to the dangers of disablement or death. And there were many who received the dreaded telegram informing them laconically that their fears had been realised. For none of them can it have been easy. But it must have been especially hard for those women whose jobs made them more than usually aware of the dangers. And none were more closely involved than the coders, plotters and others who were privy to the movements of ships and aircraft at the very moment of battle.

Ruby Garrett, stationed at Bomber Command HQ for most of the war, knew at least four Waafs 'affected by actual loss of their husbands or boyfriends. One was actually on duty at the time, and we had to pass the

166

message through to the traffic office without her seeing it.' But none seem to have cracked up. According to Ruth Anderson, an admin and welfare corporal stationed at Bridlington, Debdon, Hornchurch and Gloucester:

> There was a lot of stiff upper lip. Some Waaf were engaged to pilots and they would hear it coming through [that the plane had been lost] or they would be waiting for that particular plane to come back, and it didn't. But they would carry on knitting, or doing whatever their duty was, and wait until that last plane was in, and they never did show a thing. We never saw one of them break down during work. Very strong. It was fantastic, believe me.

Wartime Weddings

But not all wartime engagements ended tragically, and there are many accounts of quite memorable wartime weddings.

Some were splendid affairs, especially when the Navy had anything to do with it. Daisy Henderson (now Baldwin) became engaged to a sub-lieutenant who, on learning that he was to be posted to the Far East for two years, arranged for her to be shipped from Cape Town back to England. She arrived at Southampton in July 1945 'to a welcome from a Royal Marine Band playing on the quayside and my fiancé waving up at me'. Regulating PO Eve Lynch, at her wedding to CPO Eddy Canvin at the garrison church, Hamburg, was given away by the Flag Captain, the ceremony being filmed for Pathé Movietone news and seen by all her friends and family back in Britain. Wendy Batt, after her wedding to Lieutenant 'Fergy' Ferguson, was piped aboard his Motor-Launch at Newhaven for a reception attended by many of the local brass hats.

Equally colourful was the wedding of Thelma Child (now Everden) in 1943 when, as they left the church, the other NAAFI girls 'made an arch of beribboned rolling-pins for us to walk through. They were the biggest rolling-pins I have ever seen, scrubbed white.'

Others had to overcome problems of rationing if things were to be done properly. Freda Spowart was engaged when she joined the ATS and married her fiancé on his first leave home after two years in Italy.

> Food was hard to come by, but Mum put on a lovely meal for eighty guests with help from neighbours and an uncle of mine who had a shop. And – dare I say it? – Cook provided me with tins of meat and all the ingredients for a three-tier cake. Mum made it and a neighbour iced it. The guests couldn't believe it.

Sometimes a certain amount of cheating was needed. When Lilian Bailey married her soldier-fiancé Ramsay Bader friends provided them with a cake with a plaster of Paris top.

Finding a wedding dress could be another problem. Some women were lucky enough to be able to borrow one of twelve dresses – four for 167 each service – sent over by one of the Hollywood studios. Edna Smith applied for one to her ATS commandant.

> She put my name forward to borrow one, stating size, etc. At last it came. It was marvellous, very heavy material and fitted perfect. I felt like a film-star when I wore it. The day I got married I came out of the house to get in the wedding car, the driver held up the long train of the dress and he said to all the neighbours and friends standing by: 'Blimey! I haven't felt a dress like this for a few years!'

The one thing that spoiled the day was that, being May 1944, all leave was stopped as part of the run-up to D-Day, the invasion of Normandy.

> I had got my two ATS friends to be bridesmaids, and my husband's friend was going to be best man, [but] only the two getting married could have seven days' leave. So I had to get in touch with Mum to find me two girls who would be bridesmaids and a best man, which she did. We were just lucky the two dresses fitted the two girls who I had never seen before.

Others at the same period nearly had no wedding at all. Dorothy Hobson writes that

> George and I planned to be married on 17 June 1944, and five days before I was to start my seven days' leave I had a telegram from him to cancel the wedding arrangements as all leave from N. Ireland had been cancelled. Two days later I had another message 'the wedding was on again', and the day before I was to go home it was off again. I decided to take my leave anyway and when I arrived home George was already there. He'd been flown from Ireland to somewhere in Scotland and then by rail to Sheffield. We were married on Saturday as arranged, and my parents and friends had somehow managed to get enough food for a lovely tea and reception. What with the wedding being on and off so many times no one had thought about a honeymoon, until it was too late. We had to stay the night in my parents' home, which was most embarrassing.

But the prize for the most dramatic wedding story goes to Jill Carter, who in September 1945 sneaked off and got married while on sick leave.

> On the third day of our honeymoon a telegram reached me ordering 'report forthwith or consider yourself a deserter'. I returned immediately to London to be met off the train by two Wren POs who told me, 'The prisoner will fall in', and I was taken to the Port of London Authority building (overlooking the Tower of London!) and put on a charge. My fellow-prisoners were seven very small seamen, on charges of stealing, razor-slashing, etc. When the Master-at-Arms ordered us to 'Fall in and the tallest at the back' I found myself towering over them all. 'Cor blimey,' whispered a tiny little fellow in front of me, 'Snow White and the Seven f—— Dwarfs!' I found myself facing a court of senior Naval and Wren officers with a Captain as judge. I was given an immediate discharge from the Navy and told to return – to my
> husband!

Meanwhile, though some women were getting married, others were being reunited with husbands whom they had not seen for months, even for years. Some, like Dora Sibley whose husband had spent the entire war in West Africa, took up again as if they had parted the day before. Some had grown so far apart that the marriage could not possibly survive. For many, probably the majority, a great deal of readjustment was necessary, since the war would have changed both husband and wife.

This was the case in even the happiest of marriages, as Florrie Buck told us.

I was at Stanmore when I next saw my husband, in the summer of 1944. I was just outside the sick-quarters, helping a WAAF officer into an ambulance, when I saw a soldier walk into the gate. I didn't run towards the soldier, I ran into the sick-quarters where the MO was just doing a ward round, and it's unheard of to interrupt them while they're doing that; it was a lady MO, and she wasn't very pleased, and I was saying 'Ma'am, ma'am, it's my husband!' And she thought the worst, so immediately she pushes me on to the nearest empty bed, saying 'Oh, my dear, my dear!' thinking I must have had a telegram. I said: 'It's all right, ma'am; he's outside.' However, having been directed from the guardroom to the sick-quarters, he was met at the entrance by three nurses absolutely weeping, they were crying for joy for me, not having seen him for five years. You see, everyone knew about the two of us. The officers would say to someone complaining about something or other: 'Look at Corporal Buck here; she hasn't seen her husband for years, and you don't hear her going on about it.'

Anyway, he was met at the door by these girls all weeping and he wondered what was going on. Eventually he managed to find me being resuscitated, and one of the nursing orderlies brought along a cup of tea, so I said to him, 'Do you take sugar?' and he said to me: 'Do you smoke?' We'd only been married two months before he went off, and it was like being strangers again.

We had no home, so we got on the Tube at Stanmore to go to my mother's; and, you know, I was sitting there with Eric thinking: Who is this man? Who is this man who's moved into my life? After all, it was five years of a totally different life. We weren't the same people. I thought: Who is he? He's just walked in, and that's it. What am I going to do? It was very strange. And three days after, bless his heart, he said to me: 'You know, you're not the girl I married.' And I said: 'No, I'm not. I've been through the Blitz and five years of the Air Force, and I *am* different.'

ELEVEN
Peace Ever After

Early in 1944 all leave was cancelled and all duties stepped up. There was an air of anticipation, yet utmost secrecy. We thought surely we must be invading Europe soon, but when, where and how we just didn't know; so we worked hard and waited.

CLAIRE LOWRY

Preparations for the invasion had been going on for some considerable time. Since it was vital to keep the Germans in the dark there were few people – other than those involved in the planning – who were privy to the detailed arrangements. But it was not difficult to guess that D-Day was approaching. Troops headed south, unusual exercises were carried out, strange new vehicles and equipment could be seen; and despite the rash of posters proclaiming that 'Careless Talk Costs Lives' rumours began inevitably to spread.

Betty Stanbury was one of many whose units moved out at short notice in the spring of 1944.

The main body of the battery went by train. We had haversack rations for three meals: hadn't a clue where we were going. We stopped early in the morning at a large station – only people on the platform were police, Salvation Army, Red Cross and WVS who gave us tea, coffee, chocolate and biscuits. It was obvious no one was to know the troops were moving.

They eventually ended up in Dorset, where their identity-cards were called in and all details of home town, county and parents' names and nationality blacked out before being returned. Then one night

we heard heavy vehicles passing through the village and next morning we MT staff had to go to our petrol depot and service the American convoy coming through with petrol and oil. All kinds of vehicles came, some we had never seen before – looked like motor transport but they could also go across water, so the GI told me when we filled his vehicle.

At about the same time Mae Cassidy moved to a special camp ready to take up to 6,000 people at short notice. Since no one knew if these would be prisoners, refugees or our own defeated troops, it contained everything from interrogation-tents to delousing-cubicles.

On our days off we went into Worthing, which was full of troops of all kinds.

Two streets were made up as a German town, and some of the boys were dressed in German uniforms. Suddenly you'd see someone you knew. 'Tell them at home where I am,' they'd say. 'Can't. We're under the censor, too.' Then one night after lights out we heard a plane overhead; not one of ours. *Whoosh*, down came the bombs. We were under our beds in a flash. Was anyone hurt? Voices, noise, everyone shouting for their friends. We had only shrapnel in our tent, but in the first tent there were three hurt. One girl lost her legs. Our subaltern had gone to the lat[rine]s. They had a direct hit; she was blown to bits. It was a very sad camp that morning. But life goes on, and we soon picked ourselves up. Things were hotting up. We could hear our bombers going over every night. The French coast was being bombarded by the Navy. Would it be soon?

The Germans, too, were aware that an invasion was imminent and regularly sent out planes and E-boats, looking for unusual activities or special concentrations of troops. Mary Staples tells us that at HMS *Foliat*, the combined operations centre outside Plymouth, 'the word went round camp that life was to be quite normal, so hockey was played as usual. During the game a small plane appeared, very high: on went the game. The buzz went round that it was a German photographer, and certainly any pictures he may have taken showed HMS *Foliat* as normal.'

Not all the efforts to avoid detection were so successful, unfortunately. Jean Rawson was at HMS *Attack* at Portland on 'that disastrous night when the E-boats got wind of the pre-D-Day manoeuvres in the Channel. All available craft were bringing shrouded bodies into the base, and we all felt very vulnerable that the war was right with us.'

Preparations meanwhile were being made to deal with the large numbers of casualties expected when the landings actually took place: the lessons of Dunkirk four years earlier had been learned. Massive banks of blood plasma were laid in, patients in hospitals throughout the south of England were evacuated farther north, and the nurses were put on alert. One morning in the middle of May Joan Piper was

told to report to Matron's office at 9 a.m. We all lined up in front of Matron's desk. She was an imposing figure and as she rose to greet us said: 'Nurses, the call has come.' I had no idea what she was talking about. Apparently we had been chosen to go anywhere, any time we were needed. We had to pack all our uniforms and a change of clothing at once in readiness and were required to leave an address and telephone number whenever we left hospital. The first Sunday in June the message came that I was to report back. It was a beautiful sunny day and hard to say goodbye, not knowing when I might see my family again.

She left London for Sutton Emergency Hospital where, as they waited for casualties to arrive, they were told how to administer a newly developed antibiotic called penicillin.

*

Down on the coast Claire Lowry had been given a week off and spent her days sunbathing on the flat roof of her quarters.

Every day an endless stream of army vehicles, manned by soldiers, rolled past on their way to the harbour. They were practising for the big day, and I waved to them from the roof-top and they smiled and waved back. On 6 June they began to roll again, but this time it was different. The soldiers' faces were blacked up, and they sat upright in their vehicles – grave-faced. It suddenly dawned on me that this was the real thing; they were actually going to invade that day.

Moyra MacLeod, distributing last-minute orders in Torbay, had realised this the day before.

The river was crammed with landing-craft, nearly all . . . full of American troops. Jazz music splintered the ancient sunny silence of the Dart. Men, stripped to the waist, lay in the sun and shouted to us and sometimes threw us sweets. The officers hailed us and gave us last letters to post. We waved to them and felt sick at heart.

Farther east, boats crew Wren Veronica Christie (Ronnie Moody) and her oppo Barbara Smith rushed a generator out to one of the ships of the invasion fleet in Southampton Water, 'so for some naval personnel and the soldiers on deck we were the last females to wave them off and wish them God speed,' says Veronica. 'I hope we passed muster.'

By dusk the decision to go ahead had been taken, and seven Ats at Eisenhower's HQ had been working non-stop routing and transmitting the signal. Queenie Stearn, serving at a combined ops base on Hayling Island, heard about it from her friend Bridget, who had seen the signal, and they decided to go down and see them leave.

So we set off for the deserted miles of sand. As the stream of little boats began to come into view on their way to the rendezvous at NAB Buoy we waved enthusiastically and they all hooted back in salute. As the stream increased, so did the hooting, until it became a veritable cacophony. It was a wonder it didn't alert Jerry! Hour after hour we went on waving. A June dusk fell, so we got out our regulation white handkerchiefs, the better to be seen, and the exchange of salutes continued until it was too dark for us to be discerned, our navy uniforms merging into the summer night.

Jill Carter, along the coast at Newhaven, had been used for weeks to seeing the harbour

jammed from end to end and side to side with minesweepers and landing-craft. One could walk from East quay to West across the decks of these ships. I came on duty just before midnight on 5 June. The eerie emptiness of that harbour was an unforgettable shock. I knew the invasion of France had begun. An elderly PO and stores NCO were the only people at the end of the harbour – where I was told to remain on call. At around 4 a.m. we three lined the harbour and cheered the first ship to return, an RML with battered prow. She did not return our welcoming cheers, and we felt the awful sombreness of the occasion.

At the Westcliff radar site at Portland, Elsie Wood (Stamper) had witnessed the beginnings of the build-up during her evening watch. But it was not till she came off duty at 11 o'clock and saw the Portland Bill lighthouse shining bright for the first time in years that she realised it was really happening.

Things were busier at RAF Tangmere that evening, and by the time Hazel Williams went off duty at midnight

> the table was smothered with little barge models showing all the build-up, and the ops room was like bedlam, for each of the Allied squadrons had controllers for their own countries – all talking at once in their own language: French, American, Polish, Czech, etc. And masses of VIP visitors coming in to have a look. All night we could hear the noise of military traffic going down the lanes.

By dawn the plotters and radar ops could start to relax a little, and Pat Sparks remembers handing over to the incoming watch at 0800 and just tumbling into bed, too tired for breakfast. At midday they were woken up by the cooks, full of the news that the invasion had started. 'They were most disgusted when we grunted and went back to sleep, for they did not know what our work was, of course. Even my family thought I was doing clerical work, as I was described as "Clerk SD".'

For these women the most dramatic stage of their involvement with the invasion was over. For others – those whose job it was to look after the battered machinery and wounded men – it was just starting. Barbara Smith remembers that

> the craft began to trickle back battered and battle-scarred, the men unshaven and tired, glad to be back whole. Jimmy [their coxswain] took two LCPs almost to the Portsmouth boom to ferry one of our craft back, its bows were under water, props in the air; how they'd managed to struggle so far was amazing. . . . A call came for every available craft to race to one of the hospital-ships which had been lying off Netley waiting for hours to discharge their wounded. Services were dreadfully overstretched, and the men were having to be sent further away to hospitals. Seeing the underside of the stretchers soaked in blood, as they were hoisted by slings from a crane, suddenly brought the war very close.

'We certainly knew what nursing was all about then,' says Eleanor Cook. 'Men with gas-gangrene, men blinded, some already so badly injured they would never recover. I could not get the smell of blood-soaked field-dressings out of my nostrils for ages.' Winifred Brading (Phelan) found herself cutting the clothing from desperately injured young men with pallidly green skin. She remembers their fortitude and the effort to make jokes and thank nurse, the sad duty of writing home for

173

wounded men who could not write for themselves, while herself awaiting news of her husband whose ship, HMS *Swift*, had sunk in the Channel.

There was no time to sort out prisoners by nationality. The ward where Joan Piper worked

admitted British, American and German patients. The Allies were nursed at opposite ends of the ward to start with and then left to fraternise: the German POWs were on a side-ward guarded by a British soldier. During the weeks we admitted more and more. We also evacuated those getting better farther north. The senior German officer of the first intake thanked our medical superintendent on leaving for the treatment of his men. He said he could see that all our patients were treated alike. (The first penicillin injection I ever saw was given to a German POW.) When re-dressed in their uniforms for evacuation, the Germans, who looked very young to me (I was twenty-two), appeared frightened. It was said they thought they were going to be shot!

Frightened they may have been, but the Germans still had a lot of fight left in them. Within a week of D-Day in fact, from bases in still-occupied Holland, they were to launch the first of their secret pilotless rockets, the V1s, onto southern England.

Intelligence sources had warned the high command that these weapons were on their way, and those who needed to know about such things had already been briefed. Hazel Williams again:

Some time before the first V1s came over, the ops room personnel had been shown a paper describing the pilotless machines. It was a great secret, and we all kept very quiet about it. We were told to say that as soon as anyone plotting had a message to say there was one of these machines about we were to shout out 'Diver, Diver, Diver'.

One of our girls was plotting on RDF South (covering the area south of our ops-table area). She was a girl called Mabs Kent, from Newcastle. Suddenly she gave a startled look, faced the controller and said, 'Oh sir, I've got one of those Diver things!' completely forgetting that she was to shout it out three times. And so the first of the hundreds of V1s was plotted.

For those who had not been prepared, these 'doodle-bugs' or 'buzz-bombs', as they were to be nicknamed, came as a complete surprise. Mary Cook (Mercer) was in the Royal Marine Wrens quarters in Rochester that first night.

Most of us had gone to bed except two girls who were on fire watch out in the street. Suddenly we heard this droning noise coming nearer; we knew it wasn't the normal kind of German or British plane, we heard the Wren officer bring in the fire-watching girls, and when this 'thing' seemed as if it was coming through the roof we all jumped out of our bunks at the same time and made a mad rush for the lowest part of the house. By this time the sirens had gone and we stayed in the small basement nearly all night. The all-clear didn't go until we were in barracks at midday, still not knowing what these 'things' were.

When the V1s landed the warhead containing a ton of high explosive caused considerable damage. During the second half of June some 2,000 hit south-east England, half of them falling on London. 'While you could hear the roar you felt relatively safe,' recalls Blanche Davis, 'but as soon as the engines stopped everyone rushed for cover. Several times my driver stopped the bus to enable the passengers to protect themselves the best way they could. The V2s followed shortly afterwards, and I hated these more than anything. They travelled faster than the speed of sound; the first you knew of them was the explosion as they hit the ground.'

The V2s appeared in September and were fearful weapons. Silent, too fast for radar to be of much use, there was little to do but clear up after them. 'There wasn't much anybody could do,' says Kathy Gibbons. 'It blew down half the street. Mostly dead people we pulled out of the ruins, plus bits and pieces. We tried to find what we could in the debris and get people to hospital if they were still alive.'

Not all the V weapons got through, however, as Hazel Williams explains.

Some of course failed to cross the Channel due to malfunction, others were shot down by the ack-ack and, best of all, our Fighter boys learned the knack of tipping the buzz-bombs with the wings of the aircraft and turning them round so that they went back to the area they came from.

It wasn't safe to shoot them down over built-up areas, so many ack-ack batteries moved to the south coast where they accounted for some 20 per cent of all V1s that crossed the Channel. Evelyn Hambley, after years of inaction in Pembrokeshire, found herself under canvas on a cliff-top near Hastings.

I was on duty for three days and three nights, taking a nap whenever there was a lull in the firing. But we were all so excited at our high rate of shooting them down that somehow the ghastly conditions under which we lived didn't matter. I certainly learned some new words from RAF pilots who chased the V bombers from France but failed to get out of our range when nearing the English coast.

Sadie Nias describes life on her gun-site on Foulness Island as 'tough, out in all weathers, often wet through for days, particularly when we were trying to combat the V1s and V2s. As the winter came on it rained and blew all day every day, the marquees where meals were taken blew down each night, but at least we weren't bored.' And the weather wasn't all they had to face. Operation Diver – as the fight against the V weapons was called – involved the ATS in their most dangerous rôle in the war. If they managed to shoot down a V1 without exploding the warhead, there was considerable risk to themselves. One hit by Margaret Hunt's crew came down on their own gun-site, 'but fortunately it landed between the gun-pits and the Nissen huts where we lived and no one was killed or injured'. On other sites they were less lucky, and between July and September there were twelve Ats killed and a further 131 wounded.

But gradually, as the Allies moved into the Low Countries, the attacks on Britain tailed off. The Germans withdrew and, for a while, continued firing on newly liberated cities in Belgium, Antwerp alone receiving nearly 6,000 V1s between October 1944 and March 1945. To combat this menace five mixed regiments were brought over from England in the November, constituting, in Shelford Bidwell's words, 'the only deployment of women in an operational rôle in any regular army'.

Servicewomen had been following the men into Europe since late July. But the first women to set foot in Normandy were nurses, two of whom disembarked on Juno beach on 14 June, while it was still under shellfire.

The first of our informants, Mary Morris, came ashore on the 19th, despite a gale which sank more ships than were lost on D-Day itself. The beach was by now 'a deserted battlefield: smashed amphibian vehicles, the remains of concrete emplacements, a paradise of scrap metal, tin hats, broken rifles, etc.'. They set off inland towards Bayeux, along a road from which the traces of battle had not yet been removed.

> The parting of clouds of dust revealed huge tanks on the side of the road, black from burning, dozens of them with dead crews hanging half in half out of the turrets and escape-hatches. There was mile after mile of destroyed armoured cars, trucks of all kinds, and always dust, heat and the stench of decaying maggot-ridden bodies.

By the 21st they had set up their hospital-tents and were ready to accept casualties, though in conditions very different from those left behind in England. They had the new wonder-drug, penicillin, of course, which dramatically reduced the incidence of gangrene. But the sterilising equipment, she noted, was 'positively archaic. I am sure Florence Nightingale was better off in the Crimea.' And Miss Nightingale never went to bed wearing a tin hat because of enemy planes strafing the tents. All day the wounded came in, British, Canadians, Germans, Poles, the odd Free French, a few Americans, a maquisard, even a Latvian. On 25 June she records having worked six straight hours in the oppressive heat of a fly-infested hospital-tent,

> silently handing the surgeon the instruments at the right moment. He never spoke, and I had to watch carefully to mop his brow periodically. We were all exhausted by 4 p.m. and went to sit on the grass outside to have a cup of tea. The two worst cases are to come, one only twenty years old. They both have to lose a leg, and my own feelings for them are mingled with exhaustion, and the nauseating job of clearing up the blood-stained theatre

afterwards, and carrying away the legs to an incinerator and watching until they are completely burned.

The servicewomen who arrived later that summer, though not so directly confronted with the present horrors of war, were still faced with much of the aftermath. Eve Canvin, then a Regulating PO, landed at Arromanches as part of the advance party sent to prepare and establish quarters for the main body of Wrens. On coming off the landing-craft they were transported to Todt House, Courseulles, which, as she learned, 'had been used by the Germans as a labour-camp. It was bleak, blood spattered on the walls, and of course very primitive. On the roadside were many wooden crosses topped by tin hats – no name.'

Only volunteers were sent into Europe, and written permission had to be given by parents (or by husbands, in the case of married women). This was frequently refused, and several of our informants express regret that they were never able to get out of the country as a result. Those who did so could find themselves gradually moving eastward as the Allied advance progressed, into Belgium and eventually into Germany itself.

The advance was not totally smooth, of course. Mary Morris had to look after soldiers wounded at Arnhem, one of whom described the whole affair as 'a shambles, utter chaos, no communications and thousands of men from the 1st Airborne Division dead. The wounded screaming for water and stretcher-bearers – trapped between German infantry with mortars behind and half-tracks in front.'

Nevertheless by the end of 1944 things were advanced enough for recreational facilities to be widely available for troops behind the front lines. The NAAFI established themselves in Normandy from early on, and Margery Leigh remembers stepping proudly on to a Bailey Bridge at Arromanches in the October. Entertainment, too, was not forgotten. A Wren concert party, including Eileen Phelan, left Portsmouth in December to entertain the troops at Channel ports before they proceeded to battle zones.

It was a bitterly cold winter. We sailed out of Dover harbour iced up with mountains of snow everywhere in HMS *Foulness*, a mine-sweeper. Amazingly all the opera houses [in Calais, Dieppe and Boulogne] had survived. Every night we had to climb into costumes of the thinnest and briefest materials, make up our legs – no tights – then deep breaths in the wings, off with the duffle coat and go on stage to music, lights, wolf-whistles from a packed audience every night, applause – magic!

On 2 February 1945, Win Dowd left for Ostend as part of AKS ATS Overseas, with her 15-hundredweight Dodge truck equipped with twin projectors and speakers, ready to take films to the troops.

At first we sometimes did three shows a day, travelling between each one. The projectors didn't even have time to cool off at times, and on hot days it was almost impossible to lace up the film. One unit would always stay put at Ostend on rest and maintenance, and one would do the 'local' tour, from the French border to Holland. Because Antwerp and Brussels were still being attacked by V1 bombs, we took it in turn to go into the more dangerous areas.

By the end of March the launching-sites had been bombed out or captured, which made Belgium a safer place for non-combatants. In fact, by the time Mary Winter flew to Brussels that February, the V1s had stopped falling on the capital.

This was the time for the settling of scores in the newly liberated parts of Europe as prisoners returned home to reveal who had denounced them to the Gestapo. According to Mary, 'it was not uncommon to see piles of furniture and effects being burned in the road. The collaborators had themselves been denounced, and the local people were taking their revenge.'

Such reprisals went on for several months; the first thing that Shirley Aston saw on landing in Ostend late the following May was a group of women having their heads shaved. But there were two days that May when, surely, no fires were lit in anger and even the girlfriends of Germans were left in peace: the 7th, when news of the German surrender was announced, and the 8th, celebrated by the Allies as VE-Day.

Queenie Stearn, in charge of the Wren plotters at Portland when the first German U-boat came into harbour, was one of few women to be involved with the realities of surrender.

Protocol demanded that all formalities should be observed, so the Duty Commander was on edge to be ready for the occasion. I'd worked out an ETA by DR [dead reckoning], but the girl plotting that stretch of the Channel left her model of [the German submarine] apparently becalmed near Star Point. I kept asking her whether she was sure the craft was not moving, and she repeatedly assured me her plot was accurate. Suddenly, at one jump, she moved the model from Star Point to Portland Harbour bar. I rushed in to tell the DC who understandably looked furious and rushed up to ground-level, fastening his sword as he went, as courtesy demanded that he should be there first, ready to receive the surrender.

For most, however, victory in Europe meant a day of great rejoicing, with discipline relaxed, for a few hours at least.

We had some idea for about a week that the war was going to be over soon, then in the middle of the night we woke up to bells ringing and a noise outside. We quickly got dressed and went outside, and lights were on everywhere; someone had even lit a bonfire on that hallowed ground, the 'Square'. We sang and danced until the early hours, that is, until 'Ma'am' arrived and made sure that her little girls got back to their own billets. . . .

D-Day. A Leading Wren Visual Signaller flashes permission for a Fleet Air Arm pilot to take off on 6 June, 1944.

R.A.F. FORM 1394

ROYAL AIR FORCE

Brief Statement of Service and Certificate of Discharge of

Surname ..... BADER (Nee Bailey.) ..... Official No. ..... 431143.

Christian names ..... Lilian Mary.

Date of current enlistment ..... 28.3.41. ..... Terms of enlistment ..... D. of P.E.

Rank on Discharge ~~or Transfer to Reserve~~ ..... Leading Aircraftwoman.

(a) Branch of Air Force in which enlisted ..... W.A.A.F.

(b) Date of mobilisation or embodiment ..... 28.3.41.

(c) Date of Discharge ~~or Transfer to Class~~ 20.2.44 ~~Reserve~~

Cause of Discharge ~~or Transfer to Reserve~~ ..... On Compassionate Grounds under provisions of K.R. & A.C.I. 652 Clause 11.

(d) General character during service .....

R.A.F. Trade ..... Instrument Repairer II.

(e) Degree of trade proficiency :— A(i) ..... Superior. ..... A(ii) ..... --

B ..... -- ..... C ..... --

Special qualifications held ..... N I L.

(f) Medals, Clasps, Decorations, Mentions in Despatches, Special commendations, etc. ..... N I L.

DESCRIPTION OF ABOVE-NAMED AIRMAN/AIRWOMAN ON DISCHARGE OR TRANSFER.

Date of birth ..... 18.2.17. ..... Marks or Scars .....

Height ..... 5 ft ..... 1 ins. ..... Birth Mark Left Thigh.

Complexion ..... Dark

Colour of Eyes ..... Brown.

Colour of Hair ..... Black.

Airman's or Airwoman's Signature ..... Lilian M. Bader.

BRIEF STATEMENT OF TRADE QUALIFICATIONS, CHARACTER AND GENERAL CONDUCT.

An airwoman who at all times has carried out her duties in a satisfactory manner, and whose character has been exemplary.

(Signed) .....

Unit Date Stamp ..... R.A.F. STATION, 6 FEB 1944 BOSCOMBE DOWN.

Commanding ..... R.A.F. BOSCOMBE DOWN. Royal Air Force.

Name of signatory ..... D. D'A. GREIG. (IN BLOCK CAPITALS)

Attention is directed to Notes (a) to (f) on reverse.

Lilian Bader's Statement of Discharge.

Waafs parade down the Strand for VE-Day celebrations.

We were not supposed to be having the day off on VE-Day, so we dressed in best blue to go to work. (Ivy Roberts/WAAF Sgt)

We had gone to bed when late one night we heard a noise outside and there was a small 'band', a trumpet, drum, etc., and a large group of people. They told us that the Germans had surrendered and then gave 'three cheers for the ATS'. We put on greatcoats over our pyjamas and joined them, regardless of the time and lights out. We followed the triumphal procession round the streets till we reached a huge bonfire and found the men from work already there. I remember doing the Hokey Cokey – then eventually, still in pyjamas and greatcoats, we paraded back to the billet. (Ellen Jackson)

That May morning the whole camp paraded to Divisions to give prayers of thanks. I crept in at the end of the ranks of Wrens, as I had never paraded before. I don't remember very much of that day, except that all the pubs in the countryside had beer – but no glasses! (Nurse May Staples at HMS *Foliat*)

Those who were near enough made for central London, where all the lights were on again for the first time in nearly six years. Eileen Scott-Martin and the other redcaps were allowed to take off their provost flashes and mingle with the crowds around the Palace. She had 'never seen such happiness. We all danced and sang the night away. (Of course next day down to earth, flashes back on uniforms and back to duty.)' Freda Spowart and some of her friends, after visiting London to join in the fun, came back and 'did the victory sign with the searchlight, then we lowered the beam to the ground and flashed it around the field where we startled a few couples doing their own kind of celebrating.'

But not everybody was out rejoicing that night. Peggy Scott and her fellow-nurses were 'too far out of town and too tired to do much celebrating'. Not everyone, indeed, thought it appropriate to join in the celebrations. Connie Poolman 'felt too sad' to accompany her ATS friends to London 'and stayed on my own in barracks and cried. I felt there had been too many killed and injured, and too much damage done to be happy. My own brother had been killed when he was twenty-two.'

Even those out having a good time could find themselves faced with reminders of the price at which victory in Europe had been bought. Eve Sugden ended up that evening in one ancient Dorset pub 'where the walls and ceilings were covered with the signatures of all the British and American aircrew who had ever raised a mug there. The barmaid showed me a wall of photographs. "The ones edged in black," she said, "were killed and we retired their mugs."'

In the recently liberated cities of Europe there doubtless were many people with reasons of their own for mourning, but for most it was a day of simple relief and joy. Mary Winter remembers the streets of Brussels 'crammed with people, Belgians, troops of all kinds. No one wanted to work. I think we were supposed to be on duty, but I can't remember   183 working that night. The streets were decorated, everyone was singing and dancing, the bars were doing a roaring trade and so were the newsvendors.'

Throughout the world in fact, sometimes bemusing the local population, the end of war in Europe was celebrated. Kay Kerrvish was on leave in Shilong, Assam, where 'no fireworks were needed as we had the worst tropical storm I have experienced. Next morning I was ashamed of the British officers who had wrecked a fine hotel in their drunken celebrations.'

The war was still not over, however, as Peggy Skuse (Slatter) reminds us. In Cape Town, where she was a PO writer in the Admiral's Office, 'VE-Day came and went with little jubilation for us as we were more concerned with operations in the Pacific'. They had another three months to wait, until Japan surrendered in mid-August, and she was one of many Wrens and sailors who, officers and ratings alike, 'linked arms and danced and sang up and down the streets of Simonstown, after having partaken of much gin and freshly cooked crayfish in the dockyard wrennery'.

But the surrender of Germany did mean that an increasing number of women were given the opportunity to go abroad, in most cases for the first time in their lives.

The women who did volunteer for service in Europe risked finding themselves the objects of curiosity, sometimes even of resentment. Mary Winter and her fellow-Waaf were completely outnumbered by male wireless ops –

> a state of affairs which had not happened to me before, the more noticeable in that there appeared to be such animosity towards us. These men were rather proud of themselves; they were the second TAF [Tactical Air Force] (Rear) Mobile Signals Unit, they had landed at Lussy Beach Head on D-Day plus 13, they were 'heroes' and what were we doing stealing all their thunder? It took quite some time and quite a bit of leg-pulling before we broke down their resistance.

Shirley Aston, arriving in Belgium shortly after VE-Day, at first found that servicewomen were treated with hostility by the local people; 'then [we] discovered that they thought we were there for the benefit of the men! When they realised we were there to work their attitudes changed. Apparently the Germans before us had their own women in uniform.'

Life in Brussels turned out to be quite pleasant. All service personnel could use the magnificent Montgomery Club, housed in a former royal palace and run by over thirty NAAFI women with 300 local staff. There was an ENSA theatre and cinema and, for those who wished to do so, an easy opportunity to make money on the black market. Shirley more than doubled her pay by selling her cigarette ration.' "Flogging" was a way of life,' she says. 'It was never considered to be stealing. I remember a girl dragging a bed through Antwerp; she had flogged it together with the army blankets.'

Jean Wood, who ran the catering side of all NAAFI establishments in Belgium, was amazed to discover how well stocked the shops were compared to Britain and that 'coupons for clothing could be bought at the shop doorways'. P. M. Warren, another 'TAF Waaf' in Brussels, confirms in *The Best of Enemies* (1986) that

> a few bars of Lux, which we could get from the Naafi for very little, were all that was needed to get as many clothing coupons as one wanted. While a tin of 50 cigarettes – doled out to us free of charge every week – could be used to purchase any of the mouthwatering goods on offer along the glittering streets.

She only stayed in Brussels for two weeks before the whole unit packed its bags and, in early July, set off for its new quarters, at RAF Buckeburg in Germany. In those early days of the occupation there were fears of what the disgruntled civilian population might do, and all RAF personnel had to carry weapons if venturing outside.

> The order rather tickled us Waafs, for while the men were armed to the teeth we women had no means of protection whatsoever, except, of course, the men themselves. We were forbidden to walk anywhere outside our billets unless accompanied by men bearing arms.

Mary Winter, who had also moved to Buckeburg, remembers her boyfriend trying to kiss her goodnight without letting go of his sten-gun, 'which did rather get in the way, to the amusement of some passing citizenry'.

The civilian population had very little to be amused about in the summer and autumn of 1945. The British forces were based in small towns which had been spared the bombing, but there were opportunities for visits to cities such as Hanover, at this time no more than a heap of rubble with names of survivors posted up on corners to tell any returning soldiers or POWs where members of their family were to be found.

On such a trip another wireless op, Irene Boud, found herself unprepared 'for the feeling of sympathy that came over me'. This was, indeed, a commonly reported reaction, though one not shared by Mary Winter when, on the way to Hamelin, she passed the former extermination-camp of Belsen, the stench from which still reached the roadway, months after the liberation.

For their part the Germans posed no threat, and the carrying of arms was soon quietly abandoned. Some male members of the occupying forces fraternised energetically with female civilians, and it was the men who were most heavily involved in the flourishing black market. 185

Servicewomen, on the other hand, had little contact with Germans other than with those working as cooks or servants. It was clearly in the Germans' interest to be friendly, or at least neutral, towards their erstwhile enemies, though Shirley Aston writes that 'if you turned round quickly in the canteen you'd catch a look of hate from the German employees'.

But there were not many women who had the opportunity to experience life in Europe after the liberation. The number of Waaf in Belgium, for example, rose from 89 to 1,200 in the six months up to July 1945, but dropped to just over 200 following the move to Germany. A handful of women were given quick 'Cook's Tours' – the chance of a flight over the Continent for an hour or so, without even a landing – but most didn't get closer than the south coast of England.

Women who had served alongside men for months, perhaps years, could find that they were being left behind. The 1st Searchlight Regiment was ordered overseas in January 1945 and, as Janet Sykes says,

> we girls were devastated when we were told that no Ats were to be included. We said a tearful goodbye to our gunners at Canterbury and some of us lugged our heavy kit-bags, and gas-masks and tin hats to a lorry and set off for an infantry holding unit at Ramsgate.

The problem was what to do with the servicewomen left at home, especially those whose skills were now obsolete. It had, indeed, been common throughout the war for women to change jobs; rapid technological advances together with a more realistic interpretation of what women could undertake meant that there had been a steady flow of women upgrading their skills or learning entirely new ones. But once the Germans were on the retreat there were few new openings, and not all of those were desirable, as Dorothy Baker discovered. Following the disbanding of her AA battery, she found herself one of a handful of Ats attached to an RAMC unit attempting to find a vaccine against scrub typhus, a disease killing many of our troops in the East. Thousands of rats had to be injected with the typhus, then checked every hour, day and night, since they had to be opened up within minutes of dying for the vaccine to be of any use. All of this was done by ATS operatives wearing protective clothing, and if one were to cut herself the wound had to be cauterised immediately.

Most of the remustered women found themselves involved in rather more humdrum work. Margaret Hunt went into the Pay Corps, an experience which she 'disliked intensely. It seemed so dull after life on the gun-site, and I wasn't sorry when it was time for my demob.'

Demob

We were very fed up when we heard that girls doing men's jobs would be released quite quickly, regardless of their demob numbers. Obviously the

sailors returning from abroad wanted their old jobs back and it wasn't worth the Navy retraining us for other categories just to work out our time. We asked the Admiral to keep us as long as he could, and he said he would be pleased to do so, but the day came when he sadly told us he would have to let us go. He had received a signal from the C-in-C Portsmouth which said: 'If those are Wrens on your barge, demob them; and, if they are sailors, get their hair cut.'
Pamela Burningham

It was not feasible to allow all service personnel to re-enter civilian life at once, and so a strict rota was established based on age, marital status, category and length of service. Hazel Williams was demobbed in September 1945.

As a married woman I was in the first lot of women to get out. Otherwise, as a single twenty-year-old with the release number 50, it would have been a considerable time before I was released. The first part of my demob started at an ex-American base called Horsham St Faith. I had to have my medical there; we all had to have one prior to leaving the service, of course. I remember the room I had this in was still more or less as the Yanks had left it, with messages written on the blackboard showing states of readiness of their bombers! We also had to get rid of our WAAF uniform and kit, except for our No. 1 Blue (best uniform). I always remember how the equipment officer was surprised that I had lost my button-stick – a little stiff cardboard holder for placing one's buttons on when polishing them with Brasso and thus not getting Brasso on to our uniforms. I had in fact kept it as a souvenir. Next we travelled down to Birmingham to spend a day signing off, collecting our coupons for civvy street, our gratuity pay; I had the princely sum of £65, plus our cigarette and sweets ration in a large brown paper bag. There were hundreds and hundreds of Waaf getting demobbed. All shapes and sizes and married to men from all over the world, a great number of GI brides amongst them. I then took a train to Guildford to join my husband of just three months.

For Sadie Nias, being a civilian again 'was the strangest sensation. Pleasure at being free to arrange one's life, to be able to buy clothes in a shop, clothes with bright colours. I was desperately sick of *everything* being khaki.' Jill Carter found it 'new and marvellous, having come from school to married life with a war experience thrown in'. While Mary Palmer describes the day she left the WAAF as 'the happiest day of my life. We were sent to Wilmslow for this. It was a shocking place; the food was disgusting. I didn't care, because I was going home.'

But what they found there often proved unsettling. 'How strange it was getting back to civvy street,' writes Melba Clarke (Rudkin). 'We all looked forward to it so much and counted the days to our demob. However, once back in civvy street, I found there was no comradeship at all.' For one Wren, 'the experience of return to civvy street was quite traumatic. One missed the companionship of one's Wren friends, after

187

the carefree life we shared. At home one's former friends had either married or moved away from the area, so that one felt lost, if not bewildered.'

There was the hope of companionship at work, of course, and those who had been in employment before joining up were guaranteed their old jobs back. But 'the whole atmosphere was different', as Sadie Nias explains. 'Girls who had not been in the services seemed to be completely different in outlook.' Liz Sealey, back working for Gaumont British Films, found that 'those who had been there all during the war paid a great deal of attention to trivia, such as how many paper-clips one had used and suchlike. It did for a while seem rather petty after service life.' Mary Palmer returned to the Ministry of Labour where the young staff resented her as there wasn't enough work to go round. She was 'bored stiff after nearly four years of intense work and everything happening round me' and was glad to leave after three years on getting married.

Those who, like Ruby Garrett, had been in positions of authority found it particularly difficult. 'Oh dear, people started telling *me* what to do! Of course I couldn't get the hang of it, and the girl showing me said she couldn't accept my work. What a cheek! So I walked out. Then I got a clerical job in a factory. All very strange. I felt like an alien!'

The shock of entering civilian life was even greater for those just back from overseas. Peggy Skuse, in 1946, found that 'poor England and its people looked the worse for wear after the years of war. We looked healthy and bronzed and were jeered at by the porters and staff at Euston Station.'

Mary Snow soon learned that her colleagues who had stayed in England

> were not too happy at the thought of us taking over senior jobs; many envied our wartime service. No longer a nursing sister and officer but back to being just a qualified nurse. UK was a very dull place. Like many other QAs, I went to the Tropical Diseases Hospital for some specialised training and subsequently went to Kenya.

These were not the only women who chose to prolong their wartime experience. A number of servicewomen re-enlisted, especially those who had known no other form of work. (After all, as Hilda Mason says, when applying for a job it would not help to say she could operate a predictor!) Some served for several years, but this could mean merely postponing the problems of their return to civilian life.

Things could be tough outside work, too. Women who had been used to having food, clothing and housing provided, perhaps for six years, found themselves having to cope with the queues, the shortages, the overall greyness of life in postwar Britain. Above all, it meant that they were now responsible for their own future. Many had had demanding jobs, it is true, but their days had been spent within a clearly defined framework. And, as Florence Richter explains, 'though service life is full of restrictions, it is so organised that apart from the actual work that one did very little other thinking is needed. Being a civilian is very different.'

It had been foreseen that there would be problems, and the Educational and Vocational Training Programme existed to prepare service personnel for postwar life. Women were given some guidance about possible jobs, rather more about how to run a home. But a handful of lessons on budgeting and dressmaking were of little help. Lilian Shattock was one of many who found it difficult to cope with being newly married.

> Nowhere to live wasn't easy. Would you believe it, the council eventually gave us a hut in a camp in the country just vacated by POWs. Even still had the notice up, RAUCHEN VERBOTEN, and, yes, a large combustion stove like we had in the huts in the previous camps . . . the hut was divided into rooms and had an outside loo . . . ironic after serving in the WAAF.

Nissen hut or not, at least she and her husband had some privacy. Many women found themselves living with parents who, like Joan Dunhill's, 'seemed to find it hard to accept that you were no longer just a young girl, but a mature and changed adult who had learned to stand on her own feet and make her own decisions'. Married women found this particularly hard to accept, and Ruth Anderson – whose husband was still in the forces – says that her mother still thought of her 'as a small child to be watched over, forgetting that I had learned to organise my own life and do the job I had done in the RAF. I had to say where I was going, when I would be home, with whom I was going, and a small inquisition every time I went out by myself.'

So for many women – most of whom had longed for the day of demob – settling back into civilian life was a difficult process. The comradeship, the sense of achievement, the realisation that they were doing work that was acknowledged to be important; all this had gone.

Some, however, had not survived to see the arrival of the postwar world. Women in all branches of the services had been killed, though the casualty rate, it must be said, was relatively low compared with nurses, for example – or, indeed, the civilian population of the blitzed cities.

But memories do not take account of statistics, and for some women the most poignant moments of the war remain the times when they were faced with the evidence of death. For Lady Elizabeth Talbot, then First Officer Steele, the saddest thing she ever saw was

> when one of our own shells, fired from Portsdown Hill above Portsmouth during an air raid, failed to explode in the air and came down on the WRNS quarters at Lee on Solent. It exploded when it hit a rafter above the

189

dining-room where Wrens were having tea about 6 p.m. before going to a dance, and killed six of them.

And Margery Weston, a signal sergeant in the ATS, can never forget

Birdcage Walk on a lovely June day, ankle-deep in fresh green leaves blasted from the trees by the flying bomb which destroyed the Guards Chapel in Wellington Barracks, killing and maiming so many people at worship.

Coming off Sunday-morning shift at the War Office, our path through St James's Park was blocked by a silent crowd of people, all watching as Guards from the barracks, in military order, carried blanket-covered stretchers shoulder-high along the footpath. The sound of their footsteps was muffled by the fallen leaves, their faces grim and grey; but they carried their pathetic burdens with such care and dignity. Two of our orderlies were killed by that bomb as they attended morning service in the chapel. This is one memory of my war which has never faded.

But for Irene Boud the great moment of shock came after the war. During her training in 1943 she had made friends with a young woman called Lilian Rolfe, who had left her home in Brazil to join the WAAF.

As she was so far from her home, I took her to visit my parents whenever possible. We both passed out as wireless ops and I was to stay on as an instructor. A few days after the end of our training Lilian came to my billet to say goodbye as she was being posted. I remember her telling me she had transferred to the FANY and that she was leaving for London and also that she may not be able to get in touch for a little while. I never heard from her again.

What Lilian could not say was that she was one of the fifty women agents (including twenty-four Fany and fourteen Waaf) recruited by SOE to serve in occupied France. She went in by Lysander in 1944 and was among the fifteen caught by the Germans, of whom just three survived.

Irene knew nothing of this until the day when she and her husband were listening to the radio and a story in the series 'Now It Can Be Told' came on.

The one we were listening to was the story of Violet Szabo, and at the end of the story she and two of her friends were taken out by the Germans and shot. One of these girls was Lilian Rolfe. I was so shocked that it was some time before I could believe what I had heard. . . . I remember Lilian as a gentle, very slim, fragile girl, and I never stop being amazed that she also was a very brave one. I am proud to have known her.

But the survivors can be proud of their own contribution to the war, and this feeling is indeed strongly present in many of the accounts we have heard and read. One can ask, though, if this is ever mixed with any expressions of regret for the years spent in the struggle for peace. One

woman told us that she was recently asked if she would go through it again, if necessary, and said she would since 'memory erases the less congenial moments'. But one wonders how much *has* been erased. Spectacles come in more colours than rose, after all; and many, when summing up their experiences of half a century ago, refer to the bad moments as well as to the good.

Janet Sykes, for example, says that

> looking back on my time in the Army, it seems a wasted part of my life now. Our young lives were blighted by anxieties and fears; we lost most of our privacy and the pleasures young girls take for granted now – clothes, make-up, being able to go where they please. We had to grow up quickly and face unknown dangers, but there were enjoyable times – comradeship, laughter, love – which one remembers.

Freda Spowart 'in spite of the tragedies of war enjoyed every minute', while Mary Palmer 'would not have missed one minute of [her] sometimes sad, sometimes infuriating, often funny, always frozen, life in the forces'.

Eve Canvin, on a recent visit from her home in New Zealand, went over to Normandy, back to the place where she had landed with the first group of Wrens in the summer of 1944.

> We visited the beaches, children playing and crowds sunbathing. The Mulberry is just a few chunks of concrete, Arromanches and Courseulles now thriving resorts; Caen no longer carries that dreadful sickly smell of corpses, and I felt that our small contribution helped to make it what it is now. I'm proud to say 'we were there'.

Bibliography

Of public sources consulted the most useful include:

Nurses
Lucilla Andrews, *No Time for Romance*, Harrap, 1977.
Brenda McBryde, *Quiet Heroines*, Chatto & Windus, 1985. (She also wrote about her own war experiences in *A Nurse's War*.)

WLA
Vita Sackville-West, *The Women's Land Army*, Michael Joseph, 1944. (Still beautifully readable.)

FANY
Hugh Popham, *F.A.N.Y. 1907–1984*, Leo Cooper/Secker & Warburg, 1984.

ATS and FANY
Shelford Bidwell, *The Women's Royal Army Corps*, Leo Cooper, 1977.

WAAF (all by ex-Waaf)
Katharine Bentley Beauman, *Partners in Blue*, Hutchinson, 1971.
Mary Lee Settle, *All the Brave Promises*, Heinemann, 1966.
P. M. Warren, *The Best of Enemies*, Howard Baker, London, 1986.

WRNS
Ursula Stuart Mason, *The Wrens 1917–77*, Educational Explorers, Reading, 1977.
Eileen Bigland, *The story of the W.R.N.S.*, Nicholson & Watson, London, 1946.

GENERAL
John Costello, *Love, Sex & War: Changing Values 1939–45*, Collins, 1985.
Angus Calder, *The People's War*, Jonathan Cape, 1969; Granada, 1971.
Peter Lewis, *A People's War*, Thames Methuen, 1986.
Roof over Britain. The official story of the A.A. Defences 1939–42, HMSO, 1943.
Man Power. The story of Britain's mobilisation for war, HMSO, 1944.
Front Line 1940–41. The official story of Civil Defence in Britain, HMSO, 1942.